*As You Pass By*

# As You Pass By

## Architectural Musings on Salt Lake City

A COLLECTION OF COLUMNS AND SKETCHES

FROM THE *SALT LAKE TRIBUNE*

By Jack Goodman

*To Kay &
Dr. Hal —*

*Jack Goodman*

University of Utah Press

Salt Lake City

5   4   3   2   1
1999   1998   1997   1996   1995

LIBRARY OF CONGRESS CATALOGING-IN-PUBLICATION DATA

Goodman, Jack, 1913–
    As you pass by : architectural musings on Salt Lake City : a
collection of Salt Lake tribune columns and sketches / by Jack
Goodman.
        p.    cm.
    ISBN 0-87480-488-4 (cloth : alk. paper). — ISBN 0-87480-489-2
(paper : alk. paper)
    1. Architecture—Utah—Salt Lake City.   2. Salt Lake City (Utah)—
Buildings, structures, etc.   I. Title.
NA735.S34G66   1995
720'.9792'258—dc20                                        95-22070

# Contents

# Acknowledgments

It almost goes without saying that the author and artist whose name appears on the cover of this volume is not solely responsible for *As You Pass By*. Jack Gallivan, a friend of many years and now publisher emeritus of the *Salt Lake Tribune*, dragooned me into doing the weekly "City View" column some ten years ago. Harold Schindler, then the editor the *Tribune*'s Sunday Magazine, helped whip the initial columns into shape followed since by other helpful editors.

As a relative newcomer to the Utah scene (and a journalist with a life-long aversion to scholarly research) I've depended on the Utah Division of State History, its library and staff for factual matters such as dates, the names of architects responsible for buildings herein, and for much anecdotal material. Likewise the staff of the Utah Heritage Foundation and *Tribune* librarians, who incidentally helped immensely in the early stages of this book.

Happily, I've been able to consult the excellent volumes and articles on Salt Lake City and Utah architecture written by such genuine scholars as John S. McCormick, Karl T. Haglund, Philip F. Notarianni, Margaret D. Lester, Thomas Carter, and Roger Roper. Many of my ideas on style were formed after conversations with such architects as the late Lloyd Snedaker and such present-day practitioners as Boyd Blackner, Burtch Beall, Jack Clawson and Walt Scott.

Last, and far from least (fact is, she should be first on the list) is Andrea Otañez, who edited this volume, typed, checked data, hunted for missing drawings—all with great humor.

Sincere thanks to all, not excluding my wife Marjorie and son Nathaniel.

# Introduction

DECEMBER 1994

When walking the streets of Salt Lake City—or any town or metropolis—
most of us tend to look ahead and downward, understandably so because
we must avoid tripping on a rough patch of pavement. Piloting an automobile through city streets is, of course, something of a chore. We alertly look
at traffic semaphores and watch cars alongside, approaching and behind our
own vehicles. More's the pity—in heeding normal safety needs we ignore
our surroundings.

I hope this volume may persuade you to peer, hastily or at length,
at the new or old buildings nearby. Residences, business buildings, public
structures are all often enhanced by previously unnoticed architectural elements. Buildings have doors and windows placed in logical or illogical series. There are roof-rim cornices, sometimes even bits of sculpture calcu-

lated to attract the eye. All such should give clues as to the style and age of buildings encountered.

A reading of this volume may also persuade you to take heed of the scale, the size, the relationship of new or old buildings. You may begin to appreciate the role of "street furniture," lamp posts and public benches, as well as street and advertising signs. Perhaps you will take note of historic structures you suspect are doomed to make way for "progress." You may pay more heed than in the past to buildings perched on foothills or at canyon entries—and it may thus call your attention to the need for zoning meetings.

This collection also seeks to tell the story of a city—how it grew, changed and expanded as people and trends came and went. Through it all, some architectural gems have survived; many have not. Still others are rising to take their place and reshape Salt Lake City's skyline.

I hope the book will focus your attention on the complex work of today's architects—good and bad—and upon the achievements of their predecessors.

JACK GOODMAN

CHAPTER 1

# Earliest Houses Still Standing

# The Woodruff Farmhouse

DECEMBER 22, 1991

Fortunately, an unknown someone had shoveled the sidewalk clear of snow at 1604 S. 500 East. Whether a neighborhood boy had bared the walk with an old-fashioned shovel or had used a snowblower to attack the accumulated white fluff, I know not. But the pristine white farmhouse, with its snow-covered roof and rear saltbox extension, bore the look of Christmas cards commonplace before seasonal-greeting cards took on a more modern look.

Next time the weather is snowy, stroll past the house, which Wilford Woodruff built for his family in the years 1859–60. Its years make it one of the oldest surviving farmhouses in the city, although its "saltbox" addition marked by the sightly roofline from the peak of the house to the one-story level at the rear must have been added just a few years later when Woodruff's family was "extended."

5

Lest you are inexplicably unfamiliar with the history of Utah's "prevailing faith," it may be worthwhile to point out that builder Wilford Woodruff was no ordinary "saint." He served as president of the Church of Jesus Christ of Latter-day Saints from 1887 to 1898, perilous years for the faithful. The practice of plural marriage or polygamy had led to verbal and even physical warfare between Mormons and the "federals." Utah was denied statehood and church funds and lands "sequestered" as a result of an insistence upon polygamy as practiced by otherwise law-abiding saints.

It was Woodruff who told his fellows in 1890, "I am under the necessity of acting for the temporal salvation of the church," a necessity that led to his issuance of the Manifesto, which historians label the "official" declaration that proclaimed the end of polygamy among the faithful.

Making matters a bit easier for historians, Woodruff, like so many of his fellows, was a journal-keeper. On May 20, 1859, he noted that he, his son Wilford and son-in-law Robert Scholles had cut approximately 300 logs "to build a house down on the farm." The farmland in question was all in the area designated the Big Field Survey, representing a first expansion of the platted Great Salt Lake City. Woodruff's pine logs averaged thirty-five feet in length, and cutting the trees and sliding them down the Wasatch canyons was not easy. "It was the first time in my life I had labored in three feet of snow on the twentieth day of May," he wrote in his journal.

Just when the log-cabin farmhouse was plastered over with white stucco, and when the saltbox extension went on the rear (the western end), is not precisely known, nor is the date when a porch was added. The porch is off-center, closer to the south than to the north. However, architectural historians researching the farmhouse when nominating it for the National Register of Historic Places found "some evidence" the farmhouse once housed two families. There's a door between the two southernmost windows on the east-facing facade, while another front door once existed between the first and second windows from the north. The old house was once symmetrical—the four upper story windows being precisely above those downstairs.

Latter-day Saint historians show a special interest in the farmhouse, since it was Wilford Woodruff's principal home during the years 1886–92. Although he was "on the run" and living in "the underground" for much of that time, his journal shows he stayed in the farmhouse several times and for several days in succession, apparently outwitting the "Feds."

While the snowcapped house was his primary residence when he issued the 1890 Manifesto, it's well to remember it was indeed on a farm, a five-acre tract of land now central in what local residents label the Waterloo Area, or Waterloo Ward. Wilford Woodruff planted his land in corn, wheat, hay grasses and oats, grew potatoes, and planted peach, plum, apple and apricot trees. He tried his hand at almond-growing, raised some sugarcane and had a small molasses mill. In addition to church work, he was president of the Utah Horticultural Society and the Deseret Agricultural and Manufacturing Society.

There are three, not one, Wilford Woodruff houses, and the trio appears as a unit on the National Register. The farmhouse illustrated in the sketch is at 1604 S. 5th East; the second house, Woodruff Villa, is at 1622 S. 500 East; while the third, usually designated as the Asahel Hart Woodruff House, is at 1636 S. 500 East. Church president Woodruff had his villa built in 1891, just a year or so after the issuance of that all-important Manifesto. The Woodruff Villa is built of brick and stone and displays a carved stone on its east-facing facade telling all comers its name. At the Utah State Historical Society, researchers say the stone inscribed with the Woodruff name indicates Mormon leaders had come out of hiding and were to become publicly visible once again.

The Asahel Woodruff house, built on his father's land in 1907, has, like the villa, been converted into apartment use. Meanwhile, LDS historians see the three houses as indicating major phases in Mormon entry into full-scale American citizenship. The farmhouse is a reminder of the pioneer Church of Jesus Christ of Latter-day Saints battling with the federal government for sovereignty. The Woodruff Villa of 1891–92 marks the "end of the conflict and hope for the future," while the Asahel Woodruff house of 1907 reflects the life and times of a second-generation Mormon who was a successful grocer, ZCMI executive and businessman, as well as bishop of a new Waterloo Ward. (Created in 1905 on the old Great Field, the ward was built complete with a brick chapel and cultural hall, signs of new times.)

For this nonsaintly columnist, of course, the chief interest in the Woodruff houses is in the 1859 farmhouse, which, unfortunately, displays a "For Sale" sign just outside its dooryard. One hopes a new owner won't mean too many changes in the middle of the city farmhouse that has the "look" of New England or the Midwest.

# Pioneer State Park

SEPTEMBER 29, 1985

It is a stage set, I suppose, since no Utah town ever looked quite so clean and orderly, even in the days when Brigham Young could command the faithful to build their communities foursquare to the four points of the compass, with broad streets and ten-acre blocks, carefully engineered irrigation ditches, proper tithing houses and careful attention to similar civic niceties. But on an early autumn morning a visitor to Pioneer State Park's "village" near the mouth of Emigration Canyon can picture a typical Utah town as it must have appeared back in 1870 or thereabouts.

True, the few people you will encounter are joggers, dressed in garb that would have seemed odd to Utahns a century or more ago. And because the tourist season is over, the oxen and other livestock are gone, the carefully tended vegetables are picked, and the "Deseret General Store," housed in the 1858 Miles Andrus home hauled here from Crescent, Utah, is open only on weekends.

There are advantages in strolling the streets of this replica of a Utah village, of course—no mud or manure in the streets, no soggy spots where irrigation ditches overflow the wooden footbridges, no flies or skeeters, no dust, garden trash, garbage piles or similar eyesores that must have afflicted residents of Salt Lake City or outlying Utah communities long years ago. All of which, or the absence thereof, might set you to musing about such matters as "restoration," "rehabilitation," the "re-creation" of historic communities that have assumed increasing importance to historians, architects, craftsmen, artists, and, of course, tourist-minded local and state officials and business people.

The best street for strolling and learning a bit about historic restoration is the central one leading to the "pioneer" community's largest structure, the long, low, adobe and stone Social Hall. En route to the latter substantial building, trim post rail and picket fences guard the 1864 Gardner Cabin. This simple, Abe Lincoln-style affair, dating to 1864, was brought here from Pleasant Grove as a sample of the first crude structures built by newly arrived immigrants. They were familiar, of course, with such cabins in Kentucky, Pennsylvania, New York State or just about anywhere in the early blooming seaboard and Midwestern states. A few steps farther uphill is the Samuel Gauchos/Henry Draper home, built in the late 1860s in Fountain Green (the dark-roofed, wood-frame house on the right in the sketch).

Next is the Social Hall, with its rather odd entry stair, its white adobe over red sandstone walls and its generally spacious, inviting look. Built in 1852 as Salt Lake's entertainment center, it stood on today's small grassy plot marked by a tablet at the west end of the Social Hall Avenue corner of State Street. Just beyond it there's another adobe residence, this one from Payson. Built in the mid-1850s as the John Boylston Fairbanks home, it is distinguished by its twin, rather oversize chimneys. But, back to the Social Hall.

Through the persistence, foresight, herculean efforts and downright good citizenship of the late James Moyle (long-time Utah State Parks chairman and State Historical Society board member) the foundations of the long-vanished landmark Social Hall were carefully excavated, measured, and sifted for remnants of the original structure. Through careful study of photos, prints, drawings and even old-timers' memories of the vanished building, the replica you visit nowadays was erected in Pioneer State Park a half-dozen or so years ago.

It's a replica, but its companion buildings (except for outhouses, sheds, barns and such like) are the original stuff, transported from aforementioned towns. In many cases new adobe, new planking, new windows, and shingles replaced rotting, missing, or doddering parts. Rehabilitation and restoration, in other words. Expensive, too, but well done.

In season, on busy weekends—and whenever volunteers are available—guides or docents, dressed in "period" costumes, add or detract from the scene (some visitors feel such antics give the place a "phony" air). On occasion, members of the Mary M. Atwater Weavers' Guild demonstrate old-time carding, spinning and weaving techniques, which most sightseers feel are "all to the good." There are brief "musicales" or entertainments in the Social Hall, while wagon rides utilizing oxen or more prosaic horse teams give the village streets rather more life than they have at this time of year. But this, of course, is not Colonial Williamsburg, where Rockefeller funds enable year-round candle-making, cobbling, silversmithing and the like by crafts people laboring in wigs, knee-breeches, colonial dame gowns and similar "authentic" costumes. And it must be remembered that scores of fine old buildings remained in Williamsburg, Va., even before the Rockefeller family set about the historic colonial capital's restoration some seventy-five years ago. Williamsburg has matured; our "old village" is new.

One complaint I've encountered when discussing our local village with architects is the relocation near the mouth of Emigration Canyon of Brigham Young's Forest Farm House, the sizable red brick affair with an abundance of porches and fancy curlicues. Now near the western edge of the park, it once stood on the fringes of Sugarhouse, the product of a later, more grandiose period than the downtown Lion House or Beehive House. It is, to some visitors, "very out of place in a Pioneer Utah Village." Fortunately, it is separated from the majority of the village structures by the distance of perhaps two city blocks. Well screened from the street system, it isn't too jarring—to my eyes at least.

While a pleasant spot for a visit, especially so since it offers splendid views of the foothills, mountains and the city's modern skyline, today's Pioneer Village fails somewhat by virtue of being a replica, an outdoor museum piece, welcome though replicas, restorations and museums may be. Just for contrast, journey up to Heber on a busy weekend, when the so-called "Heber Creeper" is operating.

True, there's a shabby, unhistoric row of fake, false-front shops beyond the rail tracks. But the 1890s railroad station, hauled from Honeyville, where it long served the Union Pacific, is in use—as a railroad station. Patrons swarm to its ticket windows, passenger cars are being loaded or unloaded, a smoky locomotive blows steam from its petcocks, there's a smell compounded of creosoted ties, wood smoke from the station stove, the odor of popcorn and of nearby barnyards.

Or trek out to the old Wheeler Farm on 900 East in the vanishing rural lands of Salt Lake County. School kids visiting Wheeler Farm see, hear and smell bawling cows, clucking chickens, ducks, horses and such like in a nonrestored but preserved setting. The Wasatch Scenic Railroad station at Heber and the Wheeler Farm are in reality, museum pieces, but somehow they realistically operate as they did half a century or even a century ago.

Pioneer State Park is a splendid place for a stroll, for browsing and dreaming of the past, and it's a splendid concept. The State Park people are doing their best to give visitors at least a taste of how things were in the Utah we now know only through history books. But the result is somewhat like a fly preserved in amber, intriguing but lifeless.

Oh well, the village trees are growing, the paint on some of the picket fences is flaking and scaling a bit, weeds are growing along the irrigation ditches. In a few years time, when the trim-edge neatness softens, and the costumes of the volunteers fray a bit, things will look more Utah-like.

EDITOR'S NOTE: Several historic buildings are being moved from sites around the state to increase the attractiveness of Pioneer State Park, which has been renamed "This Is the Place" State Park to help spotlight the centennial of Utah's statehood.

*Drawing Courtesy of Betty and Ed Fingl*

# The Quartermaster Cottage at Fort Douglas

MAY 13, 1990

If you have tired of gardening chores and find following a golf ball across hill, dale and sand trap too enervating this weekend, venture up to Fort Douglas for a pleasant and painless stroll through history. Aside from the immediate vicinity of Temple Square, no tract of land in the state is more intriguing to the history buff or a peripatetic student of architecture than the 128-year-old military post drowsing in the summer sunshine on the benchland above the city's residential districts.

If the weather is what New Englanders label "fair to middling," it's the perfect time for peering at the sandstone barracks buildings facing Stillwell Field, gazing at the artful carpentry work enhancing the "Quartermaster Victorian style" house on or near the Officers' Circle or touring the modest Military Museum fronting the parade ground. Gothic Revival homes date from the 1870s, the Post Chapel was built in 1883. And don't miss the low-lying barracks, or the old Post Cemetery. It's the last resting place of men who fought in the 1863 Bear River battle some historians term a massacre, and of Col. Patrick Edward Connor, whose bluecoats wiped out the "warlike" Shoshones of both sexes in that melee. He was promoted to brigadier general soon after.

Civil War veterans and U.S. military personnel who saw service in the Spanish-American War, two World Wars, the Korean "conflict" and Vietnam are interred in this peaceful setting. So too are German, Italian and Japanese who died while prisoners of war at Fort Douglas.

There's no need to feel slighted if you saw action in other branches of the services. The small, surprisingly comprehensive Fort Douglas military museum reminds visitors that the old USS Utah was sunk by Japanese bombers at Pearl Harbor, the USS Salt Lake City, an eight-inch gunned cruiser, saw action in naval warfare off the Aleutians, while a not inconsiderable number of Marines, Air Corps and Air Force veterans and Coast Guardsmen were inducted at this old-style military post.

Troops who first arrived here on the barren benchland in 1862 were quartered in tents and crude cabins before existing structures were built. They were sent to Utah Territory to keep a wary watch on Brigham Young and his followers in the years when the Latter-day Saints were considered, to say the least, subversive. Indeed, the first artillery pieces at the new post were said to have been pointedly aimed at Brigham Young's Lion House. Connor and his volunteers from California and Nevada were instructed to guard the new transcontinental telegraph lines and the network of stagecoach and mail routes that had begun to crisscross the region. During their most active post-Civil War days guarding the West against "hostiles," Fort Douglas troopers included an Indian infantry unit—men of the Brulé band of the Sioux Tribe serving as Company I, 16th U.S. Infantry, largely against the Utes. The post's most noted troopers were the black "Buffalo soldiers" of the 24th Infantry, who took part in both the western Indian-fighting and in Cuba during the Spanish-American War.

The old post circle, with its barracks buildings, officers' homes, nearby chapel, flagpole and bandstand, will remind devotees of Hollywood films such as *She Wore a Yellow Ribbon,* and a dozen "oaters" in which the likes of John Wayne, Errol Flynn and even Ronald Reagan fought side by side with a celluloid George Custer and his cohorts. If westerns ever come back into style, old Fort Douglas could be rather easily "dressed" to suit a new *Bugles in the Afternoon,* although this was never really a cavalry post.

Many native Salt Lakers will report that they did indeed ride horses at the fort—as youthful members of the University of Utah ROTC and its polo teams. But by the 1930s the commanding officer's quarters and regimental headquarters had a more modern look. New brick officers' homes were built on one side of Stillwell Field and a three-level double barracks rose in 1939 for the 38th Infantry. By the initial years of World War II the fort became headquarters for the 9th Service Command, directing "operatings and activities" in much of the West, providing finance offices for all Utah installations, plus vehicle repair and salvage "ops" shops. Today remaining "red bricks" can accommodate 1,000 officers and troops and 2,000 other personnel, although holdings of the old fort have shrunk considerably.

Which is another reason to explore the historic post. In 1939 Fort Douglas still comprised 9,000 acres, chiefly housing the 38th U.S. Infantry Regiment (dubbed the Rock of the Marne for its World War I service). By midyears of World War II, the 38th was overseas, but barracks housed the 5th Airbase Group, 7th Bombardment Group and 88th Reconnaissance Squadron, plus elements of medical, quartermaster, ordinance and signal units—a total of almost 4,000 troops. Little wonder such military men as Major-General (ret.) Michael B. Kauffman have formed an active Preservation Association.

In part through the efforts of the Utah Heritage Foundation, many of the post's older structures are on the National Register of Historic Places. General Kauffman's "troops," the Heritage Foundation forces, and a host of preservation-minded military and architectural buffs have helped persuade the entire Utah Congressional delegation of two U.S. Senators and three U.S. Representatives to press a bill transferring some 55 acres of the fort to the University of Utah.* The university, of course, already received fort lands used for its Research Park, foreshortened golf course and medical center and even acquired a few remnant barracks buildings dating to that 1941–45 "war to end wars."

Under the measure there seems a good chance of transferring the museum, chapel, parade grounds and a cluster of historic homes to the university, in expectation that the U. will maintain and preserve them intact. The Army's reserve components would keep the balance of the existing 119-acre fort as we know it today. In protecting the fort's designated national landmarks and historic register properties, the Congressional delegation foresees continuation of neighborly cooperation between the university and the military. In view of pressures for budget-cutting in Washington, the plan seems a good one indeed.

In sum, the flag will still fly from the cannon-guarded flagpole at the old post, its military museum will be maintained, and the well-preserved old buildings continue in service for a new generation. Strollers, joggers and bikers will still ramble along Hempstead Road or Soldiers Circle, old locust trees will still shade the cemetery, very possibly band concerts might again be given from the old gazebo. Downhill just a bit, students will hasten to classes, upslope a short way visitors can seek out the botanical gardens at the mouth of Red Butte Canyon.

EDITOR'S NOTE: Congress transferred much of the fort to the University of Utah in 1991.

# The Cornick House on Major Street

SEPTEMBER 19, 1993

Major Street is a rather minor thoroughfare. If you've never encountered it, it's the street paralleling State and Main—a much interrupted two-lane route running north and south betwixt and between those two major arteries. Nowadays, it seems chiefly dedicated to serving the backsides of businesses lining State or Main, a street that itself seems mostly devoted to rather unprepossessing warehouses, small factories and the like.

All of which are reasons the casual visitor is surprised—perhaps "floored" is a better word—when stumbling upon 1727 S. Major Street. It's just north of the big vacant lot alongside a one-time Pykette Co. factory building, and is flanked outside its protective fence by structures one can only describe as "nondescript."

Obviously old, 1727 is a small residential-style building, not quite overwhelmed by its commercial surroundings. The one-story, peak-roofed, brick building has a tidy lawn, colorful flower beds, trees, old-style electric street lamps of a type no longer gracing many downtown corners, plus a solid-seeming metal picket fence affixed to solid-seeming brick gateposts and corner posts.

This small but handsomely painted red brick house dates to 1894. William Cornick and his wife, Margaret Ann Rigby Cornick, had the house built on two of twenty-four lots owned by her brother, Seth Rigby.

Back in 1894, the Cornicks operated a sizable farm on the Rigby acreage—this according to Floralie K. Millsaps who kindly furnished much of the information reported herein.

The house is easily recognized by architects and nonarchitects alike as copied from a "pattern book," a common source for many homes in Utah and across the nation. How much a prospective home builder paid for such a pattern-book plan I can't rightly say.

Today, as way back in 1894, the baked red brick of the house is neatly laid, stringer fashion, upon a sandstone foundation. The housefront faces west, and is marked by a triple-windowed bay. The front porch south of the bay is featured by carpenter fretwork and trim, a giveaway to the period in which the home was built.

Four large rooms and a tiny fifth room are still inside the brick walls, but a two-story barn complete with hayloft has vanished from the rear, along with a tool shed, chicken coop and vegetable garden. All in all, the complex was typical of new Salt Lake buildings near the city limits at the turn of the last century.

Time passed, as it has a way of doing. The Cornick husband-and-wife team produced three children—William Seth, who became a banker; Clyde, who studied art in Paris; and daughter Thirza, described as a "housemaker." Art is a rather skimpy producer of wealth, so Clyde Cornick became a sign painter.

More time passed, as did William, the family patriarch. He died in 1925, his wife following him in death three years later. Son Clyde and his wife, Ruby, took over the home and housekeeping chores and built an extension of brick plus a wooden sun porch. Clyde—still an artist—used a double-windowed room on the north side as a studio.

Clyde and Ruby were childless, but family nephews often visited the couple as they did Ruby, who became the lone resident after her husband died. One nephew, Norman Cornick, a professor at Colorado College, tried to keep an eye on both house and aunt. When she died, at age ninety-one in 1990 (on the sun porch), he left matters in the hands of another nephew, LaMar Gulbransen.

The house became vacant, and in poor condition, with a weak roof and weakened floors. It attracted vagrants and drug users since the neighborhood, like the old house, had deteriorated.

Enter Jerald W. Taylor, president of Taylor Electric, in search of a small house useful as an office. He hoped to form an investment company after his retirement.

Mr. Taylor and wife Edna fell in love with the deteriorated house, ignored the advice of one architect, bought the place, and hired another architect, Don Hadden, to blueprint restoration tasks. Bricks were cleaned, original wooden cabinets refinished, new bathroom and kitchen fixtures installed, along with new electric wiring. Four big streetlights were found, coming from the long-vanished Walker department store at Third and Main. The gardens were relandscaped.

And there you have it. An office manager for Taylor Investment, Jerry Wayman, occupies a front room and desk in the old house daily, and is easily persuaded to show visitors the original hardwood floors, polished fireplace and artist Clyde Cornick's paintings on the walls. You can even view an old ball-and-claw-foot bathtub—once in the Plandome Hotel.

The house is a major find on Major Street.

# CHAPTER 2

# Early Downtown—A Few Survivors

# Hotel Utah

JUNE 15, 1986

This past week the folks who own and operate the Westin Hotel Utah have been marking the seventy-fifth anniversary of this grande dame of our region's hostelries by laying on a series of breakfasts, luncheons, dinners, parades and balloon ascensions for all and sundry.

In the case of the Hotel Utah, "all and sundry" means everyone in our town—especially those of us who fondly remember such vanished havens as the lobby soda fountain, the coffee shop's speedy-service breakfast and lunch counter and the open-air roof garden restaurant of olden days.

By odd coincidence the hotel was staring me in the face as recollections danced in my head, recollections of Bill Morris who checked hats and remembered the faces that accompanied each chapeau; garageman Frank Newman who swung your car around on that 1940s turntable; the smiling coffee-shop waitress named Fern I've always recalled as the world's best waitress; cheery Jim Durbin, host at that same downstairs food spa; plus such perfectionist managers as Guy Toombes, Max Carpenter, Max Dean, Hank Aloia and Stuart Cross.

The Westin Hotel Utah was not precisely staring me in the face—but the ornate upper stories of the hostelry happened to be directly in my line of vision as I sat in an office on the eleventh floor of the Kennecott Building. Until I began the accompanying sketch, I had never really realized that a very sizable Italian Renaissance temple sits atop the topmost stories of the 1911 structure.

Along with generations of native Salt Lakers, newly arrived residents and most hotel guests, I knew the handsome building at South Temple and Main was topped with a tower that in turn is capped with a beehive. Early on, that tower and beehive were discreetly illuminated with a multitude of electric light bulbs. A bit later, during or immediately after World War II, tubular neon lights outlined the beehive, while a five-story-high illuminated sign on the corner high above the Union Pacific Railroad's downtown ticket office announced the presence of the city's best-known hotel.

In later years (I believe under manager Stuart Cross) those neon lights were deemed a bit tacky. Nowadays soft floodlighting picks out the dome on snowy, foggy or clear nights, something of a homing beacon for downtown pedestrians streaming out of Symphony Hall.

Oddly enough, original drawings for the Hotel Utah, the 1909 architects' drawings and renderings in the offices of Los Angeles architects John Parkinson and Edwin Bergstrom, don't show a beehive at all. The architects blueprinted the twenty-five-foot-high, column-fronted "temple" visible in today's sketch, setting it upon a rooftop base graced by a pair of rather sizable lions, twin shields, a coat-of-arms or two, plus the present-day vines. No gargoyles are visible—but just about every other imaginable motif was happily seized upon by architects Perkinson and Bergstrom. Thus the "temple," like the hotel's lower, middle and upper stories, was and is festooned with all manner of terra cotta decorations. But the architects provided nary a beehive.

Apparently the architects were promptly informed of this oversight. Ours being a state whose busy-bee populace likes its homespun symbol to buzz on quilts, flags, ice cream molds, pillow-cushions—and hotels—that awesome oversight was quickly righted. Not only was the Hotel Utah's tiptop tower speedily topped by a twenty-two-foot-high, sixty-foot circular beehive, but it was flanked by a quartet of eagles (complete with shields) and finished off with a flagpole from which the national emblem floats daily.

All this rich topping may sound to trendy modernists as a little too much of a good thing—making for a building that may, in some minds, resemble a wedding cake. And yet, to traditionalist minds, the Hotel Utah has lasted well, inside and out.

Inside, of course, the thirty-foot-high lobby, with its twelve rotund pillars and gleaming Czechoslovakian-crystal chandelier, plus its Empire Room, bespeak the era when stage stars who had crossed in such ocean liners as the *Mauretania* arrived in our city aboard comfortable, heavy-weight, nonstreamlined Pullman cars, entering the lobby accompanied by fitted steamer trunks and gleaming cowhide suitcases.

After all, William Howard Taft slept here, a president rotund enough to require a special bed. So too, in latter days, did Lyndon Johnson, a president lengthy enough to likewise require a special bed. Fact is, every one of the nation's chief executives from Taft's time to the present has bedded down at the Utah—and would recognize its gleaming white facade and crusty hard rolls, if not that beehive-topped tower.

Happily, when the time came to improve and enlarge the Hotel Utah, Robert A. Fowler (architect of the expansion) and manager Stuart Cross took pains to make the new wing facing the Mormon Temple grounds precisely match the old. They tracked down the California maker of the original terra cotta tiles and decorations, and happily learned that the old manufacturer had preserved not just the hotel's decorative motifs, but the old mold from which requisite new decorations could be pressed and cast. Now, if the Westin Hotel Utah people will only restore the elevator operators to their old posts, rebuild the coffee shop to its 1940s specifications and reinstate that lobby soda fountain . . .

One thing they could and should do is paint the base of the little "temple," and apply fresh paint to that beehive. Despite the efforts of the peregrine falcons, the pigeons have made the hotel's upper works look more than a mite shabby. A new coat of white paint would not be amiss, especially for those of us who view the old hotel from lofty new office buildings nearby.

EDITOR'S NOTE: The Hotel Utah was closed in 1987. After renovating the building, the Mormon Church reopened it in 1993, calling it the Joseph Smith Memorial Building. It no longer functions as a hotel.

# Salt Lake City and County Building

DECEMBER 25, 1988

Salt Lake City's citizen taxpayers will be giving themselves a belated, but very handsome and useful Christmas present come April. On April 28, 29 and 30, our town, led by Mayor Palmer DePaulis, the Utah Heritage Foundation, restoration architect Burtch W. Beall Jr. and just about anybody who is anybody, will rededicate the multispired, Romanesque Revival municipal building at 451 Washington Square.

Lest you've forgotten, the square is the landscaped block bounded by State and 200 East and 400 and 500 South. The building in the spotlight, known through most of its history as the City and County Building, now has a single owner, Salt Lake City.

Since the citizen-taxpayers habitually judge the restoration of public structures in dollars-and-cents terms, let me go on record as believing that most Salt Lakers, after inspecting their city hall's completely restored exte-

24

rior and interior, will agree their dollars have been well spent. The work now being finished was financed by a thirty-million-dollar bond issue, and work is, according to staff architect Don Hartley, "within budget and on schedule."

This may be a mite surprising to cynical citizens all too accustomed to today's cost overruns. Indeed, way back when the architectural firm of Monheim, Bird and Proudfoot blithely estimated $350,000 as the cost to build the structure they envisioned, but the construction bid was $377,978. And inflation or cupidity were not unknown in those "good old days," for when the work that began in 1891 was completed in 1894, the final cost figures totaled $900,000. However, there was some return on the city-county investment, since part of the richly ornamented building served as Utah's State Capitol from the granting of statehood in 1896 until completion of the present Capitol in 1915.

These past many months, sharp-eyed restoration watchers have seen new stonework, quarried, cut and carved by such artisans as Wes Hansen, being installed by crews from the Larry/Dean Construction Co. A major reason for the much-needed restoration was the weathering, scaling and fracturing of the Kyune sandstone sills, balustrades and elaborate stonework on the building's 300-foot-high central tower and its multitude of lesser spires. Snow and rain, freezing and thawing on the porous sandstone surfaces, plagued generations of maintenance men. Indeed, these same soft Utah sandstones were partly responsible for the demise of the Dooley Building and problems with other fine local structures.

In its heyday, the building's balconies and archways were enlivened by sculptured ornaments such as traditional acanthus leaves plus nontraditional subjects, including male and female pioneers, Jim Bridger, Chief Joseph of the Nez Perce, Chief Walkara of the Utes, Mayor Jedediah Grant, Mayor Robert Baskin and Federal Judge Jacob Blair. Masonic symbols were especially prominent because the Masonic Orders presided at the July 25 cornerstone laying in 1892. In part this was because leaders of Utah's Mormon Church were in considerable disfavor or even in prison in the wake of the Edmunds-Tucker Act prohibiting the practice of polygamy. High above several balconies, gargoyle-like monsters and fanciful creatures reminded those who glimpsed them of stonework on medieval cathedrals. Unfortunately, many exterior carvings weathered so poorly they were removed, and replacement is only partial.

Indoors restorers have done an exceptional job, despite difficulties including the demise of a Pelican Point quarry from which onyx tile for stair-well walls once came. "However, we've pretty well matched them with tiles from Mexico," Don Hartley reports.

When the building opens to the public and all its windows are illumi-nated of an evening, there may be complaints that russet-red paintwork in corridors "makes things too dark." But decorators say sconces, chandeliers and reopened domes will provide sufficient light and will serve to recall the restoration's 1890s styling.

False ceilings and acoustic tile have been removed, meaning the full 18-foot height of such rooms as the Council Chamber, the Mayor's office and old courtrooms will have a feeling of spaciousness, which was mistak-enly eradicated decades ago. Accretions such as a candy stand and refresh-ment counter are gone, splendid fireplaces stand revealed, and handsome wood paneling has been cleaned of peeling paint. There has been some nec-essary modernization—television and electronic media provisions have been made in the Council Chamber's repositioned press box, while ancient lavatories have been replaced by fine, clean, apparently efficient plumbing for public and office needs. Well-remembered artifacts have been restored, including the dozen or so old-style wall safes, bearing oil-paintings of the Wasatch peaks along with the proud hand-painted Mosler, Bachmann and Co. trademarks dated Jan. 2 1883. The life-sized painting of Brigham Young by E.W. Perry, dating from 1865, will soon be rehung in the Council Chambers.

When the building's hundred or so rooms in four full-length floors are open, ascend the broad, central stairs to the fourth floor then look aloft into the newly revealed, freshly painted central dome and seek out the paired smaller domes. All were hidden, for a multitude of years, by false floors and ceilings put in place by administrators who failed to appreciate the craftsmanship and beauty of the old-style structural masterpiece.

To architects, engineers and safety-minded citizens, a major and costly phase of the work has been earthquake-proofing the elaborate structure. Badly damaged by an earthquake in 1934, the building shook so severely that its tower-topping statues were removed. In oversimplified terms, the entire structure now sits upon a steel and concrete mattress deep under-ground, with a roller mounting that should permit the structure to ride out whatever quakes may shake the city hall in the second century.

In freshly landscaped Washington Square, considerable interest has focused on the flagpole, statues of children and fountains on the State Street side. According to the city's Phil Erickson and county archivist Robert Westby, the flagpole was raised in 1936 when every pupil in the city's schools signed his or her name on an 8½-by-11-inch document to be ceremoniously buried next to the flagpole. Not only that—each youngster also set down what they hoped to become when their school days ended.

According to Erickson, these documents were dug up in 1957 and the signatures and predictions were microfilmed by the City Recorder's office. The microfilm was then placed in the care of the Utah State Historical Society. If Gary Topping of that office can locate the microfilm for you, you may find your name listed with your classmates and read of your future dreams. Erickson, whose city office treasures a "hard copy," tells me that virtually all schoolgirls of 1936 wanted to be wives, mothers and homemakers but the boys were variously inclined. Sam Skaggs (supermarket owner extraordinaire) wanted to be a chemist. Frank Wilkins (retired judge) wanted to be a newspaper reporter. As for Will Fehr, editor of the *Salt Lake Tribune*, he, like many of his schoolmates, hoped to be either an aviator or a G-Man.

My own youthful residence in Brooklyn denied me the opportunity for Salt Lake time-capsule immortality, but in my boyhood I wished to skipper an ocean liner, or at least a Staten Island ferryboat.

# The Elegant Peery Hotel

JANUARY 5, 1986

Unfortunately, local records tell us little about Charles B. Onderdonk and his work as an architect here in Salt Lake City or elsewhere. But if the estimable Mr. Onderdonk is looking down at us from some vantage point in the heavens, he should be pleased by the very thoroughgoing job of restoration being completed at the old Peery Hotel, on the northwest corner of 300 South and West Temple. He might even rip out a harp string or two at news that the re-do bears a three-million-dollar-plus price tag, since the elegant-for-its-time hostelry he designed cost just over $150,000 to build back in 1910.

You may remember the building best as the Miles Hotel, named for hotelier Harry Miles, who owned and operated it along with the vanished Congress Hotel on State Street, which it resembled. The Peery, in its original guise, was one of the city's major hotels in the days when trolley cars

28

or high-sided taxis took visitors from the Denver & Rio Grande or Union Pacific railroad stations to its handsome lobby.

The Peery or Miles outlived many contemporaries, including the Wilson Hotel on 200 South, east of the ex-J.C. Penney parking terrace; the Moxum at 400 South and State (southwest corner), the Cullen Hotel (across from the Capitol Theatre) and the aforementioned Congress Hotel. The Newhouse Hotel, a giant in its day, vanished in a spectacular cloud of dust some three years ago. And the Little Hotel on Main Street has been refurbished as an office building, which is quite justifiable because it began life as the home of the *Salt Lake Herald*.

The Grand Hotel, one of the larger tourist havens of its day, still welcomes guests at 400 South and Main, while the Plandome, up the block at the State Street corner, also remains.

With hope, the restoration of the Peery Hotel will prove as much of a commercial success as its neat-but-not-gaudy outward rehabilitation. Niels Valentiner and Associates, the rehab architects, have decked it out in a coat of warm, russet-brown, chocolaty paint and have shaded the street-level lobby entrances and the Shenanigan's restaurant with dark blue, burgundy-edged awnings, which add to the building's "period look." The rather deep projecting cornices have been repaired and painted, with the paintwork quite properly emphasizing quoins enhancing the corner edges of each of the hotel's three wings.

If you visit the Peery (where a branch of the Trolley Square Pub will shortly be installed) take time to stroll through the ground-floor lobby, which has a dignified front desk and a broad staircase, both gleaming illustrations of the fact that polished hardwood is far handsomer than any plastic yet devised by the world's chemists and engineers. While I'm in no way qualified to comment upon restaurant or bar-room viands or fare, I can report that the Shenanigan's Restaurant, on the east side of the hostelry, seems a very pleasant spot indeed. Fact is, it has the rather indefinable look and feel of a San Francisco eating and drinking haven. As for the guest rooms, they've been reduced in number from the former Hotel Miles' 105 rooms to just 78 rooms in the restored Peery. Not only are the rooms more sizable—all have baths, which was not the case in many of the vintage hotels mentioned above.

Even a cursory glance at the outside of the Peery Hotel will show Salt Lakers how times have changed. The south-facing facade, at 110 W. 300 South, is indented by a pair of rather deep "light wells," giving the building's upper stories an E-shaped plan. The windows are huge by today's standards, meaning the old hostelry's rooms were comparatively light and airy. Times being what they are, the Peery has been air-conditioned, but the huge old windows have been replaced with new ones of equal dimension—windows that can be opened by guests who may want to sample the outside air. As I've tried to indicate in the adjoining sketch, the Salt Lake Sheraton is nearby, with the twin American Towers even closer at hand. Both of those rather severe white giants lack any outward decoration, but are rich in row upon row of rather small-appearing windows. Both look about as hospitable as the Valley Bank and Trust offices just across the way from the Peery.

Not that the Sheraton Towers or the twin American Towers are deliberately cold and sere. They are gleaming white and clean as a hospital and no better or worse than similar structures elsewhere in the city, the nation or the world. The problem, to this observer at least, is that such hotels and apartment buildings seem to have been designed by engineers, seem to resemble file cases in which humanoids store themselves for a night or two. At such places as the Sheraton, the Hilton, Marriott and, perhaps, even the Westin Hotel Utah, a guest feels himself to be merely a number. He or she registers—using a plastic credit card, then rides a computerized elevator. Where, by the way, have elevator operators departed to, along with their uniforms and gloves? Said guest enters a look-alike room on a look-alike corridor. Little wonder weary guests can't quite recall whether they are in Columbus, Ohio, or St. Louis, Mo.

When the nearly forgotten Charles B. Onderdonk designed his hotel for David Henry Peery, it was not as glamorous as San Francisco's Palace, New York's Plaza, or Denver's Brown Palace. But he gave commercial travelers and tourists visiting our town a convenient, long-lived, light and airy, well-heated establishment. It came complete with the requisite dining room, bar and well-upholstered lobby chairs in which a guest from ranch country, a mining town or the big city could enjoy a few moments of relaxation and conversation with his peers. A bellboy paged him if there was a message—no flashing light on a bedside telephone. The newsstand in the lobby doubtless carried our city's four dailies, as well as the *Saturday Evening Post, Collier's, Liberty*, plus an assortment of other magazines. There was a selection of cheroots, nickel "ceegars," pipe and chewing tobacco, along with a favorite package of coffin nails.

Obviously, quite a few of the above one-time necessities of a traveling salesman's life won't be available at the "new" Peery. I neglected to ask partner-owner Vic Kimball or decorator Rich Assenberg whether there's a television set in each room. But there is a satellite dish adorning the building, a certain sign of changing times, even in an elegantly restored old-era hostelry.

# Hansen Planetarium

APRIL 6, 1986

A week or two back, Robert Ruff and other members of the Hansen Planetarium's directors' board reported that the 1905 building now occupied by
our local stargazers is in need of considerable repair work. Knowing Bob
Ruff and several of his colleagues, I think we Salt Lakers who give thought
to the look of our city as well as the heavens can be pretty well assured
that the necessary work will be carried out thoughtfully, when funds are
found, and that the building at 15 S. State will continue to grace the pleasant block between Social Hall Avenue and South Temple for another
lengthy span of years.

    All you need do is examine it for few minutes to assure yourself that
outwardly it is a one-of-a-kind gem. If you step inside even briefly, you will
quickly realize it is a prime example of the manner in which an aging structure can be put to new and very practical uses.

32

As a considerable number of Utahns will remember, this gracefully decorated building served as Salt Lake's major public library for fully a half-century. When writing of the neighboring Alta Club a while back, I mistakenly asserted that the club's architect, Frederick A. Hale, also had designed the library. A check in John McCormick's *Historic Buildings of Downtown Salt Lake* showed me my mistake. Hale was the "supervising local architect," but the design was by a very prestigious New York firm, Hines and LaFarge, and a very handsome utilitarian building resulted.

Then, as now, a pair of spiral stairways led from the entry lobby to an upstairs area where gleaming glass cases housed specially guarded volumes, and to a small auditorium suitable for meetings by such organizations as the League of Women Voters and a variety of fine arts groups. There was, of course, a children's library where the bookish promise of "infinite riches in a little room" proved to be true to many incipient devotees of the printed word.

When the George T. Hansen family made possible the provision of one of those newfangled planetariums in our town, the far larger and more modish library on 500 South was completed and has more than proved its worth. But so has the remodeled local haven for youngsters and oldsters intrigued by the parade of the planets, by adventuring in space and in the predictability of Halley's sky voyager. Architect Wesley Budd, who designed the additions and reconstruction work necessary for converting a public library into a public teaching aid concerned with the heavens, did a splendid job. The old, polished woodwork of the staircases, the oak walls upstairs and down, remain largely intact—and yet the gleaming Foucault Pendulum, mezzanine displays and the planetarium auditorium itself all fit snugly into the old structure.

Outside, one hopes your eyes will be sharp enough (despite having absorbed a multitude of library volumes) to see the details above the classic Beaux Arts portico of the old building. A very large third-story window is centered above the triple windows and doors of the entry lobby. Above this big-paned window a carved wreath very properly and proudly encloses an open book of carved stone. A balustrade above the portico gracefully curves above the rounded walls defining the twin stairways.

And, in addition to hedges and plantings softening the base, a very playful, very ingenious fountain donated by Obert C. and Grace Tanner reproduces, in sprays of water, the shape of our globe. At this season of the year kids by the droves alight from big yellow school buses outside the planetarium, and the fountain, one observes, has become almost as much an attraction as the big globe and the space-shot exhibits inside.

If the library-turned-planetarium has a flaw, it is that it was built of Sanpete limestone, a yellowish, off-white stone called oolite in the geology textbooks. Unfortunately, it is, for limestone, rather soft, spalling readily in our climate of alternate hot sun and frigid, icy, snowy winter. The Governor's Mansion (the former Kearns Mansion) on South Temple, is built of similarly troublesome oolite, while some of the problems of the Salt Lake City and County Building also center around the negative qualities of equally soft Utah stone.

The old public library has another link with the City and County Building. Back in 1898, when there was no truly public library, the new state legislature permitted the utilization of a special tax for public libraries. Salt Lake City, its coffers thus legally enriched, spent $1,400 to purchase a library from the Grand Masonic Lodge of Utah, a library estimated to be worth $24,000 by the knowledgeable scholars of that period. Having no library building, those books were housed in the big new City and County Building in Washington Square park. The Ladies Literary Club was then credited with "persuading an eccentric mining millionaire" named John Q. Packard into donating both the site and construction funds for the 1905 building on State Street.

One wonders whether he was any more eccentric than multimillionaire Andrew Carnegie, who was concurrently sprinkling public libraries throughout our land.

# Historic Judge Building

APRIL 16, 1989

While strolling down the city's chief business boulevard one superlative spring morning, I was caught up short—and saddened—by a "closing business" sign in the window of the Chas. Felt men's shop, perhaps the last establishment in Salt Lake that could properly be designated as a "haberdashery." Previously, this genteel gentleman's clothier's shop at 307 S. Main was owned and operated by Howard Collins. Howard turned the latchkey over to employee Charles Felt when he, Collins, retired at least a dozen years ago.

Now with the equally knowledgeable Mr. Felt retiring, gentlemen wishing well-fitted garb of a certain quality will be forced to seek jackets, vests, trousers, ties, belts, shirts and handkerchiefs in the menswear section of faceless, vast, midmall department stores. No more Fife's, Frank's or Hibbs.

Alas, elderly suits bearing their memorable labels remaining in my closet won't button round my increasingly rotund midsection, and my suits from Chas. Felt may suffer a similar fate.

However, while my haberdasher is fading like the last rose of summer, the Judge Building next to his emporium stands sturdy, handsomely renovated and well maintained at 8 E. Broadway, where it has lasted since 1907. Through the years, its seven stories of shops and offices have held an intriguing mix of major and minor tenants, and that's still the case today.

Before my time in town, the major street-level space now occupied by the U.S. Bank was the busy headquarters and ticket office of the Denver & Rio Grande Railroad, a location convenient to the rail line's big station a half-mile west on 300 South.

Of course, the most notable—and unfortunate—event in the Judge Building's long life came to pass only recently, when a blackguard named Hofmann delivered a bomb to the office of a young businessman named Christensen. The explosion brought death to the latter, a life sentence for the former, and a trio of much-discussed nonfiction books expected to produce a spate of movie films and television specials before many more months have passed.

But the Judge Building is, in the main, a cheerful place, especially if you seek out the bright and gleaming Judge Cafe, back of the office building's main lobby. The Judge Cafe, lest you've never entered same, is the favorite gathering place of some members of the Utah Jazz. Players, staff, fans, media folk and autograph seekers meet in this setting of polished wood, smooth white bar and clean-swept tile floor to discuss victories, defeats and multimillion-dollar plans for a new arena. One added note concerning the cafe's decor: some two dozen pairs of autographed sneakers, worn by such worthies as Karl Malone and Darrell Griffith, are neatly aligned atop the pantry closets back of the bar—and well out of reach of even the tallest prospective sneaker-snatcher.

Who was the interior decorator? Frank Layden? He denies it.

Now, as in its heyday, the Judge Building's upper floors are a haven for lawyers, accountants and even court reporters.

The most intriguing name among the barristers currently listed is a rather improbable one—a chap named Daniel Boone. But mention of the Judge Building to an attorney "of the old school" will bring on nostalgic memories of legal lights aplenty who once graced the Judge Building's halls. "That's where I first practiced back in 1937, in an office on the seventh floor," Clifford Ashton reports. The famed firm of Rawlings, Wallace and Black (well known for its clout in Democratic Party circles) had major offices in the building. Likewise Dan Shields, Vern McCullough, Fred Finlinson and other students of Blackstone.

Ladies interested in high fashion, rather than divorce, came to the Judge Building to patronize the long-vanished Beau Monde Shop, where millinery and fashionable wear were rivaled only by an outstanding set of stained glass windows. Ladies—or gents—could likewise indulge a sweet tooth in the gleaming white premises of See's Candy Shop, or purchase big, heart-shaped boxes of chocolate creams, caramels or luscious bonbons when Valentine's Day approached.

The Judge Building, as designed by architect David C. Dart, came into being at the command of Mary H. Judge, whose real estate interests were financed by a substantial tonnage of silver flowing from Park City's Silver King and Mayflower mines. A lessee of the latter and part-owner of the former, John Judge led an interesting life, to say the least. As a lad in New York State he worked in iron mines, then fought in the 2nd New York Cavalry in the first years of the Civil War. He was captured, imprisoned, managed to escape—but was recaptured by Confederate prison guards who tracked him down with bloodhounds.

Whether or not John Judge was intrigued by prisons, his first job in Utah when he came West was as a guard at the territorial prison in Sugarhouse. He soon sent for his wife, Mary, and their five children.

But after "striking it rich" in Park City, Judge died of "miner's consumption" in 1892 at the age of forty-two. Fortunately, his wife "invested well," chiefly in real estate, including the Judge Building. Her charitable contributions were many, including generous gifts to the Cathedral of the Madeleine. Just before her death in 1909 (when her estate was valued at three million dollars), she paid for construction of a home for aged and ailing miners. The building, never used for its intended purpose, was converted instead into the initial building of today's Judge Memorial High School. And, of course, the still very serviceable Judge Building at Broadway and Main continues as a long-lasting testimonial to one of the city's first businesswomen.

# Refurbished Pierpont Avenue

JUNE 8, 1986

Cities, like oceans, seem to have an ebb and flow all their own. At the moment the tidal stream in Salt Lake City seems to be moving east and west, meaning you can chart a rising tide of office construction east of Main Street, while a swirl of building and remodeling work for hotels, restaurants and night spots occurs on the city's west side.

The west side's most ambitious project, the cause of much hammering, troweling and partition-placing, is occurring on Pierpont Avenue, just beyond the oddly truncated parking terrace serving the Shilo Inn. The buildings being renovated, refurbished and restored for a reported sum of 1.5 million dollars are located at 126 and 140 Pierpont, a pair of once doddering structures that most folks would hardly have deemed worth saving.

Not so, Tom Seig and his ambitious, upbeat associates who, having placed seafood spas and clubs in the old New York Hotel and a 1300 East firehouse, have opted for a Mexican beanery at the Pierpont Avenue address. Did I say beanery? From the look of things, when the Pierpont Cafe opens in July or thereabouts, the old buildings with luck will have been transformed into things of beauty and joy forever. If the culinary delights match the newly renovated buildings, we will be well serviced.

The side-by-side structures have a curious history, having served respectively as a railroad station, our town's first high school, a National Guard armory and the long-lived home of the Western Newspaper Union. German-born Carl Neuhausen designed the right-hand, or easternmost building in 1897 as a depot and headquarters for the new Oregon Shortline Railroad, which extended north from Salt Lake City through Idaho to the Columbia River country. Until recently, some Union Pacific locomotives and freight cars still carried OSL markings, although the UPRR bought the small road at the turn of the century.

When the Union Pacific expanded its system, it likewise built a far larger station, giving passengers a handsome red brick affair at the end of South Temple close to today's Triad Center. Meantime, in 1898 Neuhausen also designed the westernmost structure, taller and rather more ornate, as seen in the accompanying sketch. It accommodated the Salt Lake High School, whose pupils must have been hard-put to study, what with the coming and going of OSL locomotives and trains on the Pierpont tracks. When the first structure now utilized as West High was built, the two rather modest buildings were used as a Utah National Guard headquarters, and the school gym became a drill floor.

By the time World War II erupted, the National Guard moved up to Fort Douglas, and the presses of the Western Newspaper Union were anchored on big concrete foundations in the basement of the structure. Trucks arrived with rolls of newsprint and rolled out editions of many of the region's weeklies.

Those concrete press foundations were to cause considerable grief for the FFKR architectural firm, better known as Fowler, Ferguson, Kingston, and Ruben. Its principals were not only charged with inserting a club and a cafe into the buildings, but they've been completing a galaxy of handsome offices on both the upper and basement levels of the refurbished structures.

The only outward change in the building visible from the street, the trio of rather odd triangles visible above the second floor of the smaller structure, are windows lighting some of the new offices in an area adjacent to a lofty galleria extending through much of the building. Fact is, the interior is so nicely illuminated by natural daylight, the architects have themselves taken up quarters in this Greenwich Village-style loft.

Meanwhile, as is often the case when thoughtful restoration or remodeling occurs, the entire square block adjacent to West Temple and Pierpont seems likely to benefit. Louis Ulrich, one of the architects involved, reports that sidewalks are to be improved, trees planted—and we may soon see an outdoor cafe on Pierpont Street. The Peery Hotel, with its Pub Club and Shenanigans Restaurant, is less than a block away. However, the big parking lot across the way could stand some improvement, such as shade trees, or possibly a hedge of the sort that now hides at least a portion of the parking lot alongside the nearby New Yorker.

Only a few of the buildings in this long-lived commercial neighborhood are embellished with detailing of the sort the sharp-eyed stroller can spot on the facade of old Salt Lake High. Its cornice is topped by a pediment that has lost the easternmost upper ledge of its detailed molding, but the triangular pediments topping the central windows in each bay as well as the little Roman arch above the central window and doorway all show architect Neuhausen's classical training.

One supposes the high arched entryway soon will be restored to its former style. Meanwhile, the paired buildings gleam with fresh white paint, giving this extremely down-at-the-heels street a new air and flair. Several sizable factory and business buildings close by, such as Sweet Candy Co. and Patrick Dry Goods have been spruced up and repainted in the past few years. If architect Neuhausen (who also designed the Cathedral of the Madeleine) is looking down upon his restored handiwork, he must be pleased.

# The *News* / KSL / Union Pacific Building

JANUARY 1, 1992

Our town's Central Business District begins, according to municipal map-makers, just opposite South Temple from the Hotel Utah and Temple Square. On one side of Main Street, the Kennecott Building and ZCMI are its anchors. But across Main, its ground floor occupied until recently by the Citicorp Bank (and temporarily by Zions Bank), there stands a modern-appearing building sheathed in vertical bands of black and white metal.

If you are old enough to recall the years before and immediately after World War II, you will remember its original version—looking much like the six-story structure in today's sketch, a drawing made from a *Salt Lake Tribune* photo dating from 1960.

The rather unfortunate black-and-white facade applied to the building in 1965 or thereabouts was, it seems to me, the first such major modernizing of an elderly structure in the downtown district. Applied by the construction firm of Horne and Zwick, the smooth, shiny, monotonous front completely hides the 1899–1902 efforts of architect Richard Kletting to give the city a superior office building in the then-popular Richardsonian Romanesque style.

The initial facade of the building, before the Walgreen's Drug Store gave the ground floor a partial black-and-white appearance, was russet in color. Its surface of rusticated stone was deeply pierced by tall windows, with two groups of such windows topped off on the Main Street side by stone arches, while three groups of windows on the South Temple side were also embellished by arches.

Occupying a historic Church of Jesus Christ of Latter-day Saints site, the building was variously identified by visitors according to use. The *Deseret News*, being an initial major occupant, called it the News Building. Radio station KSL, with twin towers topping the roof in graceful style, usually referred to it as the KSL Building. Since the major downtown offices of the Union Pacific Railroad were housed on several floors, railroaders called it the Union Pacific Building. Those tenants are all gone now, but those readers with failing memories might want a brief review.

Those being the days when the UPRR was a major player in the state's power structure, journalists such as the *Tribune-Telegram*'s business editor Bob Bernick made frequent treks to the offices of Joel Priest, the railroad's public-relations man. His office was, if memory serves, one or two floors above a big marble and wood-paneled lobby.

If Mr. Priest chanced to be traveling to Boise, Las Vegas, Omaha or even Ogden, his efficient secretary, Gwen Hovey, could usually answer most queries. Alas, Mr. Priest is no longer with us, but Mrs. Hovey is still extant, serving as a board member of such worthy organizations as the Friends of the Marriott Library at the university.

But it is as "headquarters" for 50,000-watt radio station KSL that the disguised building at Main and South Temple was best known to most Salt Lakers. KSL, lest you've forgotten, had its beginnings in 1921 in this very building, on the city's 132-foot-wide Main Street, long before the sidewalks were rebuilt, long before angle parking was abolished. Fact is, there may have been no parking meters on the street back in 1921, when one Earl J. Glade put KSL on the air—from the basement of the six-story "skyscraper."

By 1940, when much of Europe was aflame with Hitler's war, Utah had, the statisticians tell us, fully ninety radio sets for every one hundred families. How many were Atwater-Kents, how many were Stromberg Carlsons or Philcos I know not—but certainly very few bore "made in Japan" labels.

Meanwhile, at some point in its career, KSL quit utilizing its tall rooftop towers and switched the transmitters to the shores of the Great Salt Lake. By that juncture, of course, you could hear broadcasts of music by the traveling "big bands" from Saltair, not far from the new transmitter. And you could, especially at New Year's time, hear our local broadcasts "direct from the rooftop" or ballroom of the Hotel Utah. The hotel was just across the way. A wonderful thing indeed, that entertainment medium called radio.

KSL and CBS were then, and are now, among the leaders in a region that boasts forty, not four, radio stations.

Time passed, announced hourly on radio stations of course. Not "railroad time," but newfangled daylight-saving time. The Union Pacific, which had its ticket offices across the way in the Hotel Utah, was persuaded by business needs to move its passenger offices to a new (and reputedly drafty) building at 400 South and Main, where the First Security Bank had also installed new offices.

And by 1969 or thereabouts, just a few years after the old Union Pacific Building was "restored" with its new, modern-style sheathing and necessary air conditioning, the railroad moved most of its operations to the big station at the foot of South Temple.

Meanwhile, at date uncertain, the *Deseret News* had moved its editorial offices to a modest building near 100 South at Regent Street, adjacent to the pressrooms of the Newspaper Agency Corporation. Strike off another tenant from the list at the six-story stone fortress.

Down the block you could still have lunch at the Utah Cafe or shop at Adrian and Emily's. But not for long—a mall would arrive almost before you could say John Bogis, that being the name of the gentleman who owned the Utah Cafe.

Simultaneously, another new era had its beginnings over on Social Hall Avenue, a thoroughfare you once knew as "Automobile Row." In 1950 or thereabouts, KDYL-TV, with the late Bennett Larson and Danny Rainger as manager and program director, respectively, opened new studios under the ownership of Time-Life Corp. Not to be outdone, KSL-TV, hiring Paul James and Bob Welti from their rivals as sportscaster and weather-man, respectively, likewise built new studios, as did KUTV.

The old Main Street building had lost its radio station, its newly weaned TV station, the newspaper offices and the railroad. No wonder the building is hard to recognize or recall. And of course KSL is no longer on Social Hall Avenue—it having moved again, this time to the Triad Center. Nothing is permanent, certainly not radio—nor the look of a station's first home.

# The Century-old LDS Temple

MAY 9, 1993

This being the one hundredth anniversary of the completion and dedication of the Church of Jesus Christ of Latter-day Saints' Salt Lake Temple, it may be a proper time to give serious thought to the six-spired granite structure and its look.

Of course, one hundred years is scarcely a moment in the long existence of major ecclesiastic structures around the globe.

If not notably old, why does the rugged, honest look of the 186-foot-long Salt Lake Temple hold so much of our interest? Cyrus Dallin's gleaming conception of trumpet-bearing angel Moroni stands atop a 210-foot-high east central tower. That's a considerable altitude, but many spires, such as the ornate High Gothic crossing tower of England's Canterbury Cathedral, are taller.

Not age, nor size, nor height, yet many Utahns are seeing the temple with a new, appreciative look. Hugh Garner, a Salt Lake City attorney and member of the Utah Historical Society board, recently told me: "I happened to round the Main Street corner last night just as the floodlights on Temple Square came on. The sight of the temple was gorgeous. I was overwhelmed."

Scores of Utahns must be descended from the workmen who laboriously cut the great granite blocks from Little Cottonwood Canyon's walls, drove oxen and wagon teams that hauled the heavy stones down the steep canyon, dug canals used for the task, or piloted rail cars in latter years of construction. Workmen built scaffolding and operated derricks, masons troweled the stones securely—after they were cut and fitted into place. Their progeny must look at the temple with understandable and special pride.

Watercolorist Sally Howe Rosenblatt reminded me one day that her grandfather and great-grandfather, whose Davis-Howe Foundry and Machine works once stood on West Temple, had cast the framework for the famed oxen that support the temple's baptismal font. George Edward Howe is "a family legend and hero," although many of his descendants have only seen the oxen in photographs.

Another intriguing interest in the structure's present appearance can be found in the temple's secure place in local art, history and photography. Camera-work historian Nelson Wadsworth has produced a fascinating volume on the construction and history of the rising structure. An equally absorbing exhibit of drawings, plans and photographs of the temple is at the church's art museum.

An artistic example can be seen in a pleasant watercolor by Al Rounds. It shows the temple as few still alive ever saw it. Its spires rise above and beyond Brigham Young's Beehive House, and above an unpaved road occupied by two team-drawn wagons.

Mr. Rounds must have painted from old photos, old drawings—and from his imagination, imaging the scene so many of us believe must have existed before the century's turning.

Now is an especially good time to walk around the temple block, between flower beds, past Temple Square's statues and fountains and to study the thick-walled, sturdy temple.

Hopefully, you will give some thought, and much credit, to church architect Truman O. Angell. Of course LDS prophet Brigham Young claimed he envisioned the temple. But it was Angell, immured in a tiny office, who drew the plans.

There are, of course, the requisite Moon Stones and Earth Stones, Sun Stones and seven stars carved to represent the Big Dipper. Inspiration for these and other religious symbols came from LDS scripture and the destroyed Nauvoo Temple.

But there are no carved saints, no Jesus, no gargoyles—suchlike are reserved for cathedrals.

It was Angell who gave the temple its unity. It has buttresses—but is not Gothic. It has parapets not unlike those of the Tower of London—but is not an English or Scottish castle.

A week or so ago, a Holladay resident, in the *Salt Lake Tribune*'s letters to the editor, took issue with my appraisal of the new San Diego Temple, in part because I did not venture inside. Dear reader, there is no need to enter the Salt Lake Temple to appreciate it. Its towers and the major structure are unified.

What seems most important is that Angell did his work well. As the old WPA *Guide to Utah* points out, this monumental edifice "represents more the inspiration and theologic functionalism of its founders than any one architectural style."

Its architect and the men who spent so many years building it were diligent and honest—in the tradition of Abbot Suger at St. Denis, or Jean de Chelles, who basically designed Notre Dame in Paris (circa 1258). He and his fellows were directly in the traditions of the unknown and unsung men who designed and built the great cathedrals through the centuries across all the Western world.

CHAPTER 3

# Where People Lived—
# Magnificent Mansions and Homes

# The McCune Mansion

AUGUST 23, 1987

By the turn of the century—that is to say, by 1900—our city's premier residential "boulevard" was lined with the very sizable mansions of a dozen newly minted Utah millionaires. Known as Brigham Street in the rags-to-riches era during which precious metals flowed from Park City, Bingham Canyon and Eureka, the tree-lined thoroughfare which we call East South Temple had its beginnings as the prestigious residential street of our town when Brigham Young ordered construction of the Gardo House across the way from the Beehive House.

According to historian Margaret D. Lester, it was to be used "for social purposes," with Brigham's twenty-fifth wife, Amelia Folsom, slated to serve as hostess to entertain visiting dignitaries. He died in 1877 before its completion, and the structure, popularly known as Amelia's Palace, was sold to the "Silver Queen" Susanna Egeria Bransford Emery Holmes, who ordered it enlarged and remodeled in Second Empire style.

Meanwhile, sizable mansions such as the Thomas Kearns residence, the Dinwoodey home, the Judge mansion, Dern mansion and Matthew Walker home rose on Brigham/South Temple. But it remained for one Alfred McCune and his wife to decide bigger could be better, and apparently, to reason that by building uphill on Main Street, they could "look down" upon the nouveau riche of the community. After all, McCune had been born in India where his army-officer father helped maintain the British Raj. Very possibly the family fled the heat of Calcutta each summer for the high, cool, hill country. In any event, the McCunes built their mansion uphill at what is now 200 N. Main, on an elevated site still providing a sweeping view of the city, valley and mountains.

Most East South Temple nabobs had employed such very competent, but local architects as Carl Neuhausen, Richard Kletting or Ware and Treganza to design their pretend palazzos or castles. But the McCunes, no pikers they, sent their architect, S.C. Dallas, to distant Europe to be more fully versed in overseas culture and styles. On his return, and in part following the lines of the Fifth Avenue mansions his clients had glimpsed in New York, Dallas blueprinted a huge (for Salt Lake City) turreted, tile-roofed, veranda-rimmed building of a style many nowadays associate with the Newport, R.I., summer homes of East Coast multimillionaires.

Built of dark red brick on a heavy brownstone base, and occupying a very large corner lot, the mansion featured a rotunda-topped, circular entryway on its southwestern extremity. As a result, imaginative members of the present generation can envision spanking teams of carriage horses circling beneath the canopy to disgorge, or even debouch, high-styled, tightly corseted ladies coming to take tea with the McCunes in their not-so-modest bungalow.

Then as now, visitors enjoyed the opulence of rooms in which newel posts, columns, moldings and window trim were solid oak or mahogany. Bathrooms were tiled to a fare-thee-well and given a further "air of class" through a plentiful use of "genuine marble." Cut glass or crystals were affixed to chandeliers, the walls were covered in brocade, and the third-story room inside the curved turret had, in addition to a sweeping view across the city, a frieze painted by an artist (now unsung) of the sort of forest scene most often associated with Fragonard.

The McCunes, who moved in in 1901, did not take root for long in

Salt Lake City, moving to the gentler clime and more exotic life of Los Angeles in 1920 or thereabouts.

As they departed, the McCunes made a generous gift of their very sizable mansion to the Church of Jesus Christ of Latter-day Saints, in the belief that it would serve as a new home for LDS presidents in years to come. But according to historian Margaret Lester, the mansion was considered "inappropriate."

Perhaps it was feared in that simpler era that tithe payers, often simple rural folk, might resent their First Family living in a style better suited to a mining millionaire—or even a traction company magnate. For, parenthetically, Alfred McCune, besides a considerable interest in mining and forest products companies, owned the local trolley car system prior, I believe, to its operation by the UP&L's traction interest.

Instead of housing church presidents the mansion was then occupied by the McCune School of Music and Art. The school used the building for well over a quarter century, until, in 1951, Brigham Young University took it over as headquarters for its extension courses. A decade later it was converted for use as business offices and for receptions and the like.

However, for many young and old Salt Lakers the building is best remembered as the headquarters and studios of a most remarkable woman, namely dancer-educator Virginia Tanner. One feature of the mansion was and is a very sizable ballroom, complete with hardwood floors and walls lined with oversized mirrors. Miss Tanner, nationally known as an educator as well as a dancer, was of the opinion that very young children could not only learn to dance in the classic and modern manner—but could choreograph their own works.

As a result, tykes wearing "Ginny gowns," simple flowing garments resembling old-fashioned nightgowns, daily circled the big ballroom in long lines and short lines, in precise or imprecise patterns, dancing up a storm, very often to the works of Mozart, Bach and Tchaikovsky. Down through the years, both before and after the Virginia Tanner Dancers moved to the university campus, the organization won national awards and acclaim, appearing in Washington, D.C., being seen on that newly arrived medium called television and in the pages of *Life* magazine and other publications.

Virginia Tanner, is, unfortunately, no longer alive, but the dance movement she did so much to foster remains part of the Salt Lake scene, in particular the Children's Dance Theatre which she founded at the U. of U. some years ago.

Many of the small-fry who danced around the mirrored ballroom of the McCune Mansion went on to join the Utah Civic Ballet, Ballet West, Repertory Dance Theatre and the Ririe-Woodbury modern dancers, or groups beyond the borders of Utah. Thus the McCune Mansion remains a building of happy memories for the parents of budding dancers, as well as their offspring.

# Salt Lake's First All-electrical Home

SEPTEMBER 29, 1991

As most walkers in our town know, the cityscape in the neighborhood where the Avenues blend into the Federal Heights district is one of the most pleasant of sights these days, with mums and impatiens still in full bloom in many yards just as sycamore, maple and oaks are tinged with autumn color.

Strolling along Third Avenue at its intersection with Alta Street, the pedestrian—or leisurely motorist—can't help but be struck with the unchanged quality of a section of town that has retained its status among the finest in the city for many years. It's nearly a century since some of these spacious-appearing homes were built, while a majority have stood solidly in place (and price) for at least fifty years.

While most such big, old, tree-shaded dwellings reflected the prevailing taste of comparatively wealthy Salt Lakers who avoided the new and

55

the conspicuous, not every such "revival" home lacked innovations—interior innovations not visible from the street. The biggest surprise came with the discovery of a booklet concerning the two-story, red-brick home at 1348 Third Avenue that noted this outwardly typical building was our town's first "all-electrical home."

Back in the early 1920s, there was a Rocky Mountain Electrical Cooperative League, an organization including the Utah Power & Light Co., Edison Electric Appliance Co., Fairbanks Morse Co., Walker Electric Supply Co. and Wasatch Electric Co. among its major components. This league sought, among other things, to inform the public "regarding the possibilities for correct illumination and the convenient use of appliances in the home, office or industrial plant through the proper wiring and location of electrical outlets."

That being the case, when railroad man L.B. Swaner decided to build a suitable family home on upper Third Avenue, he decided, or was persuaded, to make his new dwelling the town's first model "electrical home."

What's more, "through special arrangement with the builder, the Electrical League has planned and installed all the electrical features found in the home from the wiring to the selection and furnishing of electrical appliances and fixtures."

As one result, this three-bedroom home had—and possibly still has—some 150 electrical outlets and nearly 50 switches between its full basement and its rooftop ridgepole.

A dining room, breakfast room and a kitchen all were well equipped for push-button electrical living of the day.

In those long-gone days, a proper electrical home such as this was fully equipped with a well-lighted "reception hall," a rear hall (which had a refrigerator outlet), porch lights, cornice lights and yard lights. The main-bedroom plan shows few surprises with the exception of a phone-extension outlet, but it boasted six bracket lights. By the by, the living room downstairs had a full quota of seven bracket lights. There's no sign, in this musically equipped household, of a special outlet for the Christmas tree or electric trains.

The booklet, detailing the finer points of the Swaner home, is full of timely advice—as welcome today as way back when. "Do not consider the kitchen complete unless you have an exhaust fan. . . . It keeps kitchen odors out of the house, keeps the kitchen cool and saves deterioration of hangings and upholstery. . . . It may also be used to ventilate sleeping rooms on sultry nights by closing all downstairs windows and running the fan . . . to draw a current of air through all bedroom windows."

And, advises the Electrical Co-op, installation of at least one side-wall fixture over the sink and another over the range "will save much china breakage and speed the work."

Despite all such good advice, Mrs. J. Robert Stewart, who, with her husband, "much enjoys the house," has redone the kitchen, one reason being that the old mid-wall outlets were unsightly. The kitchen "was of course designed for a maid or cook," and the present occupants have neither. But otherwise, the interior is little changed—although the early monitor-top GE refrigerator is long gone. "We've redone the porch-sunroom on the east side," the owner says, and the maid's "apartment" in the basement has been transformed into spare family rooms.

Just three families have occupied the home in its 65-plus years—the Swaners, the David Lawrence McKay family and the Stewarts. The coal-fired furnace apparently vanished in the McKay years, with a gas-fired forced air system as the replacement. Being a home in which light, bright colors were utilized rather than dark brown-stained wood finishes, its interior look remains much the same as when the Swaners were its occupants.

But furniture styles have changed a great deal, meaning the all-electric home of today has an airier "look." And at least one partition, that between the kitchen and breakfast room, has vanished.

According to the present Leland (Lee) Swaner, this Third Avenue all-electric house was a happy family home indeed for some twenty years. His father, who did considerable traveling for railroad companies, had seen many differently styled homes in many cities and chose the plans to be followed according to his own and his wife's taste.

"In fact, Dad became so intrigued he also designed and built the house at the Alta Street corner (124 Alta) directly to the east." It's an equally large, well-styled, red-brick affair.

Lee Swaner can remember just one single fault with the now elderly house—and that fault did not concern electric power. "Dad planted most of the existing trees," recalls Lee. "The most bothersome was that big sycamore—still standing. Did you ever try to rake sycamore leaves when they fall? They are like iron—and weigh a ton apiece."

JACK GOODMAN '90

# The Kahn House, a Victorian Showplace

APRIL 1, 1990

What with specially installed asphalt channels, doubled turn lanes, sema-phore arrows and similar engineering aids designed to speed traffic flow and prevent traffic "friction," the intersection of South Temple and 700 East is so efficiently busy that motorists are rarely foolhardy enough to halt even briefly for a glimpse of the nearby buildings. As a result, while you've kept your fenders intact, you may have never taken note of the wondrously pic-turesque brick and wood edifice at 678 E. South Temple, a structure en-riched by "gingerbread," leaded glass, shingled gables, a graceful tower, shady porches, artfully managed brick chimneys and other Victorian ele-ments.

Designed by Henry Monheim, and dating to the 1880s, it is known to locals as "the Kahn House," and serves to remind knowledgeable Utahns that today's tiny hamlet of Corinne (near Brigham City) was once a commercial center of considerable "gentile" significance.

Nowadays, the turreted building is no longer a residence, and the family of owner Emanuel Kahn, once sizable and prestigious, has vanished with the valley snows. Fortunately for those of us who enjoy the "look" of Victorian mansions, the businessmen who now own 678 E. South Temple have preserved it in meticulous style. In fact, when extending it a dozen yards south, they artfully built a wooden addition that precisely imitates the main section of the elderly brick structure. But, back to Emanuel Kahn and Corinne.

According to an account of the Kahn clan found in Margaret Lester's excellent book *Brigham Street*, the first member of this Jewish family to reach Utah was Prussian-born Samuel Kahn, who settled in Great Salt Lake City in 1859, where he promptly became a partner of Nicholas S. Ransohoff in a dry goods firm. About the time Ransohoff departed for San Francisco (where he established a long-lived department store) a younger Kahn brother, Emanuel, arrived on the scene. The brothers then joined forces with one George Bodenburg to establish a wholesale and retail grocery and dry goods business that was soon serving customers in the mining towns of Idaho and Montana as well as Utah. The Bodenburg and Kahn emporium was a one-story affair that stood, as early as 1863, on the northeast corner of Main and First South, flanked by the rival Hooper, Eldredge and Co. shop and a good-sized liquor store and tavern.

A few years later older brother Samuel Kahn married one Sarah Cohn, while Emanuel married her sister Fanny Cohn. Bodenburg, like Ransohoff, then disappeared from the local commercial scene—and the firm of Kahn Brothers was formed in 1867 to become a major force in the wholesale grocery trade. Shortly afterwards another large dry goods firm came into being when the Cohn brothers, Louis and Alexander, opened a store on Main Street. Nowadays, quite a few old-timers, including Simon Frank, remember it as a "minidepartment store." The family relationships being so closely knit, it seems likely the Kahns helped the Cohns set up their increasingly flourishing business venture.

While that remains conjecture, it is true the brother-sister bonds were so tight that when architect Henry Monheim designed a home for the Emanuel Kahn family, he did the same for the Cohns. Very soon there was a Louis Cohn house at 666 E. South Temple, an Alexander Cohn house at 670 E. South Temple, and the aforementioned Kahn mansion at 678 E.

South Temple. The two Cohn homes, a mite smaller than the Kahn place, were demolished in 1975, for, I believe, the parking lots east of the Masonic Temple. If you are at all interested in local genealogy, it's intriguing to note that the Cohn brothers also married sisters, Carrie and Jennie Lippman.

So far as I can learn, no descendants of Emanuel Kahn or his older brother Samuel remain in the Salt Lake area. But some of their good works linger. For example, Emanuel was active in the formation of the Congregation B'nai Israel, which has melded into today's Jewish Congregation Kol Ami. He is also listed as a member of Wasatch Lodge Number 1 of the Masonic Order. And Margaret Lester (herself for years the librarian of the Utah State Historical Society) reports Emanuel Kahn was "the originator of the Masonic library in 1874." That library, in its turn, was one of the progenitors of the present Salt Lake City Public Library.

And what of Corinne? The Kahns were, alas, among the "gentile" merchants who incurred the considerable wrath of Brigham Young, who disliked otherwise faithful members of his flock purchasing foodstuffs and goods from nonmembers of the Church of Jesus Christ of Latter-day Saints. As one result, Mormon merchants were banded into the Zions Cooperative Mercantile Association, today's ZCMI. As another result, following the established wagon train and railroad routes to points north and west, the Kahns and other Salt Lake merchants set up shop in Corinne in the expectation that the lively "burg on the Bear" would soon become a major non-Mormon commercial center. That never happened, in part because ever astute Brigham Young instituted construction of church-financed railroad links between Ogden, Salt Lake City and other centers, effectively countering the effort to make Corinne the region's major freighting center.

Many gentile merchants removed themselves and their trade stocks from Utah when the Corinne effort failed, but the Kahns (and Cohns) revived their Salt Lake business efforts and flourished until at least the 1890s, when they occupied their costly new homes on East South Temple. When the last of Emanuel Kahn's family vacated 678 E. South Temple I know not. True, there was one prominent man of the same name hereabouts in post-World-War II years, but I'm told this gentleman, Jake Kahn, who headed the local General Electric Co., was not connected with the home in question.

*Drawing Courtesy of Don Rosenblatt*

# The Prairie Style Cameron Home /
# The Haven

MAY 8, 1988

Shortly after the turn of the century there was a considerable vogue, even in the Intermountain Region, for building large homes in the "Prairie style." Still easily recognized, these were and are low-roofed buildings characterized by a "look" and outward detailing significantly influenced by Frank Lloyd Wright's justly famous Robie House in Chicago. Among Utah architects who were somewhat smitten with the style were the principals of the Salt Lake firm of Ware and Treganza.

Among the half-dozen or so homes Walter Ware and his partner did in the style then in fashion, the Cameron house at 974 E. South Temple remains outwardly unchanged despite its very different usage as "The Haven," a rehabilitation home for alcoholic men and women.

Dr. Peter Goss, one of Utah's best-known architectural historians, points out that predominant Prairie style elements at The Haven, easily spotted by observant nonprofessionals, include the hipped roof with its very wide overhangs, rows of indented brick alternating with the normal facing, stone banding beneath some of the windows, plus the very typical deep, well-shaded front porch. Not so typical of the period are the geometric stucco inserts placed within the brick at the second story level, squares now painted in a rather unharmonious pinkish-cream color.

The home was built for Frank N. Cameron, who, without the urging of a gubernatorial commission, established his Cameron Coal Co. in the Carbon County coal fields after coming from his native Pennsylvania in 1902. Then, while serving as a director of the Utah Savings and Trust Co., he and his wife decided to build a city home on prestigious Brigham Street, now East South Temple. The original plans, much revised, were filed with the city in 1908—and called for a "brick, iron and concrete" house of eight rooms, costing fully $9,000. The Cameron home soon took shape, with the usual hardwood flooring, decorative leaded glass, well-detailed banisters, and an up-to-date (for the time) kitchen and pantry. A large living room and dining room opened on each side of the entry. There was the requisite breakfast nook, and, upstairs, five bedrooms, two baths and a "sewing room." At some later date, a trio of bedrooms was added in the basement, very possibly for servants. When the Camerons departed, the late Dr. Milton Pepper had his office and reception room on the main floor.

The Pepper family has continued to own the house for some thirty-five years. Since 1969 when Kearns McCartney helped establish an experimental and unique "boardinghouse" for alcoholics, the old home has been leased by The Haven for use as a rehabilitation center.

Meanwhile, another mansion on old Brigham Street, the 1917 William Edward Fife home at the corner of I Street serves a somewhat similar purpose. The latter, a handsome building of black brick set off by stark white corner quoins and located at 667 E. South Temple, is "for men only" and is largely funded with state dollars. The Haven continues to be largely dependent upon contributions. True, some of its men and women guests pay for board and room, but others lack funds to do so.

By the by, if memory serves correctly, Mr. Fife operated a fine men's haberdashery on Main Street vying with Arthur Frank and Hibbs for the carriage-class downtown trade.

The Cameron home gained its measure of fame in the 1930s when Jack

Dempsey, the boxing world's famed "Manassa Mauler," bought the home for his mother, Cecelia, and his father, Hyrum. Somehow, the house took on a considerable local aura as "the home Jack Dempsey bought for his mother," his father being rarely mentioned in the sports page clippings in the *Salt Lake Tribune* files. The yellowing clips tell everything you might wish to know about Dempsey and considerably more. They include data on his sixty ring victories, comparatively few words on his early losses, fat paragraphs on his 1919 title victory over Jess Willard, accounts of his punchout of the "Orchid Man," gorgeous Georges Carpentier, and details of his "long count" bout with Gene Tunney.

According to those *Tribune* files, Jack visited his ma and pa at 974 E. South Temple on May 15, 1939. During the same trip the exchamp reported "the cows on the family ranch in Murray look swell." From the family's Murray home at 5030 Naylor Lane, Dempsey shipped prime turkeys and prize celery to his busy restaurant on New York's Great White Way where the likes of Walter Winchell and Billy Rose dined late and often. It was Rose, according to *Tribune* yarns, who, with Ira Gershwin, wrote "Cheerful Little Earful," the ditty vocalist Estelle Taylor sang before she became the second Mrs. Dempsey. For the record, Dempsey first caught the eye of local sports writers when he fought John and Jim Hancock on the same night at the old Salt Lake Hippodrome in 1914.

Dempsey, who died in 1983 in New York at eighty-seven, held the heavyweight title for seven years and recalled being paid sixteen dollars for his first Salt Lake bout. But the files don't tell us how much he paid for the Cameron house, when he bought and sold it, or what sort of renovations Cecelia Dempsey made in its interior. One clipping says "he was a fearsome presence in the ring, known for his fists of concrete and his surly demeanor." Another sportswriter, equally given to hyperbole, told *Tribune* readers he was "generous to a fault and gentle as a lamb." Someday, perhaps, the Utah Heritage Foundation or the Utah State Historical Society will set a plaque in place outside 974 E. South Temple, or on Naylor Lane in Murray, or at the humble abode where Hyrum and Cecelia Dempsey briefly settled in Price with their Colorado-born six-year-old.

*Drawing Courtesy of Mrs. Kearns McCartney*

# English Reproduction on Haxton Place

MARCH 10, 1991

Even when a skiff of snow decorates its trees and lawns, Haxton Place hardly needs a cloud of fog to give it an English air. Fog or smog, the London look should not be surprising, since Thomas G. Griffin, a transmuted Briton himself, designed this small but prestigious real-estate development as a reproduction of London's own Haxton Place. The latter—although I've never seen it—would be just one of many similar cul-de-sac neighborhoods in Old Blighty that were so popular in the early years of the eighteenth century.

Haxton Place, if you've never found its tree-shaded walks, runs south from East South Temple between 900 and 1000 East. To be more precise, it is entered at 940 E. South Temple, and a short distance down the block, you can study the twin gateposts you must thread if you are afoot. The brownstone gateposts (I've drawn one as best I could in the appended sketch) are topped with curvaceous bent iron or steel members that remind one not of London, but of Paris, where rather similar design elements mark the early underground stations of the Paris Metro.

To my way of thinking, this Art Deco metalwork atop stone posts makes for far more handsome street decoration than that odd modern concretion installed atop the pedestrian walkway on 100 South between State and Main last year to enhance the streetscape.

Haxton's four stone posts with their bent metal tops lead down an extremely pleasant street that had its beginnings when dentist James T. Keith bought the 2.5-acre plot of land in 1909. Keith promptly divided his acres into lots that remain occupied today by three homes on the east side of the short street plus an equal number of homes on the west. Its principal landmark is the very sizable-seeming single house that closes off the Londonesque backwater at the south end. The talented Thomas Griffin was hired by Keith almost simultaneously with his purchase, and among Griffin's first moves was to design the broad, low brick structure as two residences—virtual twins. The structure, now almost completely covered with ivy, has a solid facing, but according to Margaret Lester, author of *Brigham Street*, the "units have a seventeen-inch space separating them." Thus they are indeed two houses, each very nearly a mirror of the other.

For many years the Griffins occupied the home on the east, while Keith and family lived in the western sector, separated from his English-born neighbor by those scanty seventeen inches. During later years and contemporary times, the double house and the trio of dwellings on each side of Haxton Place have been home to families bearing such names as Bamberger and Burt, Dugan, Pearson and Pomeroy, Schubach and Strange, Whitney and Van Cott. Best remembered, to this columnist, was Olive W. Burt, who, besides being a *Deseret News* staff member, wrote well over a score of books and stories for youngsters. Olive and her husband lived in—I believe—the right-hand, or western, half of the big residence seen in the drawing. In that not-too-distant period, the interior of the home was made interesting to interior decorators by a handsome staircase that was rich—like adjacent walls—in heavy wood paneling.

Since all the Haxton Place homes abut sloping lawns, stand behind many elderly trees and shrubs and are of very nearly equal height, the little neighborhood has a unity despite the architectural variety displayed in its individual units. One home is a two-story brick structure with particularly broad porches rather reminiscent of Frank Lloyd Wright's "prairie bungalows"; another, which stands alongside the "twin houses" (numbered 34 and 35) at the end of the short street, is a half-timbered affair unsuccessfully recalling much earlier English cottages. In addition, there's a red brick neo-Colonial, while still another home is hard to assign a style.

But the entire Haxton Place, the *tout ensemble*, is very successful indeed.

One reason must be that no utility poles or lines crisscross the neighborhood—this must have been one of the first local blocks in which power lines were all placed underground. And of course the fact that traffic on the block is at a minimum helps keep the street something of a backwash—a pleasant place for folks who don't wish to succumb to too much progress. There are, of course, similar cul-de-sacs or dead-end streets in the city's new suburbs, just as there are short blocks similar to Haxton Place in other, larger cities. At least a few such entities have deteriorated. But by and large, placement of such enclaves as Haxton Place seems to have resulted in more peace and quiet for residents, even in the heart of larger cities.

*Drawing Courtesy of Arthur T. Swindle*

# Italian Vice-consul's Residence on Ninth East

JANUARY 13, 1991

Now and again, in checking the history of a rather average-seeming Utah house, facts emerge that surprise, or even confound and confuse, the researcher.

Such is certainly the case with the neatly painted, well-kept, creamy-white residence at 164 S. 900 East, a house not too unlike others in this neighborhood of well-kept homes.

Occupying a portion of this building's front yard was a distinguished-appearing, rather sizable snowman—a frigid bit of contemporary sculpture topped by an orange-hued rubber traffic cone. "Obviously the work of a talented but little-known team of erudite designers," I mused.

The modest home was marked by an at-first-unseen bed-and-breakfast sign reading "The Saltair." Of even more importance, a wade through the snow revealed a plaque indicating this house holds a coveted place on the Utah State Historic Register. Indeed, a spate of research gave positive proof the building deserves its distinction. After all, not every Utah house once sheltered heavyweight fighter Primo Carnera; was the one-time residence of a prominent Utah cigar merchant; was built by a carpenter-turned-contractor; and, primarily, was the long-time residence and office of Fortunato Anselmo.

Lest you've forgotten Signor Anselmo, he was Italy's vice-consul for Utah and Wyoming for fully forty-five years. He thereby performed useful duties for residents of Italian birth or heritage in those two states at a time when such duties were of considerable significance in the political, legal and civic lives of a goodly number of Utah and Wyoming residents. And such disparate bigwigs as William Jennings Bryan and Benito Mussolini played significant roles in his life.

A carpenter, Silas B. Wood, built the box-style, quasi-Victorian home in 1903, when the nine-room residence cost an estimated $4,000.

Topped by a hip roof and two-window dormers, the house is distinguished on the street-front by a porch supported by three pairs of twin wooden columns. A modest attempt at first- and second-story bay windows and a new porch railing complete the ensemble, giving today's bed and breakfast a modest but very pleasant look.

Wood, pleased by his effort at home building, soon joined forces with architect John A. Headlund in establishing the Salt Lake firm of Headlund and Wood, Architects. That was in 1907, two years after Oscar G. Hemenway and wife Rebecca took possession of the home. The head of the household helmed the well-known firm of Hemenway and Moser, dealing in wholesale cigars at 73 W. 200 South.

According to local records, the next owners were Frank and Emma Gawan, who lived in the 900 East house from 1908 until 1920. Mr. Gawan, it appears, was asphalt plant superintendent for the P.J. Moran Co. on Canyon Road.

In 1920, Fortunato Anselmo entered the scene. A native of Grimaldi, Italy, he settled in Pueblo, Colo., circa 1905, where he served as a reporter for *Il Vindice*, an Italian American newspaper. He moved to Salt Lake in 1911, shortly after marrying Anna Pagano. Opening a wholesale food business featuring imported "old country" items, he likewise established *Il Gaz-*

*zett Italiana*, which helped him become a spokesman for the Italian community of the region.

In 1915, he was appointed Italian vice-consul for Utah and Wyoming by Secretary of State William Jennings Bryan, designated in some history books as the "silver tongued orator from the Platte." Anselmo's job was no sinecure—the vice-consul passed, signed, stamped and sealed requests for passports, visas and business import and export documents requiring the official approval of the Italian government. In those days of heavy immigration, native sons and daughters of a foreign land sent all the dollars they could spare to families left behind in European cities. Many often made trips to see the old folks, or "bring out" their relatives. In another capacity, Anselmo was the official local representative of the Bank of Naples, handling the money orders and cables of that large and old institution.

As time went on Anselmo—and his home—figured large in local Italian American affairs. In 1920, the Anselmos first entertained an Italian ambassador to the United States, one Vittorio Rolando-Ricci.

In contrast, Primo Carnera (a heavyweight of huge dimension and Italian parentage) was the family's guest in 1930. Notables whom the vice-consul greeted at the Salt Lake Municipal Airport or railroad stations included Cardinal Eugenio Pacelli—who became Pope Pius XII a few years after a brief 1936 stopover in Utah. He must be counted as the only future Pope of Rome to ever set foot in the Mormon mecca. Archbishop Francis J. Spellman of New York, later named a cardinal, was another personage greeted by Anselmo, as was Count Enrico Gallazzo, a nobleman who has faded rather completely into the mists of time.

There were major changes overseas in Italy, not altogether to local liking. A new premier, Benito Mussolini, made Italy's trains run on time, wreaked war upon the hapless Ethiopians, and, of course, installed an increasingly oppressive and warlike fascist regime. Anselmo had become a naturalized American citizen in 1923, although he later proudly became a Knight of the Crown of Italy and accepted a decoration as Officer of the Crown of Italy. His loyalty to the older regime was, however, apparent, and may have been the reason he was later ordered by the fascist government to resign his consular post. But he was also asked to remain on duty until a new successor could be appointed. Thus Anselmo was still de facto vice-consul in July of 1941, when the U.S. government ordered vice-consulate business to cease and the office to close.

Seals, stamps and documents were sent to the Italian Embassy in

Washington in proper diplomatic fashion. However, in 1950, five years after the end of World War II, Anselmo was reappointed to the post by the new democratic government. He served until his death in July of 1965, having given a total of forty-five years to his post as consular agent, much of it in the house at 164 S. 900 East.

The family had moved from the home in 1950, which was sold to Hilda Beer and later to Ronald L. Beer. Now, as mentioned, the house serves as the Saltair Bed and Breakfast establishment, owned and operated by Jan Bartlett and Nancy Saxton. They, presumably are to be thanked—and congratulated—for that unique snowman in the front yard of their distinguished Salt Lake residence.

# The David Keith Mansion

OCTOBER 15, 1989

Christmastime 1986 was a bleak, dark season for Salt Lakers who cherished the old David Keith Mansion at 529 E. South Temple. At the start of the holidays on the night of Dec. 23 a roaring fire, partially stoked by a large Christmas tree and other yuletide decorations in the mansion's richly paneled octagonal rotunda, charred and blackened much of the building's handsome interior.

Those who inspected the wrecked interior were sick at heart. The richly colored Tiffany glass skylight high above the mezzanine, one of Louis Tiffany's acknowledged masterworks, was shattered. Delicate metal work of its decorative chandelier had melted, and much of the lustrous cherrywood paneling was irretrievably lost.

Outwardly, however, the mansion seemed to have sustained little damage. The four tall Tuscan-stone columns flanking the South Temple entrance and the array of smaller stone pillars of the first and second story porches on the west facade seemed undamaged. Smoke escaping through shattered windows had darkened some of the white Sanpete County sand-stone walls of the mansion, but the building's sturdy exterior was largely unharmed. But, alas, chief glory of the structure had been its interior. Two full years, 1898 to 1900, had been needed for the building's construction because of its intricate interior and rich, indeed ornate, built-ins, designed by Frederick A. Hale.

Cornell-educated Hale had come to Salt Lake from Denver to design such notable buildings as the Alta Club, the Methodist Church at 200 S. 200 East, and the Salisbury home that later became the Evans and Early Mortuary on 100 South near 600 East.

The three-story Keith mansion, with its ballroom and notable octagonal rotunda, had fifteen lesser rooms, most of them paneled with Honduran mahogany and native birch. Built at a cost of $35,000 in those long-gone times, the mansion may have been given its opulent styling in a effort by mining magnate David Keith's wife to outshine one just completed for Daniel Jackling, and another under construction by Keith's Park City mines partner, Thomas Kearns.

Margaret Lester's handsomely illustrated book, *Brigham Street*, reports fully on the Keith mansion's "splendid woodwork," the massive skylight, and another shattered glass masterwork by Tiffany enriching the east window on the stair landing.

Long before the disheartening fire, David Keith and his wife had died in 1918 and 1919 while living in more modest quarters in the Hotel Utah. His reclusive daughter Margaret had died rather mysteriously at her Beverly Hills estate in 1934—a suicide, according to Ms. Lester's account of the socialite's tragic life.

However, happier times followed for the mansion when Salt Lake Mayor Ezra Thompson and his family purchased the home. Living there from 1919 through the late 1930s the Thompson family enhanced the front entrance with the present elaborate wrought iron grill protecting its heavy, glass-paned doors. A son, Clyde Thompson, occupied bachelor's quarters on the third floor, utilizing the ballroom as part of his apartment. Norinne Thompson, a daughter of the mayor, and her husband, H. Ross Brown, occupied the mansion from 1939 until 1969. Then they leased it to Terracor, a land-development firm.

At the time of the blaze in 1986, Terracor had become an arm of Ian

Cumming's Leucadia Corp. Fortunately, top officials of the firm had learned that the dignity, as well as the utility, of the mansion and its adjoining carriage house, had lent prestige to the firm. In addition, Cumming and Terracor president Bruce Miller had pretty much fallen under the spell of the mansion and the environment it provided.

"There was no consideration given to anything but its restoration after the Christmas fire," Miller reported.

With Max Smith as project architect, a six-month study of damage was undertaken. According to building historian John McCormick, experts from the Society for Preservation of New England Antiquities came to help develop the detailed restoration plans. Tim and Skip Hoagland of Resource Design and Construction Co. began work in mid-1987 on an eighteen-month project that brought the treasured building to its present, better-than-former state.

Bob Baird, an expert glassworker and artist, duplicated the lost Tiffany skylight and window. Violin-maker Paul Hart duplicated the original hand-carved wooden decorations. Furniture-makers Geoff Fitzwilliam and Mac Finlayson rebuilt the curving staircase in some ten months time. Smith found it necessary to replace a few major beams and rebuild a portion of the roof. But, what with new wiring and insulation, the one-time home of David Keith and family is said to look better than new.

In addition to the mansion in which company offices are handsomely housed, a flanking, back-of-the-grounds gem is the two-story carriage house (partially visible on the right in the accompanying drawing). Perhaps the largest such structure in the city, it has also been carefully remodeled to serve as company offices. As with the mansion proper, the integrity of the carriage house has been tastefully preserved.

*Drawing Courtesy of Arthur T. Swindle*

CHAPTER 4

# Where People Lived—
# Neighborhood Nooks

# Artesian Well Park

JUNE 30, 1991

On a hot June afternoon, a walker in the city will likely find at least a few thirsty Utahns enjoying the shady "minipark" at 802 S. 500 East, while they wait to fill their water jugs at the artesian well from which the tiny park gets its name.

Just about every city in the world grew up around a village well, and Salt Lake City is no exception. Legend has it that the "City Well" was used by the valley's initial Mormon pioneers soon after July 24, 1847. Some local historians insist cooling waters from the old well quenched the thirst of oxen hauling granite blocks from Cottonwood Canyon quarries to the Salt Lake Church of Jesus Christ of Latter-day Saints Temple. However, the late Fisher Harris of the Salt Lake Metropolitan Water District wrote that the well was not drilled until 1890, a year marked by severe drought.

Any mention of the 500 East well brings memories pouring forth (pardon the pun) from elderly or middle-aged local residents who insist its non-chlorinated water "tasted better" than the aqua pura (or nonpura) from household taps.

"We never had enough gasoline ration stamps during the war," recalls Jayne Cook. "But mother [Mrs. Norma Benson] loved that water. We lived at 300 South and 900 East, so she would start the car and coast downhill to the well carrying a half-dozen jugs."

Presumably, they pushed the car back uphill to save gasoline stamps.

"That was good water," says Lew Ellsworth, who lived in the Harris Apartments a block away. "We kids were sent down to fill the jugs—which were heavy to carry all the way back."

One recent day in the Alta Club grill (where other liquids besides water might be served), Salt Lakers Jim Beless, Wes Hamilton, Joseph Rosenblatt, Don K. Irvine and Si Frank all reported fetching the family water from the well a half-century ago. "It was a social event—you always met friends in line," said Irvine.

Cliff Ashton, while living in Holladay, drove to the well because his wife Myriel "so enjoyed the water." Ashton's brother-in-law, the late Joe Kjar of KSL, "kept his refrigerator full of that water. Or was it an icebox?" Ashton has another reason for remembering the City Well. "An uncle, Brigham Lindsay, ran a candy and ice cream store across the street. Best candy in town—we always got some when we came for water."

Many Salt Lakers may recall when the city's well figured in a heated controversy concerning chlorination of municipal water supplies. Shortly after World War II, the League of Women Voters and the State Health Department insisted local water supplies should be treated forthwith. Salt Lake's water reputedly was so poor that the federal government threatened to ban it from railroad trains and passenger planes. J. Bracken Lee, as both governor and mayor, termed federal standards nonsensical—but treatment plants were soon installed to handle Deer Creek, Parleys, Cottonwood, and City Creek water.

However, Dallas Richins of the Salt Lake City Water Department points out that the water flow in what is now called Artesian Well Park has never been chlorinated or treated. "That well flows the year round. It has a higher than ordinary mineral content, and the Health Department takes two samples a week and monitors it carefully," Richins says.

For the scientifically well versed, Salt Lake City water contains potassium, silica, aluminum salts, calcium, iron "and many other minerals," according to the water superintendent's surveys. Rated by "hardness per million parts," City Creek water is the hardest, followed by Parleys and Big Cottonwood supplies, while the City Well water comes off hardest of all (but remains untreated).

No matter. To those who come to the park from as far away as Tooele, Midvale and Bountiful, water from the ever-flowing artesian well is "just perfect." Its advocates have little use for statistics dredged up by Dallas Richins or the rather snide opinions of longtime city public utilities director Charles W. Wilson, who ranked the well water as "only fair" back in 1979. Scientists may spout their "1.3 NTU turbidity, calcium 130 milligrams per liter, total dissolved solids 760 milligrams per liter" at the drop of a water flask. However, folks filling water jugs in the shade of the park's aspen and oaks scorn statistics—and tell reporters "it's pure and tastes good, really good."

Visitors to the City Well who have short or long memories are all pleased with the ninety-thousand-dollar minipark the city installed there in 1979. Until then, the single curbside waterspout at the street corner made for a considerable traffic jam when a dozen or so bottle-toters arrived simultaneously to draw water.

At the behest of the Central City Community Council, federal and local funds were allotted for today's Artesian Well Park, trees were planted on the purchased corner lot, and the old well, with modern taps, was placed in a neatly contoured concrete base—flanked by neat brick walls, slatted park benches, concrete steps and stylish lampposts. John Swain was the landscape architect, and the Ralph L. Wadsworth Construction Co. handled building chores. Park superintendent John Gust and Mayor Ted Wilson found the public so approving that Richmond Park and Tauffer Park were added to the city park system nearby on both 600 South and 300 East Streets. These vest-pocket parks provide play space and grass—but offer no spring water.

Thus far, no one has suggested sending a bottle of the local aqua pura to the White House for the use of Mr. and Mrs. George Bush.

Nor have we had any reports of Bolshevik or anti-Mormon well-poisoners either.

JACK GOODMAN '94

# The Avenues Anderson Tower

MAY 15, 1994

If you have ever hiked up A Street to enter the steep road that dips into City Creek Canyon, or if you've ambled along A with the "old house" enthusiasts of the Utah Historical Society, you may have noticed a narrow flight of a dozen or so "steps to nowhere." Actually, they extend into a seemingly empty patch of grassy woodland opposite the beginning of Sixth Avenue. To the north, if you peer through the tangle of bushes and trees, there's a good view of the State Capitol just across the canyon.

If you had strolled this way before 1932, the view would have been different—since you would have been at the base of the granite tower seen in the illustration. It was a prominent local landmark from 1884 until November 1932.

Chatting with elderly acquaintances who lived and played on the Avenues, you'll find they remember the tower especially well. Teenage boys, or so-called "tomboys" of the feminine gender, tell scary tales of climbing the tower, sitting on window ledges perilously or dangling legs over the roof-top. In fact, it was the hazardous games of neighborhood kids that brought the demise of the sturdy stone tower, a structure bearing the now almost-forgotten name of the Anderson Tower.

Robert R. Anderson, builder of the fifty-four-foot-high, twenty-five-foot-diameter granite tower, came from Scotland to Utah in 1867 and became an early settler of the city's north bench. Anderson's memory, laced with a portion of nostalgia, focused on his boyhood home—where such stone towers were fairly commonplace. Many had been built as watchtowers within sight of the English border and the Scottish firths. But quite a few were rather purposeless, simply serving as "view towers," locally known as "follies."

After fifteen fairly prosperous years in Salt Lake City, Anderson ventured into tower-building on his own, reasoning that property he owned at 303 A St. would be perfect for a telescope-equipped tower. His hillock provided a sweeping view of the city, the nearby canyon country and the Wasatch Range.

Anderson's "connections" enabled him to obtain possibly flawed but useful granite stones from the six-spired Church of Jesus Christ of Latter-day Saints Temple then under construction. The gray stones were carefully "laid up" in circular fashion into the equivalent of a three- or four-story building. The tower's walls were pierced by windows of considerable size, plus a sizable arched doorway reached by a small flight of steps. A winding wooden stairway led past the unglazed windows to a parapet or observation deck, on which stood that comparative rarity—a telescope.

When it was completed, Anderson charged a small fee (a sum not known to this columnist), and those admitted could climb up to use the telescope and enjoy the 365-degree view of the city and countryside.

Alas, the tower was never a monetary success. According to a Sons of Utah Pioneers bronze tablet put in place in 1992, Anderson, perhaps deeming his venture a real folly, then opened the tower to the public—gratis. All would have been well—and the tower, which was rugged enough, might still be standing—except for children and vandalism.

Anderson, who lived at Fifth Avenue and A Street till the time his tower became a menace, once told a youthful H.Z. Lund, "I kept the tower boarded up, since I cannot stand guard over it constantly—it attracts children, and if anything happened to a child, I would have no defense."

According to Zack Lund in a missive on file with the Utah Heritage Foundation, "the most treacherous places in the tower were the big front windows whose sills were almost level with the floor. I once saw a kid on the top of the tower, running around on the very top of the wall. Fortunately he was well coordinated and leaned inwards!"

Lund, a relative, said that after the tower was boarded up, forcible entry could be made through a window on the northwest, not visible from Anderson's home. Or just "attach a rope to the high point of a boarded window and with other kids run laterally until the boards pulled free and we could enter."

No one seems able to recollect any slogans painted on the stone walls. Today, of course, there would be three or four floors worth of graffiti, with spray paint proclaiming the names of gangs and clubs. Spray paint had not been invented in the good old days.

Zack Lund recalls asking Anderson why he built his tower, only dimly remembered by older Avenues residents.

"I wanted to show the people in the valley we had something up on the hill," he replied. In addition to offering a view, Anderson and his wife, Elizabeth Holland Anderson, had sizable real-estate holdings and may have seen the tower as an advertising centerpiece attracting customer holdings.

Now the tower has vanished, except for a modest monument of its old stones. And there's no other such view point in the valley.

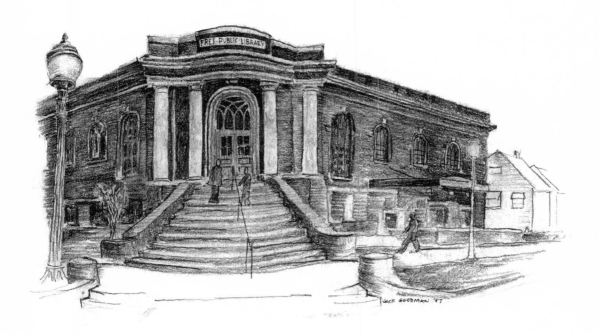

# The Chapman Library

JANUARY 1987

Now and again, in almost any large city in our land, an observant tourist is likely to encounter a not overly impressive building having an oddly familiar look. "I've never been here before, but that building reminds me of home," you may muse. Chances are you are not suffering from deja vu or paramesia—that odd feeling of having been in this place and time before.

No psychic phenomenon, this. Chances are, what you are seeing is a Carnegie Library, and there are scores of these look-alikes across the nation.

Salt Lake City is blessed with six libraries, and county residents are served by another fourteen repositories of fact and fiction, large and small buildings in which you can sit for a while and browse through newspapers, magazines, volumes of your choice, or borrow books, recordings, videotapes or favorite films.

But there's just one Carnegie-endowed library in our city, the Chapman Branch of the Salt Lake City Library System—and it's a minor gem. Located at 577 S. 900 West, it's not overly large. Fact is, I think it could be shoehorned into the largish atrium of the bulky new block-square Salt Lake County Building at 2100 South and State. There might even be room to spare.

Half a dozen reminiscing residents or former residents of the city's west side have told me the Chapman Branch was well worth inspecting. What they failed to predict was that such a visit would give me a severe case of nostalgia for my beloved boyhood days in Brooklyn, when I was a devotee of the Brevoort Branch Library a mile or so from famed Ebbett's Field. The dark red brick of the Chapman Branch, its curving steps, those four pillars flanking the entry doors may, or may not, precisely duplicate the facade I dimly recall from the era when my Bedford-Stuyvesant home neighborhood was a somnolent section of the city of New York's "borough of churches." But today's neighborhood small fry climbing the front steps, and the warm—even cozy—look of things inside, bring recollections of pleasant years for me, as they must for hundreds of Chapman Branch "graduates."

Just inside its big, well-varnished oak doors, smiling head-librarian Renee Pierce occupies a curved desk, accepting and dispensing volumes for card-holding adults and youngsters. Four highly polished wooden pillars gleam inside the entry, and at least a score of leafy or flowering plants decorate window ledges. The light streaming through Chapman's oversized windows shines upon bookshelves containing some 30,000 volumes. And, as in other places and at other times, a troop of youngsters swarming into the warm reading room shed parkas and sweaters to follow assistant librarian Martha Spear to a basement "multipurpose room" for a film show.

Given its old, wooden, schoolroom-type of clock ticking opposite the circulation desk, and the mild hissing from the steam radiators, Chapman patrons of ancient age might drowsily be induced to imagine themselves as children in this same sunny setting—at any time since May of 1928 when the Chapman Branch was dedicated.

And, not to be forgotten, just off the lobby a handsome bust of the bearded Andrew Carnegie peers down from a central perch upon a bookshelf at the wooden, brass-handled card index files, the hardwood tables and the not-too-soft wooden chairs. Carnegie, a Scottish immigrant who became a millionaire steelmaker, viewed the free public library as the "poor man's college" and endowed his still existing Carnegie Foundation with funds enough to build libraries throughout the land—including $25,000 for this branch.

Carnegie gained national fame through his bookish generosity, although steelworkers and iron puddlers at his mills argue he might have spent less on libraries and more on his employees. The name "Chapman" bestowed upon the building memorializes Annie E. Chapman of the Pioneer Library Association, who headed the city's new public library system from its inception until her death in 1903.

Our city's first library books, mostly translations of Greek and Latin classics plus some notable English works, had arrived in town under the auspices of the Church of Jesus Christ of Latter-day Saints. Most of these are now in the University of Utah and the Supreme Court. But a group of "literary women" organized the Ladies Library Association, opened a public reading room in the First National Bank Building—and apparently ran out of steam in 1876.

Perhaps their husbands said "enough literary nonsense. Take care of the kids and kitchen!"

In 1877 the Masonic Order established a Masonic Library, gathered 10,000 volumes—but soon donated the job of running a free public library to the city fathers. After Utah achieved statehood, a law was passed establishing a Free Public Library on the top floor of the new City and County Building. There Annie E. Chapman, librarian of an interim Pioneer Library Association, took charge of the free library's 11,900 volumes.

In 1900 John Q. Packard (the Q. stood for Quackenbos) donated site and funds for a grand new library on State Street, now housing the Hansen Planetarium. Joanna Sprague, the city librarian who succeeded Ms. Chapman, opened five branch libraries—three in public schools with fifty volumes each, one in the Western Union Telegraph Office and another "in the drink dispensary of the Warm Springs Sanitorium."

Soon afterwards a 1,500-book branch was housed in the Horsley Department Store Building at 610 W. North Temple. These books moved to the bright new Chapman Branch when the city received $25,000 from Mr. Carnegie's Foundation.

Enough of dust-dry ancient history.

Today's Chapman Branch looks much as it did when new although it has been "lightly remodeled." A covered ramp on the 600 South side now accommodates handicapped visitors. There's a small elevator inside, and the twin reading rooms extending off the central lobby have fluorescent lights.

Unfortunately, space age progress has been creeping in. Neither Ms. Pierce or Ms. Spear use yellow wooden pencils topped by those ingenious date-stampers of yore. A laser beam in a mysterious box now "reads" bar coded labels on the patron's library card and on the books. And a computer tells librarians where in the city system a book being sought is located. Not unlike a supermarket and warehouse, alas.

Outside the quiet neighborhood seems unchanged, despite the freeway viaduct cutting across town a block or so away. Small homes, the Revelation Baptist Church and the Best Cleaning establishment are the library's near neighbors. But something of an architectural mystery centers about the Chapman. Its architect was Don Carlos Young, one of Brigham Young's several grandsons. That being the case, why does this Carnegie Library look so much like other Carnegie libraries scattered across the land? Did local architect Young merely follow a "ready-made plan" fitted to the Salt Lake corner site? Why does the interior so precisely resemble the interiors of those sibling libraries elsewhere?

Nowadays, the Chapman Branch is a literacy center for the foreign born, for new immigrants—welcoming Vietnamese and Tongans and Spanish-speaking residents.

One imagines both multimillionaire Carnegie and librarian Chapman would be pleased.

EDITOR'S NOTE: Renovation of the Chapman Branch Public Library, completed in 1994 following a serious fire, featured complete repainting of the interior, new emphasis on heating and ventilation, access for handicapped patrons and new space for community functions.

# Wasatch Springs Plunge /
# Children's Museum of Utah

OCTOBER 4, 1987

Long, long before members of the present generation began dunking in hot tubs and slimming their bodies at our town's heavily advertised spas, early arrivals in our valley did likewise in the lee of Ensign Peak. Utah's pioneers soaked trail-weary, toil-worn limbs in the hot mineral spring they found rising, bubbling and scenting the air along the Wasatch fault near the north end of the Jordan Valley.

But long, long before the first white explorers and settlers arrived, those same hot springs were used by bands of Shoshones, Utes and Paiutes who periodically camped nearby.

Nowadays, bands of schoolchildren descend from big yellow school buses to visit the once rustic scene of long-forgotten aboriginal ablutions.

They are bound for a sizable structure known to grandparents or great-grandparents as a warm springs bathing resort. The long, low white building at 840 N. 300 West has been transformed into the Children's Museum of Utah, a very useful but struggling institution enjoyed by thousands of youngsters plus a considerable corps of adults these past four years. The museum utilizes a modest 12,000 square feet of the block-long concrete and tile-fronted building. Best known as the Wasatch Springs Plunge, the structure has considerable architectural and historic significance. More of that later, as the television commentators say.

The museum has been funded (and, I fear, underfunded) by the Bennett Family endowment. Renovation architect Joseph W. Linton of Linton, Bingham, Inc., donated much time and labor, while Salt Lake City makes the building available on what is virtually a rent-free basis, and Parks and Recreation crews tend the grounds. Which brings us, gentle reader, to the aforementioned matters of history.

As you approach the Children's Museum from points south, you gratefully discover that the big tile-roofed building is located adjacent to a small but well-tended city park, shaded by tall old trees. The scarred hillsides of Ensign Peak are on your right, the red-brick, glass-front of the one-time St. Mark's Hospital is across busy 300 West, while the Union Pacific Railroad shops and a prime collection of oil refinery tanks and stills block off the other horizon.

Reminding the visitor that this must once have been an almost idyllic scene, a historic tablet, set in place in the quiet park by the Daughters of the American Revolution, reads, "Fur trappers & traders were the first white men in this locality. William H. Ashley & his men arrived in the spring of 1829. James Bridger, discoverer of the Great Salt Lake, & Jedediah S. Smith trapped streams in this region in 1824 and many subsequent years."

A second tablet, placed by the Daughters of Utah Pioneers, sounds another sort of historical note: "Warm Springs, July 26, 1847. Brigham Young and others descended Ensign Peak and located sulphur springs. A bath house 15 × 30 was dedicated Nov. 27, 1850, and a grove of locust trees planted."

Neither tablet relates a much sadder tale noted by only a few historians. In 1847–48 Indians met settlers here and caught measles. An epidemic followed. According to Mormon journalists, "They assembled in large numbers at the Warm Springs, bathed in the waters and died."

Most pioneers were unperturbed. Documents at the Utah State Historical Society report that by the 1880s "there was a large lake, surrounded by hotels, boat docks and houses of prostitution on the northwest shore." Salt Lake City, to combat mosquitos, if not vice, began draining the lake, putting a granite sewer system in place in 1892. By 1915 the visible springs had pretty well vanished. As early as 1848 pioneers had placed an adobe structure over one major pool. As buildings and picnic grounds, hot tubs and stone-lined pools were added, the city sought title to most of the springs, which led to another tragedy.

The assistant surgeon at then Camp Douglas, Dr. J. Ting Robinson, filed a claim on the land and pools himself, saying Mormon deeds for the area were invalid because no proper federal filing had been made. And Dr. Robinson proceeded to build a saloon on "his property." The City Commission ordered him and his building "ejected." Dr. Robinson went to federal court—which decided against him.

One October night in 1866, Dr. Robinson was lured from his home on the pretext of a medical emergency and shot to death. An investigation failed to uncover the perpetrators, but historians generally attribute the attack to the tensions between "Mormons and gentiles."

The city, having secured its title, ordered the first street railway tracks laid in 1872 to run from Temple Square to the Warm Springs. Meanwhile, one John Beck developed a rival pleasure spa to the north, which served as a major resort until it went up in flames in 1898. Beck's Hot Springs, however, remained in partial use until 1953 when Utah acquired it for a new highway.

Salt Lake City built the building now serving as the Children's Museum in 1923. Fronting on what had become Beck Street and 300 West, the structure and its pools became major tourist attractions. Designed by Lewis T. Cannon and John Fetzer, the two-story building wrapped around two big pools, one 50 feet by 120 feet, the other 25 feet by 50 feet. The high, curved roof arched overhead to span the now-empty pools and a grandstand. The two-story lobby housed a small cafe, men's barber shop and masseur, and there were "seven individual warm soaking tanks."

A masseuse and hairdresser occupied part of the upper floor, while the upper floor in the north wing had five bedrooms for overnight guests. Several hundred lockers, dressing rooms and showers for all comers were other facilities.

The sulphur waters were considered so healthful that devotees of spas and such came from many parts of the nation to ease lumbago, neuritis and other afflictions. Ted Burnett, a retired local businessman, reports his father came down from the Seattle area annually for an invigorating stay at what the city then labeled the Warm Springs Municipal Baths. "The place was always busy." Burnett recalls. And, sulphuric odor or not, quite a few patrons learned to swim in the big plunge.

The heyday of hot-sulphur-springs bathing ended abruptly in 1946 when the Utah State Department of Health contended the bacterial count in the plunge made for health hazards. Pools were ordered chlorinated—but the chemical produced a damaging precipitate. In 1949 the city converted the two largest pools into chlorinated fresh-water pools of the common variety. However, they continued to pump thermal water into small private baths for sulphur devotees. Alas, a portion of the concrete roof atop the big pools caved in in 1970, leading to a heavily debated $93,000 remodeling job.

But the old plunge was finally shut down in 1976 for reasons of economy, and the vacant buildings were soon badly vandalized. Four years ago the Utah Children's Museum took over—with the pool areas carefully locked off from the exhibit spaces.

# Prestigious Federal Heights

SEPTEMBER 14, 1986

Real-estate copywriters, a breed not given to looking into dictionaries, love to advertise expensive city homes, condominiums or suburban dwellings as "prestigious." While my own dog-eared copy of Webster's tells me a prime meaning of the adjective is "of, relating to, or marked by illusion," I must admit that the Federal Heights district is among the most "prestigious" neighborhoods in our valley—especially so if judged by the bank accounts or social standing of its residents.

But are Federal Heights homeowners really aware that they are living in what was once Popperton? Do they realize their very proper neighborhood was Salt Lake City's slaughterhouse district?

Our city is, arguably, different, a perverse and peculiar burg. To this day, Chicago's stockyard neighborhood never has become the prime residential neighborhood of even Mike Royko's dreams. And, until a few dozen years ago, only New York's Dead End kids bravely lived in close proximity to Manhattan's slaughterhouse district.

It's an odd fact of history and geography that the first settler to purchase a major tract of land on the spot we now call Federal Heights was Charles Popper, identified as one of the Territory's first Jewish butchers and ranchers. This immigrant from a not-yet-unified Germany came to the United States in 1850, settled in Utah in 1864 and opened a butcher shop on what became Salt Lake City's Main Street.

He bought, raised and slaughtered cattle—and obtained the contract to provide beef for the troops at Fort Douglas. Thereupon he purchased a tract of 150 acres at the mouth of today's Dry Canyon. His acreage apparently extended from just beneath today's mountainside concrete "U" to a spot very near the upper end of today's East South Temple.

Obviously, this was a prime spot for holding cattle, slaughtering same and hauling carcasses to Fort Douglas. A local history written by Leon L. Watters in 1952 makes Popper's benchland acquisition somewhat mysterious, this being acreage "for which he obtained title by a special act of Congress." It was, I suppose, part of the original fort set up to guard Utahns from the Indians—or to guard western gentiles from predatory Mormons.

In any event, butcher Popper "established a slaughterhouse, soap and candle factory," an odiferous industry in what is now a district of curving streets, fine old trees, green lawns, well-tended gardens and gracious homes, built on what must have been a less than prestigious chunk of real estate.

The owner of 1465 Sigsbee Ave., the rather typical gray-frame home in the adjoining sketch, very kindly let me study the abstract and deed to the turn-of-the-century home. Popper vanished from the scene, along with his slaughterhouse, about the time of the Spanish-American War, at which point the acreage was "federalized."

LeGrande Young, who was, I suppose, a descendant of city-founder Brigham Young, took title to the site of 1465 Sigsbee in 1906, and the land was annexed to the city in 1907 "from Ft. Douglas," which makes for some confusion concerning Mr. Young's title. Nevertheless, he built the pleasant multibedroom home that still stands today.

George Romney is listed as the next owner, followed by H.L. and Edna Callaghan. It next passed to Col. Dicks, whose wife Matilda is reported to have been a sister of George Dern, the same chap who became Utah governor and the U.S. Secretary of War under Franklin D. Roosevelt.

The neighborhood was obviously considered pleasant when Salt Lake

City, no longer an "urban village," was growing uphill as well as into the valley flatlands. The home's next owner, a gentleman named Muir, said to have been the superintendent at the U.S. Smelting Co. works, could have commuted by the South Temple streetcar—but instead he drove one of those newfangled automobiles. After all, the stables behind the homes on such streets as Sigsbee and Wolcott could accommodate a motorcar just as well as a horse and carriage.

William Cope, dean of the nearby School of Engineering at the University of Utah, was the next householder prior to the purchase of the big, rambling, multi-porched home by its next owner, businessman Herman Bernstein.

Quite a cycle. From soap and beef to church, to government, to mining, to the military, to a university dean, and back to business once again. Meanwhile, the homes sheltered kids who organized clubs, went sledding, climbed nearby hills—and grew their own youngsters.

In any event, architects of yore designed spacious, pleasant houses in a variety of styles. These still stand sheltered by big old trees on those hard-to-find winding streets. Prestigious or no, Federal Heights remains a pleasant neighborhood.

# The Ambassador Club

JANUARY 19, 1986

Once it was pristine white. Now it's a rather sickly shade of pale green and its cornices and moldings are accented in an even more woeful, more livid greenish hue. In its prime, just prior to World War II, the building at 145 S. 500 East functioned as the Ambassador Hotel. Later the brick and stucco six-story heart of the building, along with the two matching five-story wings, housed apartments, studios and even a rather swank penthouse or two, while the lower floor gained citywide publicity as the Ambassador Club.

Now from the look of its increasingly decrepit-appearing exterior, the Ambassador Club building has outlived its usefuness. No longer deemed viable, the once pleasant dining rooms, dance floor, bar and meeting rooms will fall to local wrecking crews. The club's doors were shut, seemingly forever, in late 1985, leaving the remaining club members to their fond

94

memories of pleasant luncheons and dinners, card games with old or vanished cronies and meetings on municipal and state matters.

However, the Ambassador should be remembered for another and very different reason. It was, in its unique way, the first federal housing project in these United States. This odd bit of history turns back the calendar to 1889 when the records tell us a generous Congress appropriated some $50,000 to "properly house" Mormon women who were expected to abandon polygamy—or who were expected soon to be abandoned by their fleeing exhusbands.

In 1887, Congress had passed the Edmunds-Tucker Act in an effort to wipe out polygamy and its evils. The Church of Jesus Christ of Latter-day Saints had been disincorporated and its properties confiscated. Church President John Taylor had "died in exile" up in Kaysville while a much-sought fugitive from federal justice. Polygamous church leaders and lesser brethren fled to Mexico, to Alberta in Canada, to Arizona territory and to Cohab Canyon in Southern Utah. Or were wearing stripes in the state prison at rural Sugarhouse.

The considerate congressmen, giving thought to the multitude of wives and children certain to be "cast off" by the nefarious "polygs," kindly appropriated federal dollars sufficient to build them a spacious, hotel-like apartment house on 500 East. It was designed to house a hundred or more women and children. But as you and Robert Burns well know, the best laid plans of mice and men have a way of going awry.

According to local legend, only three women took advantage of the offer of low-cost or even rent-free housing! The housing project was abandoned after the building stood vacant for well over two years.

As so often is the case with nonfunctioning, nonprofitable Salt Lake properties, the building was purchased by LDS officials as a private venture and opened as the Fifth East Hotel.

So much for ancient history—scrupulously researched or otherwise. I should remind local historians the federal government in reality has built other "housing projects" including buildings on Indian reservations, hospitals for Civil War veterans and quarters for officers and wives at naval establishments and army posts, including Fort Douglas.

Which is why, I suspect, the unnamed architect who designed the Ambassador blueprinted a building that looks to me, at least, rather like an old-fashioned Army hospital or the Carlisle Indian School back in Pennsylvania. In any event, the old building functioned in its several roles, although it seems unlikely it will achieve the century mark.

The passing of the Ambassador Club, if not the passing of its building, provides an opportunity for musing a bit about the general problem of our city's clubs. The old Alta Club flourishes on its South Temple at State Street corner, its members unshaken by legal action being taken by an adventurous woman seeking nondiscriminatory admission to the membership rolls.

While the Alta Club remains a masculine Gibraltar (by the by, why doesn't a male seek to join the completely feminine Town Club?), most downtown clubs have faded away or seem to be in their death throes. The University Club is a shadow of its former self. The Elks Club shuttered long ago.

Members of today's up-and-coming generation of business persons find it convenient to do their eating and drinking in such coed spas as the New Yorker, the Haggis or Green Street, where they need not pay to maintain the equivalents of the old Ambassador Club. Country clubs still flourish in the suburbs, but in Salt Lake, as in many cities, downtown men's clubs seem to be fading from the social scene. I suspect that admitting women to membership in once sacrosanct havens of the male establishment won't reverse the ticking of the time clock.

But halt a moment. Because the building formerly housing the Ambassador Club was initially built for women, perhaps some of you upwardly mobile women would like to found an all-feminine social and athletic club and take over the old 500 East building before the big iron ball starts swinging.

EDITOR'S NOTE: A restaurant and bookstore are being constructed where the Ambassador Club once stood.

CHAPTER 5

# Downtown Becomes a City

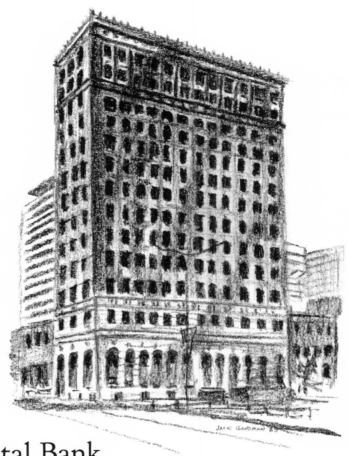

# Continental Bank

MARCH 19, 1989

As thousands of depositors and borrowers must have realized down through the years, the thirteen-story structure housing the Continental Bank is something of a "Plain Jane" among Salt Lake's major bank buildings. Nary a Grecian column decorates its facade, there's a noticeable lack of fancy marble and of exuberant, expensive hand-carved acanthus leaves or other classical motifs. Indeed, it's quite possible to imagine bank founder James E. Cosgriff ordering architects George W. Callum of San Francisco and Frederick Hale of Salt Lake to "build me a building that works—none of your fancy stuff for me."

From what our town's oldest old-timers recall, that would have been characteristic of this outspoken sheepman turned banker. After heading west from Vermont in 1890, Cosgriff soon became one of the leading sheepmen in Wyoming and Utah, owning 100,000 head by the turn of the century. He began buying small-town Wyoming banks soon afterward. Moving into Salt Lake City in 1905, he purchased the Commercial National Bank, merged it with his First National Bank of Wyoming and then acquired the National Bank of the Republic. The latter was located at 200 S. Main, where the present Continental Bank was to rise in 1923–24.

By 1920, the Continental National Bank and Trust Co., into which James Cosgriff had consolidated his individual institutions, had gained a considerable reputation as the city's "non-Mormon bank." Zion's, Deseret and Utah Savings were deemed "church banks" in the eyes of most "gentiles," but banker Cosgriff, a Catholic, was said to be less apt than the brethren up Main Street to inquire about your tithe-paying proclivities when you sought funds for a reaper-binder, money to mechanize a mine or cash to open a new cigar store.

When ordering his tall new bank structure at the southwest corner of Main and 200 South, the erstwhile sheepman supposedly did one rather unpopular thing—according to some locals possessed of long memories. The lower two floors featured by high, arched windows, carved heads and modest cornices, were faced with local stone, but he ordered the rather drab, gray brick of the eleven upper stories shipped from a midwestern brickyard, much to the disgust of a home-grown Utah industry. This had a curious result in later years when, soon after World War I, son and successor, Walter Cosgriff, wanted a modest, rather box-like annex affixed to the west end of the original structure. According to contractors still extant, the midwestern brickyard had long since gone out of business. Thus son Walter's addition had to be faced with nonmatching brick of a more brownish hue.

All of which, of course, is beside the point, especially because Walter Cosgriff is remembered in the community for many other deeds and reputed eccentricities. It was, I believe, during the Truman Administration that he went to Washington to assist in the banking affairs of the federal government but became more than a little disenchanted with the direction in which Uncle Sam's fiscal policies seemed headed. He returned to Salt Lake City rather hastily, promptly issued a scathing statement decrying Federal Reserve policy—and speedily pulled his Continental Bank from under the umbrella of the Federal Reserve. This move brought a slew of financial reporters and columnists to town to interview the then-youthful Utah banker who dared to take on the previously sacrosanct Federal Reserve Board. News columns soon filled with dire warnings that no sizeable bank could stand without dealing with "The Fed." But obviously the Continental Bank Trust flourished.

In his spare moments, Cosgriff continued to play golf and support Salt Lake's floundering minor league baseball teams with unusual generosity. While he became something of a legend in local sport circles, his wife, Enid, became an initial strong supporter of Willam Christensen's newly fledged ballet. Although there was an understandable doubt as to whether Walter Cosgriff ever attended a ballet performance, Mrs. Cosgriff in later years did more than her bit in the effort to keep the Salt Lake Bees buzzing at Derk's Field.

One oddity about banker Cosgriff was apparent to his fellow financiers, to Main Street shopkeepers and even newspaper reporters. For reasons never publicly stated, he hated parking meters, and carried on his own unceasing warfare with same. He parked his own car at Ernie Osterloh's Ramp Garage on Broadway, but daily as he wended his way up Broadway and thence north along Main to his desk on the raised banking floor of his multimillion-dollar institution, Cosgriff would vigorously kick and cuff any parking meter showing a red "violation" flag. He did this so skillfully and with such aplomb that the flag signaling a violation would disappear—as would minions of the law seeking to write tickets under his stern gaze. If he couldn't make the flag drop, he was not averse to putting a nickel or two in the offending meter, especially those outside his bank.

Times have changed, of course, and an Idaho bank holding company now owns Continental as well as the Tracy Collins Bank and Trust a block distant on Main. Indeed, there seems some likelihood Continental's headquarters will be moved into the swankier-appearing red-brick, mansard roofed ex-Tracy Collins structure. However, visitors to the tall, narrow, utilitarian Continental Bank Building at 200 S. Main will find it largely unchanged. The big clock that long hung on an outrigger at second-story level has inexplicably vanished. But the lobby and upper floor corridors, as well as the area where Continental tellers greet depositors, look much as they did back in the 1950s when people gathered for a morning cup of brew in Marie DeMann's Coffee Shop on the fourth floor. During the Utah uranium boom, the coffee shop was especially popular as stock traders and brokers met their clients and customers, set up new penny stock issues and concluded their deals over coffee.

In the '60s, Kathy DeMarco took over the little diner and, in 1975,

Mon O. Hom (who "Americanized" his name to "Ben") became the proprietor of Ben's Cafe at 401 Continental Bank Building.

Indeed, if you should hunger for coffee and a sweet roll, or an exceptionally hearty breakfast or lunch at exceptionally modest prices, Ben and his wife are still turning out viands at their old office building stand. Still equipped with a half-dozen counter stools and a half-dozen tables covered in period-piece wheat-colored plastic, Ben's still serves its mix of lawyers, bank employees and even publisher George Gregerson—whose financial weekly headquarters in the solid still-viable building the Cosgriffs built.

One oddity should be reported. The dull gray brick walls of the sixty-five-year-old Continental Bank building have been enhanced—at certain hours—by the presence of that shiny-sided, ovoid customer newcomer to Main Street, the First Interstate Bank on the intersection's northwest corner. When the sun shines from east or south, its light reflects from the First Interstate's walls and windows. This gives Continental's "Plain Jane" a patina of sorts that's pleasing to the eyes of pedestrians—although it very likely bothers office workers who must haul down their shades to avoid the reflected or refracted light.

EDITOR'S NOTE: Ben's coffee shop no longer operates, and the upper floors of the Continental Bank Building are vacant. The weekly newspaper now offices in the Kearns Building.

# The *Salt Lake Tribune* Building

JANUARY 24, 1988

There are two oddities concerning the building at 143 S. Main worth noting before I begin waxing overly sentimental about the structure or—more properly—about its past and present denizens. While virtually all comers refer to it as the *Salt Lake Tribune* Building, this ten-story brick and steel edifice designed by Pope and Burton was constructed in 1924, not for our city's largest daily, but for businessman Ezra Thompson, and it bore his name until 1937.

Commenting upon Thompson's achievements, the *Tribune* noted he was a three-time Salt Lake mayor, including a term when he was elected as candidate of the vigorously anti-Mormon American Party. More to the point, perhaps, he was a millionaire real-estate man with considerable interests in the famed Cardiff Mine, the Daly West Mine and the Peerless Coal Co.

103

According to John S. McCormick's excellent study on the city's historic buildings, the Thompson/*Tribune* structure is one of the few hereabout students of architecture cite as illustrating the transition between the Beaux Arts/Classical Revival styles and the late-arriving Art Deco/Art Moderne period. If you look aloft at the terra cotta cornice above the three-hundred-fifty-thousand-dollar building's tenth story, its Art Deco ornamentation remains easily visible, while the brick piers rising from the mezzanine level stress the verticality so popular during the 1920s and 1930s.

Happily, the building's lower floors have proven suited to the *Salt Lake Tribune*'s and former *Salt Lake Telegram*'s purposes, and from 1937 to the present the building has been the centerpiece of all manner of public events related to the state's largest circulation newspapers. Each year when the time arrives for the Days of '47 celebrations, a platform erected outside the *Tribune* serves pioneer folk dancers and provides seating for dignitaries watching the floats and paraders.

Utah veterans have used the same spot outside 143 S. Main when buglers sound taps to mark what we once labeled Armistice Day. Here officials without number have gathered for more Christmas seasons than one can remember to throw the switches setting Main Street and the "Tribune community tree" lights aglow. Nowadays, thanks to the persistence of Publisher Emeritus John W. Gallivan and Publisher Jerry O'Brien, a living, growing tree stands outside the building's door. Until a decade ago, a new tree was cut in the valley annually, hauled to the *Tribune* building and set in place. There are traditionalists among us who feel we may have lost something when ecologists triumphed over the tree-cutting ritual, watching a towering tree being hoisted into place was good fun—and an enormous "photo opportunity."

However, the best remembered *Tribune* display, one that drew large crowds to Main Street annually, was the newspaper's "Old Ironsides," a huge electrically lighted baseball field layout, erected just outside the second-story windows at World Series time. Lest you've forgotten those pre-television days, sports editors and columnists Phil McLeese and John Mooney, and such minions as writers Bill Coltrin and Don Brooks, would listen through headsets to radio broadcasts of the October classic taking place at such distant sites as Yankee Stadium or Wrigley Field. When Mel Allen or his peers reported a pitched strike, ball or foul tip, a base hit, run, walk or error and the like, McLeese, Mooney and Co. would swing into action using homemade (by the newspaper's maintenance department) relay circuitry to show the path of the "ball" by lighting the bulbs in sequence on "Old Ironsides" while the crowd cheered in the street below.

McLeese and Mooney, hands clad in rubber gloves to prevent electrical shock, labored each day of the series, clicking away the innings, the room in which they worked a cloud of blue smoke from Phil's chainsmoked cigarettes and John's stogies.

Perched out on the window sill, meanwhile, other sports staffers like young Tom Korologos, would keep the inning-by-inning line score updated with large numeral-cards. Nor was the *Tribune* alone in providing such marvelous electric gadgetry to keep its readers informed—newspapers ranging from Philadelphia's *Public Ledger* to the Brooklyn *Citizen* did much the same.

The big plate glass windows fronting the ground floor business offices in those days also offered useful attractions. One duty of every well-trained copy boy was to set the day's bulletin matter in large type, printing same on long sheets of newsprint from press remnants, then posting this synopsis of the late news in those windows. During World War II, pedestrian traffic crowded the sidewalk in front of the building to read of sea battles in the Pacific, of Hitler's buzz bombs slamming London and of the battles on Utah Beach in Normandy. Shortly after the war, the *Tribune-Telegram* cooperating with KALL, set up a "newsroom studio" in those same windows, so not-so-blasé Salt Lakers could watch announcers Paul Sullivan or Mal Wyman read a noon or 5 P.M. newscast. Live!

Since 143 S. Main has been the province of newspaper people for fully a half century, those of us who have toiled in the building as "ink-stained wretches," as advertising men, circulation department employees, artists, telephone operators, pressmen, and even as proverbial "little merchants," often view the building with affection overlaid with nostalgia.

Hustling through its doors, we who have grown gray, bald, or more than necessarily stout during our years in the Fourth Estate can't help but remember all manner of guys and gals who worked with us therein. To be scrupulously truthful, many who labored in the City Room, the Photo Department, or in the "Back Shop" entered the building via Regent Street—it being closer to the parking lot and the old Mint Cafe. And, of course, the linotypes, presses and other such items of the craft were housed in the separate, noisy quarters redolent of printer's ink across a windy alleyway used by newsprint trucks. There, Charlie McGillis, cigar clamped between his teeth, and Dewey Whatcott supervised "newsies," those crews of kids and agéd gentlemen who once roamed the downtown streets shouting "Extree! Paper, read all about it!" Alas, television has robbed us of all that.

Of course, the front doors were not sacrosanct. Murray Moler of United Press, Jerry O'Brien, then of Associated Press, and Ted Himstreet, who ran a one-man International News Service Bureau, entered up front to ride elevators to work and glom onto *Tribune* story carbons in the City Room.

On almost any election night during the '50s and after, George Dewey Clyde, J. Bracken Lee, Wallace F. Bennett, Arthur V. Watkins and other politicos of note, could be seen taking the elevator to the *Tribune*'s innards to learn how ballots being tallied by the newspaper's election service team were trending. Along with Mayor Earl J. Glade and Gov. Herbert Maw you might glimpse visitors from downstate such as Congressman Walter K. Granger or Ogden's J. Aldous Dixon crowding around the desk of the *Tribune*'s sagacious political editor O.N. Malmquist.

As you neared the stairway in the 1950s, you might be swept off your feet by a rush of photographers and reporters en route to assignments. George Bettridge, Van E. (Hypo) Porter, Borge Andersen, Jack White, Frank Porschatis, Brandt Gray, Carl Reynolds, Earl Conrad and Ross Welser would be carrying the weighty Speed Graphic cameras of the period. Then there were reporters Walt King; Al Ferguson, who quietly covered the old Federal Building and its courts; Stan Bowman, handling weather stories; police reporters Harold Schindler, Jim Baldwin and portly Maurice (Mike) Jones. Salt Lake County expert George A. (Gus) Sorensen carried only a pencil, a sheaf of copy paper, and insight into affairs that mattered.

On any busy day, one might have seen the arrival of Medical Editor William C. Patrick, just back from Ogden and a state surgical meet, while Robert W. Bernick departed for an interview with First Security President Marriner Eccles. Roy Hudson would be heading upstairs, while staffers Jim Fitzpatrick and Tommy Mathews clattered downstairs for a cup of coffee at the Mayflower Cafe—no coffee machine in the City Room in that era—while Don Howard held down the fort.

Readers of the paper's sports section would be more interested in the comings and goings of McLeese and Mooney, Brooks and Coltrin, Jimmy Hodgson, Jack Schroeder, Marion Dunn, Jim Grebe, Ed (Lefty) McFadden, Ollie McCullough and Bob Williams as they headed to and from such distant spots as Cheyenne, the Country Club, Derk's Field or the Fairgrounds Coliseum on their coveted assignments.

As if to prove that there was no bias (oh yeah?) against "newshens," a *Tribune* elevator might contain reporter Melba M. Ferguson, society editor Grace Grether, super-efficient librarian Leah Beckstead, vivacious Hazel Parkinson, Mary Pappasideris or Jackie Woolf.

My memory being what it is, the *Tribune* building remains peopled as it was circa 1950. National news editor Jim Walsh sits a bit aside in the City Room, Bill Smiley, cigarette in hand, is answering a phone alongside Art Tholen. Cigarettes would "do Bill in," and Tholen squinted even then, showing the beginnings of an increasingly serious eye problem. Hays Gorey, Bob Ottum and Will Jarvis are ever on hand, in mind's eye, before departing for Time-Life and *Sports Illustrated* posts in Washington, New York and Boston.

Jim England, then news editor, is forever wrestling with problems caused by an overabundance of news and "too small a hole" left by Herb Price and other eager advertising salesmen.

Before any day was well under way, editorial writers Erne Linford, Herb Kretchman and Ted Long would have marched across Main Street to the Kearns Building to discuss matters of prime importance with publisher John F. Fitzpatrick, whose eyes seemed able to peer through the windows—and walls—of 143 S Main. Later Bob Blair (the "Colonel") and Harry Fuller joined the editorialist ranks.

There are other names, other bylines, many Utahns will remember: Dan Valentine, now, alas, confined to a wheelchair; Roy Robinson, Clarence (Scoop) Williams, Keith V. Otteson, Bob Ellefsen, Ham Park (the "Senator from Sandpit"), who with many of the stalwarts mentioned, has gone to greener pastures. And, of course, the last one to board a late-night down-bound elevator was, very often, Executive Editor Arthur C. Deck, referred to otherwise by staffers as "the Man." Prowling back and forth across the City Room, Art would have peered across his glinting spectacles, would have fixed Will Fehr, or Jack Schroeder, or Jack Goodman with a piercing icy stare—and would have asked, "How come you're moving late copy?"

# The Original Salt Palace

MAY 31, 1992

During past weeks, Salt Lakers cheered loud and long when members of the Utah Jazz plopped cantaloupe-shaped objects into fringe-decorated hoops, and groaned loud and long when the Jazz gents missed. Meantime, sections of Los Angeles inexplicably burst into flames, Haitians went sailing in leaky craft and residents of Josef Broz Tito's "Yugoslavia" shot each other in awesome numbers.

One evening, mythical Murphy Brown had a mythical offspring, discomfiting our nation's not-so-mythical vice president. And a few Salt Lakers noticed an item in the *Salt Lake Tribune* stating it would be cheaper to tear down the "drum" of the existing Salt Palace and build anew for an expanded convention center than 'twould be to remodel same.

While cogitating on such matters, plus the city's seeming inability to replace old-with-new seating at Derk's Field, Salt Lakers could wonder whether Mayor Deedee Corradini has been ingesting too many beans even as they questioned whether a multimillion-dollar, Olympic-size ice oval should replace the battered, unfinished row of low-cost apartments on the city's west side.

Patrons of the Greek Orthodox cathedral and the Japanese Christian Church registered opposition, while patrons of centers providing food and shelter to the homeless remained silent—silent reminders that joblessness and homelessness prevail in Ross Perot's time as in the days of H. Clark Hoover.

All this also reminds one that folks who neglect history are doomed to relive it—and its mistakes. Hence the choice of today's sketch of our town's long-vanished "Temple of Amusement," the old Salt Palace completed Aug. 21, 1899, on 900 South between State and Main.

Lest you've forgotten, the Delta Center cost some sixty-six million dollars. Tearing down and expanding the present twenty-year-old Salt Palace will cost half that sum. Things were different in 1899. When civic-conscious private citizens led by W.A. Nelden beseeched the Utah Legislature and Gov. Heber M. Wells for an $8,000 appropriation to help build their "temple," the answer was a flat "no."

Mr. Nelden and his half-dozen cohorts saw their planned palazzo as a national attraction—as glossy as the splendid Ice Palace in Minneapolis, as corny as the Corn Palace in Sioux City, Iowa. Not to be thwarted, when the Nelden team learned state funds would be lacking, they raised necessary dollars by emptying their own pockets, borrowing at local banks and even by selling advertising on the fence surrounding their site.

Originally the promoters planned their Salt Palace at Liberty Park. Instead, members of this civic- and profit-minded band donated the 900 South site rent-free "for a number of years," replacing a "market garden."

Their chosen architect, Richard K.A. Kletting, designed a pavilion capped by a huge dome, with thirty flagpoles and a sculptured work depicting Liberty rising from ornate bases on the building's cornice.

Kletting, who also designed the original Saltair structures, later was the victorious architect in a Utah Capitol competition. Indeed, his designs for the 900 South palace anticipate the Beaux Arts Classicism of his handsome governmental center.

The core of attraction of the "Temple of Amusement" lay in the materials used for construction. Linda Thatcher of the Utah Historical Society reports it had "a wooden frame, then spraying powdered salt under pressure over the surface . . . large interior wall panels were made by immersing boards in ponds of super-saturated brine that in time deposited salt crystals all over the wood." When thick enough, deposits were installed in the building. Meanwhile, rock-salt slabs, chiefly from Salina, were cut, shaped and placed as footstones, porch pillars and arches.

When completed, the building cost $60,000, with much of that sum going to a Coney Island-style electrical system. Inside the circular auditorium under the dome were 900 light bulbs partially concealed by salt crystals to give an iridescent effect. Outside on the dome, porches, paths and other buildings, another 3,000 bulbs made night-time admission easily worth the twenty-five-cent charge.

The Salt Palace contained a dance floor, a stage for plays and concerts, and a sizable square exhibition hall for the display of Utah products.

The circular, 108-foot-diameter auditorium was on the third floor, window-ringed and brightly painted. Outside grounds featured a miniature railway, a merry-go-round, a "Streets of Cairo" and a "Temple of Isis," doubtless sheltering appropriately garbed "natives" of the female persuasion. There were benches, a pond and possibly a bandstand. But the best-remembered attraction was not the "Captive Passenger Balloon" nor the Circle Swing, nor the baseball diamond. It was, of course, the Salt Palace Saucer.

Designed by Truman O. Angell Jr., this wooden, steeply banked track was rimmed by seats for 4,000 spectators who cheered as the nation's best bicyclists and "locals" sought amateur and professional records. Carl Smith, the "hard-riding Mormon"; Hardy K. Downing, who later "discovered" Jack Dempsey; and the speedy Iver Larson are mentioned in Ms. Thatcher's research records. Larson's world record of 23.9 seconds for a half-mile still stands—I am told. It was set in 1911, after an Aug. 29, 1910, fire had destroyed the Salt Palace, but not the track.

That was several years after the original builders of the great Pleasure Temple had lost their shirts, dollarwise. The Salt Palace couldn't pay its $20,544 of outstanding debt when completed. O.D. Romney bought the whole shebang in 1900 for $18,000 at a sheriff's sale.

The Salt Palace itself lasted just 11 years before burning. But in 1912, Joseph Nelsen and J.E. Langrod built a large open-air theater on the Palace site, later expanding to a skating rink, dance floor and pavilion called Majestic Park. The bicycle track operated 'til 1914, when it burned down. The pavilion collapsed after a record 1916 snowstorm.

All of which is history. Recalling the troubles—and the glory—of the first Salt Palace may assist today's public officials, county commissioners and taxpayers to recall another maxim: There are people who both read history and look forward to the past.

# Rio Grande Machine Shops / Eimco Building

MARCH 17, 1991

Half a century ago, when railroads serving Salt Lake seemed far more important to the city's well-being than they've become in this era of over-the-road trucks and high-flying airliners, workers who entered the vast shed-like space of the structure shown in today's sketch were machinists, boiler-makers, sheet metal workers, pipefitters and the like. The machines they labored to keep rolling efficiently were, in the main, giant steam locomotives, although they also built and repaired freight cars.

This example of Vulcan's forge—twentieth-century style—served as the locomotive repair, boiler shop and car-building establishment of the Denver & Rio Grande Western Railroad. It was noisy, the air inside was laden with smoke, coal dust and ash. It was hot in summer, frigid in win-

112

ter—but then, so was almost any job on any railroad. Except for those held by the "big brass," of course.

The shops boasted a pair of fifty-ton overhead cranes that could hoist the boiler, cab and pilot off the running gear of a mammoth Mallet or a speedy passenger-hauling 4-8-2. The shop stood near the intersection of the Western Pacific rails and Rio Grande trackage, a block-long, brick-and-concrete affair between 200 and 300 South dating from 1910 or thereabouts. Unlovely, noisome and smoky it certainly was, but it had its own history. For example, one of the shop's employees—when the building was new and steam ruled the rails—had been young Walter P. Chrysler. A native of Wamego, Kansas, he was—like hundreds of skilled machinists and boiler-makers—a journeyman.

Chrysler was not unusual in his beginnings. Born in 1875 he began his railroad career at five cents per hour as a locomotive wiper at a Kansas roundhouse of the Union Pacific. But the wandering railroader (his middle name, by the by, was Percy) didn't stay at the local Rio Grande shops very long. The huge steam locomotives on which Rio Grande crews labored to "turn wheels" and repair tubes and grates didn't last forever either. Steam operations on that road came to an end on Dec. 26, 1956, while the last gondola car was built in those same shops at about the same time.

A bit of "name spending" might set the stage for older Utahns who recall the heyday of the railroads. There was Judge Wilson McCarthy, for example, who brought the road out of bankruptcy in the wake of the Depression. The passenger traffic manager was Harold F. Eno; general passenger agent was Dan Heiner. Well-remembered local executives included Knox Bradford and Henry Riggert. All played sizable roles in local civic affairs in an era when railroad executives were major figures in the city's power structure.

Nowadays very few Utahns know—or care—who heads the D&RGW or UPRR. In fact there's some uncertainty as to whether the Rio Grande owns the Southern Pacific or vice-versa. Currently the Western Pacific's tracks are used by the trains of its one-time rival, the Union Pacific.

One might even wonder if anyone (aside from shippers or ancient newspapermen) recalls the Ogden Gateway Case, which kept attorneys and railroaders in such a tizzy and tangle for years until Eimco's Morris Rosenblatt was victor. Which brings up the matter of the name on the concrete block office building attached to the north end of the old Rio

Grande shops, shops now partially covered with a blue-colored sheath. Eimco purchased the railroad's establishment shortly after growling diesel locomotives completely replaced the more picturesque steam giants—in an era when the manufacture of underground mining machinery was a major employer on the city's west side. Alas, most firms in our local "rust belt" have vanished.

You can still see the Eimco name on the shop offices, of course, but the old Eimco building on 400 West is closed, along with its adjunct American Foundry and Machine Co. headed by Simon Rosenblatt and the Structural Steel and Forge company run by Morris Rosenblatt.

The last brother of the trio—younger brother Joseph R.—ran Eimco when the firm employed fully 2,000 Utahns, plus a sizable batch of overseas men. But the company actually dates back to the father of the three executives cited—Nathan Rosenblatt, who came to Salt Lake as a young immigrant from Russia in 1889. The two generations built their international mining machine firm from Nathan's original Utah Junk Co. and were in need of considerably more plant space when offered the opportunity to buy the Rio Grande's locomotive shops.

Eimco was sold by the Rosenblatt family to the Ogden Corp. in 1957, after which it passed to Envirotech and then eventually to today's owners, Baker-Hughes. Hughes, by the by, is part of the old Howard Hughes enterprise. Company names are odd things— I recall asking Nathan Rosenblatt what "Eimco" means, and being told "it was Eastern Iron and Metal." "Why Eastern, way out here in the West?" I inquired. "Well," the seventy-five-year-old founder of the firm replied, "those days, no one would buy anything from a firm named western. But eastern—that was an important word."

Today's engineers, welders, metal fabricators and machinists concentrate on the manufacture of Eimco's industrial filters. These are hefty devices used in water treatment, chemical operations, sewage treatment and the like. It's not a new line either—the firm shipped stainless steel filtration equipment to Oak Ridge during World War II when atomic bombs were being made. Those were the days when shop "super" Hudson Francom, foundry foreman Eckley Keach, inventive Burt Royle, supersalesman Jim Russell and other Eimco men would meet to eat with opposite numbers from Silver Electric, Pioneer Fence and a half-dozen now-vanished westside plants.

The cafe at the Rio Grande station was a favorite spot for burgers, beans or meat pies. Today the cafe is a Mexican restaurant; one wonders whether any of the new crowd ever saw an operating steam locomotive.

EDITOR'S NOTE: The address of the former Rio Grande Railroad machine shops, now housing the Eimco Process Equipment Co., is 669 W. 200 South.

# The Sweet Candy Factory

AUGUST 13, 1989

Now and again, when passing the four-story factory building at 224 S. 200 West, you may realize that all forms of air pollution should not be verboten. Indeed, the airy odors wafting from this white and gray structure's red-framed windows will likely alert taste buds to past and future delights, will set gastric juices flowing and even will cause oldsters to recollect days long since past, when they peered into glass-fronted showcases in vanished confectionery stores to ponder the options: chocolate, "jaw-breakers," licorice whips or brightly colored jelly beans. If a gracious uncle crossed your palm with a whole nickel, you left the candy store of yore with a paper sack full of all of the above and more. If in possession of a single penny, you could still exit the shop with a mouthful of chocolate caramels with a decision yet to make—should you first lick off the chocolate, then chew the chewy stuff or crunch through the entire caramel with a single bite?

116

The brightly painted structure at 224 S. 200 West is, of course, the locale of the most aptly named business in our town, the Sweet Candy Company. This three-generation enterprise has occupied its light and airy concrete, brick and steel quarters since 1911. Architects Walter Ware and Alberto Treganza, once among the state's most prestigious members of their profession, designed the factory for Leon Sweet. Born in Visalia, Calif., in 1871, he came to Utah from the San Francisco Bay area at the turn of the century after first joining forces with one Louis Saroni to establish a small candy-making factory or two in or near Portland, Ore.

By 1911, when Ware and Treganza blueprinted the initial section of today's plant, Leon Sweet had opted to make his headquarters in Utah's capital city, a community then as now renowned for its collective sweet tooth. His son, Leon Jack Sweet, entered full into the family business in 1931 or thereabouts, to be followed a dozen or so years ago by grandson R. Anthony Sweet. Unlike some of the region's other candy makers, the Sweets never operated retail shops. Down through the years, sugar, nuts, raisins, chocolate and similar ingredients have poured out in boxes, in paper wrappers or nowadays, in plastic bags.

Local delivery trucks move the candies to Logan, Payson and towns between. Other larger vehicles leave daily, carting taffy, jelly beans and the like to merchants throughout the western states.

Wandering through today's plant (after first donning a mandatory hairnet) and guided by Leon Jack Sweet and candymaker Dorothy Swearingen, this columnist learned from the current senior Sweet that two additions, built in 1922 and 1953, were required to flesh out its present 200,000-square-foot size. A visitor likewise comes to appreciate that a 1911 building, if designed by such experts as Ware and Treganza, can function efficiently down through the years. Old machines can and have been replaced, old techniques (including hand-dipped chocolates) can become outdated. But oversized windows help keep a factory such as this light and airy. A flow-sheet in which raw materials begin uptop, and are moved down as completed and wrapped, helps keep even an elderly building efficient.

Outwardly the plant lacks decorative details except for a few touches atop its fourth floor and on its bay dividers. From the standpoint of passing pedestrians or motorists, the Sweet Candy Co. plant has looked more "modern" than ever these past few years, due to a splendid paint job enhancing the 200 West facade.

However, I've a hunch management would appreciate more room for truck maneuvers, plus more parking for some 200 employees and daily visitors and larger elevators for palletized cargo.

Times, tastes and prices have changed in the candy marketplace since the late W.W. Cassidy (who came west with the Kearns-Tribune Corp.'s John Fitzpatrick) joined the Sweet clan in managing the firm. "You no longer can give your best girl a $1.50 box of our 'Renown' candies," Jack Sweet notes a bit sourly. "In fact we discontinued our box candy line some years ago. No hand-dipped, hand-packed boxes. But in spite of none-too-truthful propaganda concerning teeth and calories, we Americans continue to consume eighteen pounds of candy per capita each year."

In an office decorated with old apothecary scales, fragile souvenir hand fans advertising Sweet's products and equally old posters, Jack Sweet recalls an era when the Hotel Utah, Schramm-Johnson Drugs and Keeley's were among major customers.

Upstairs, where copper kettles slowly twirl and jelly beans roll merrily into a multitude of boxes, storage rooms are carefully kept at forty degrees, fifty-five degrees for chocolates. Old favorites still being produced might still attract the pennies of your childhood and mine. "Fresh As a Sea Breeze" Salt Water Taffy is a current best-selling item moved for shipment at the factory's loading dock. "Jelly beans popularized by Ronald Reagan are a big item," Sweet reports. "He did great things for us." And such old-line attractions as lemon drops and rock candy are still shipped to chain stores including Sears and Woolworth, or for display on racks in supermarkets.

One upscale favorite remaining in production gained favor long ago on the dining cars of such trains as the old California Zephyr.

"Our chocolate-covered orange sticks—remember them? The know-how for making them is something of a trade secret," Sweet says with smile.

There remains one noncandy-related item to report concerning the west-side factory. Almost diagonally opposite, at the southeast corner of 200 South and 200 West, stands an equally large, one-time factory building—a red-brick affair recently modernized by the installation of large-paned bay windows. Examine the brickwork details above its upper story and you'll realize they match the patterning atop the Sweet factory. Which is logical since this building was designed by Ware and Treganza as a near twin of the candy-making plant. Its initial occupant was the now vanished Schramm-Johnson Drug Co., once one of the city's largest such firms.

# The Commercial Club

FEBRUARY 21, 1988

Before today's Salt Lake Chamber of Commerce came into existence, a pre-decessor organization known as the Commercial Club was engaged in drum-beating efforts to bring new business and industry to Utah's metropolis. Whether Commercial Club's officers or members succeeded in their chosen task, or how long the organization functioned, I know not. When I turn back my own mental clock, I see the likes of Gus P. Backman, Gen. Maxwell E. Rich (Ret.), and Fred Ball heading up the Chamber of Commerce drives to lure business this-a-way. Now and again they marched off to lead parading "Salt Shakers" down the main drags of Idaho Falls, Grand Junction and similar outlying centers of trade, pied pipers seeking to convince assorted outlanders that Salt Lake City was and is a business as well as a religious mecca.

Whether or not members of the long gone Commercial Club caused new payrolls and patrons to tilt in our direction or not, its largely forgotten leaders and members certainly built an opulent headquarters for themselves. Today, fully eighty years after its completion, the old Commercial Club Building at 32 Exchange Place remains one of the handsomest in the city.

The Salt Lake Chamber of Commerce "poor-boyed" it in rented quarters in the Salisbury Building (site of the long-vacant J.C. Penney store), then leased modest quarters in the Walker Bank parking terrace tower, and, at present, occupies a portion of the shiny but unlovely City Centre on 400 South at 200 East.

As if to illustrate that progress-minded local businessmen had a trained eye for excellence in architecture, their old Commercial Club Building on Exchange Place remains one of the best-decorated, best-proportioned commercial structures ever to grace our city. Six stories high, its style is a bit reminiscent of a Florentine palazzo. Historically, this seems quite all right, since the princes and dukes who made Florence a center of Renaissance civilization were, in the main, merchant princes, members of families that were the wealthiest in Europe in their day. In truth, the structure is not quite patterned upon Florentine models—some architectural historians decry it as "Second Renaissance Revival," but why argue the fine points? It is, as a visit will prove, constructed of a warmly tinted red brick resting upon two lower stories faced with terra cotta.

There are rather fanciful designs of mosaic tile and polychromed terra cotta, while inlaid panels ring the building just above the second story. The cornice is especially broad and elaborate. Protruding balconies, a high entrance lobby on Exchange Place and a series of fluted columns gracing the sixth floor all enhance the edifice. Those columns form a sort of loggia for occupants of the upper-story offices—providing a shadowy, Italianate porch for Salt Lakers.

The architects, Walter E. Ware and Alberto Treganza, were among the city's best in their day. Very possibly, Treganza was of Italian ancestry, hence the style and detailing. And, if the memories of old-timers are correct, Ware and Treganza sought to give Commercial Club members a headquarters equivalent (except in size) to the New York City Athletic Club, then being hailed as the finest in the nation.

When it opened in 1908, the building boasted a sizable swimming pool, several dining rooms, an especially handsome banquet room, game rooms, a host of offices and what was described as a "ladies parlor." Alas, the building seems to have been vacated by the busy businessmen a decade or so after completion. Fiscal matters then ran downhill for a number of years. By the 1960s it was chiefly occupied by a portion of the local staff of the U.S. Department of Interior's Bureau of Reclamation. The swimming pool was but a dingy, tile-walled vacant ruin, the dining rooms were abandoned. What the federal folk at the General Office of Accounting, who were among its landlords, thought of the decaying remnants of vanished luxury one can only surmise.

Fortunately, a decade or so ago, about the time the Exchange Place Historic District was formed, a gallant band of newly arrived young businessmen carried the torch (dollarwise) for the Commercial Club building, the nearby Newhouse and Boston buildings and the old Salt Lake Stock Exchange. These structures were among those erected between 1903 and World War I, chiefly through financing provided by mining man Samuel Newhouse. Along with a large group of "gentile" businessmen, Newhouse sought to counteract the very visible growth of Mormon businesses clustered around the Main Street corner of Temple Square. Newhouse, whose now vanished hotel was planned as a principal "anchor" for the lower Main Street district, "broke his pick," as miners were wont to say. He was forced into bankruptcy and lost his holdings (which had included the land for the Commercial Club he donated to the organization), sending the district into a slump from which it has never fully recovered.

The recent upgrading of the area, which included new brick walks, tree-planting and installation of the controversial triangular sculpture at the Main Street corner, has converted the area into one of the city's most attractive business settings. The Commercial Club building, refurbished in period style, is now occupied in the main by law offices and brokerage firms. The shady minipark between it and the Newhouse Building is a pleasant place for brown-baggers when the weather is warm.

The Commercial Club Building, I hope, will last another two decades and achieve the century mark. On its merits it deserves to survive—and thrive.

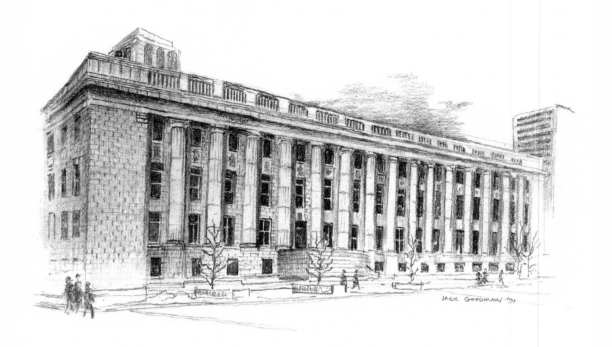

# The Federal Courthouse / Downtown Post Office

DECEMBER 29, 1991

Way back in 1903, architect James Knox Taylor, in the pay of a burgeoning federal government, designed our town's first really sizable Neo-Classic Revival structure. The combined federal courthouse and post office building that resulted has presented its handsome Greco-Roman facade to the public on Main Street between Post Office Place and 400 South since its initial "completion" in 1906.

Some two weeks ago, to properly mark the 200th anniversary of the Bill of Rights, the judges of the U.S. District Court for Utah invited the public to hear a distinguished panel discourse on the Bill of Rights—and to inspect their handsomely remodeled U.S. courthouse.

An inspection of what is now officially designated the Frank E. Moss

United States Courthouse showed visitors what our town's legal lights already know—the post office has vanished without a trace. No stamp or parcel windows, no lobby newsstand, and, alas (for that day at least), no trace of the ghost of Judge Willis W. Ritter, said to haunt these federal premises.

The building underwent some earlier major changes. A rear addition was built of buff brick onto the original west side in 1912. A final addition to the south end went on in 1932, funded, I believe, by the WPA as a form of make-work project that might be welcome in our community today.

The post office has, as most Salt Lakers must be aware, moved to 230 W. 200 South in the ExpoMart building, which means there's no need to drive by the street boxes on Main Street or Post Office Place when the deadline for filing income-tax returns rolls 'round.

In the main-floor lobby, a gleaming metal plaque recounts the services of former U.S. Sen. Frank Moss, for whom the structure is now named. One wonders, because the Federal Building at State and 100 South is named for retired U.S. Sen. Wallace F. Bennett, what can a grateful government name for Sen. Jake Garn when he retires?

On a more serious note, visitors to the courthouse agree the renovation has been handsomely done. Indeed, when out-of-state attorneys, federal commission members, important evildoers and the like come to town to do business at court, they should be properly impressed by new wainscoting, tilework, wood paneling, carpeting and so forth throughout the building's multitude of courtrooms. Offices, courtrooms, library—all have both a pleasant and a dignified look. One can't be quite sure how a federal suspect hauled before, let us say, Judge David Sam will enjoy his surroundings. But even the jury rooms look comfortable enough for a lengthy stay.

Chief Judge Bruce Jenkins, Judge David E. Winder, Judge J. Thomas Greene and the newest appointee, Judge Dee Benson, all seem to be well housed indeed as regards both courtrooms and chambers. Senior Judges A. Sherman Christensen and Aldon J. Anderson both have equally impressive, yet not overly plush, quarters. In every case, there is access for the handicapped, the lighting seems good, and decorations are sparse yet excellent, in what might be termed the "modern federal" manner. Ventilation and heating have all been attended to, and, one suspects, the sound system or general acoustics will prove at least acceptable.

The last matter is raised, of course, in memory of the late Judge Ritter. Members of an earlier generation of journalists will remember that the sometimes-irascible jurist ordered United Press bureau chief Murray Moler into the slammer for contempt of court. The judge went to considerable lengths to bar cameras, especially TV cameras, from building corridors. Not exactly a display of freedom of speech or press as guaranteed in the Bill of Rights, was it?

Judge Ritter often had cause for his erratic actions, including the occasion when I reported for the *New York Times*, on its front page: "Neither snow, nor rain, nor dark of night can stay these couriers from the swift completion of their appointed rounds, but a federal judge can, and did so today." The reference was to Judge Ritter's enraged action shutting down handling of mail in the post office beneath his courtroom and his hauling Postmaster Dave Trevithick to his bench.

Air vents unfortunately connected Ritter's courtroom to the vast spaces where bundles of mail were sorted at all hours. Now and again the dignified hush of the courtroom was shattered by cursing, swearing and the thumpings of mail sacks coming and going to points east and west. If I recall correctly, the judge sent his marshal to the scene of the noise—and the latter gentleman returned with a postal supervisor who was chained to a mail sack he was duty-bound not to leave behind. He also carried a pistol, holstered of course. Outraged by the sight of a potential gunslinger in his courtroom (plus the lackey's refusal to order a halt to mail-sorting), the indignant judge enjoined the Postal Service from handling mail beneath his courtroom. He also summoned Postmaster Trevithick for a "talking to."

The matter ended peacefully—but it may be the ghost of an errant postal worker, not the judge, who haunts the multipillared Frank E. Moss United States Courthouse.

# Auerbach's Department Store

DECEMBER 4, 1994

Doing your Christmas shopping? Don't look for the many-windowed department store in today's sketch. It exists only in the memories of middle-aged and elderly Salt Lakers.

The building is, or was, the Auerbach Department Store, which stood at 300 S. State (the corner of Broadway) for many profitable and busy shopping seasons.

First, a bit of history. The structure enhanced by angle-parked cars at the State Street curb was not built for the Auerbach merchandising clan. Instead, it was constructed in 1911, at a cost of $168,000 turn-of-century dollars, by the Jarvis Stewart Co. and leased to the Keith O'Brien Company, which ran the department store therein until 1924. The building's owner, from the start, was Evelyn Brooks Auerbach.

While Keith O'Brien occupied the building, Jarvis Stewart Co. made a $35,000 alteration when the big structure was barely a year old and made a second alteration in 1914 for just $5,000. Just across the street until that juncture, the Auerbach Company assumed occupancy in 1924 and its glory years as Salt Lake City's premier department store began.

The story of the Auerbach family could—and has—filled a book. Suffice it to say, Auerbach's became one of the few department stores in the nation remaining under a single family's ownership for more than a century. Frederick and Samuel Auerbach were the founders and Herbert, a son of Samuel, took charge after his father's death. According to *Salt Lake Tribune* records, ownership did not pass from family members until 1977, when Alvin Richer bought the business.

By that time, Auerbach's had seen many more alterations. In 1958 it opened a $1.5-million parking terrace entered from State Street. The store had been air-conditioned earlier, with improved lighting also fitted. In 1960 came a major new exterior look—the multiwindowed structure in today's sketch was completely hidden by a new white concrete panel facade. Designed by Carpenter and Stringham, the new exterior was the work of Tolboe and Harlin Construction. The new facade of Mosai stone sheets was literally hung over the steel and concrete frame of the old store. Aluminum and glass doors led, when opened, to a glittering gold and white interior.

Heeding the trend to the suburbs, Auerbach's opened a new store in Fashion Place Mall in 1971 and a second unit at Cottonwood Mall in 1976. But word came, shockingly sudden to most shoppers, that the downtown store would close in February 1979, due to eleven years of declining volume.

After Alvin Richer bought and briefly operated the big store, the building was again remodeled, this time into the red-brick, horizontal-windowed structure you can see today. The building, which today has such tenants as First Security Bank, served as a temporary City Hall while the multitowered City and County Building was being restored and earthquake-proofed.

Enough of the building's history and Auerbach's woes. This columnist, never a "shopper," has been intrigued by the reports from my wife, female relatives and all manner of local women concerning the esteem in which they held Auerbach's. Many report that countless women "enjoyed walking the circle" down Main Street from ZCMI, across Broadway to State Street and into Auerbach's, where they lunched and shopped. After which they window-shopped State to South Temple, where, if there was time, they visited Makoff's.

According to one such localite, you parked at the Hotel Utah garage to start your window-shopping tour. Such ladies swung through ZCMI briefly. "But it rarely showed the latest in fashion," according to my frau. Women then crossed Main, peered into specialty-shop windows, and possibly remarked at the odd sight of menfolk eating lunch while standing in the Grabeteria. Younger misses next excitedly ogled fresh styles at Adrian and Emily's fashion house and walked on to study the "coming attractions" at the Utah Theatre. One or two entered Hibbs', Fife's, Rosen's or Frank's to buy a tie, shirt or handkerchiefs for hubby or the boyfriend.

Pressing south, the ladies encountered the opulent Leyson-Pearsall's jewelry store, where diamonds, watches, pearl necklaces and the like were discreetly displayed. Many then sought out Walker Brothers, at Main and Broadway, housed in a building that later briefly held Sears Roebuck and then the Darling Store. A few women had entered Sam Weller's Zion Book Store to purchase such an item as *Gone with the Wind* while others sought out jewelry shops such as Schubach's (famous for diamonds). And don't neglect the United Cigar shop at the Broadway corner, where female nonladies could purchase sinful cigarettes.

Broadway (300 South) boasted a Bon Marché shop, Jerry Landa's millinery, women's shoe stores, the Paris Store, Pembroke's stationery and Keith O'Brien's.

But the real goal was Auerbach's. There the ladies had favorite salespersons, and tried on fashionable bargains. Those were the days, my friends. Who thought they would ever end?

# CHAPTER 6

# The Initial Suburbs

# The Avenues Historic District

NOVEMBER 3, 1991

Is that old mansion, farmhouse, church or business building a structure in the Gothic Revival style, or is it more properly designated a Queen Anne, Victorian, Colonial, shingle, American vernacular—or a more modern Prairie or Art Moderne house? Do you somehow enjoy gazing at the building—but do you wonder why? And what is the approximate date of its construction?

Happily, you need not take a formal class in the history of architecture to acquire at least a modicum of information concerning architectural styles. A walk through the lower Avenues of our town will help you acquire a basic knowledge of the subject.

A stroll along even a single Avenues street (First Avenue is a prime favorite) is certain to show even the casual observer why the area between South Temple and Eleventh Avenue, and Canyon Road to Virginia Street, was properly designated our town's "Avenues Historic District" back in 1976. A sharp-eyed observer can also learn more than a little about the efforts of local businessmen to help the city grow—and to profit thereby. A stroll of a mile or so will also indicate that being designated "historic" has led to more than a little neighborhood pride in the area, meaning the average sidewalk is well-paved and swept, the average lawn and shrubs are trimmed, and the average home, a century old though it may be, has been carefully painted, roofed and kept tidy in recent years.

Having said all that, how is it that the dwelling I've chosen to sketch, at 1007 First Ave., is far from the neatest on the block? Perhaps it's the odd color. This hundred-year-old home is a slightly faded blue color, with a few brown shake-shingles looking out of place on the walls back of its porch.

The history of the house is intriguing, at least to this columnist. At the State Historical Society library, a reference book indicated that one Claude W. Freed had been its second owner, beginning in 1916. Chancing to meet Richard Freed at lunch the day I found the reference book, I asked if he had ever known a Claude Freed, one-time occupant of 1007 First Ave.

"He was my father," Dick Freed said rather pointedly. "I was raised in that house, lived there while I went to Wasatch School with my brother Charles." Lest you've forgotten, the Freeds operated the Chrysler automobile agency at the east end of Social Hall Avenue until the business closed a few years ago.

"That was some house," Dick Freed reported nostalgically. "There was a full-sized gymnasium on the top floor. Every kid in the neighborhood played with us up there. A great place for growing up."

The faded blue house at 1007 First Ave. was designed by Walter Ware and Ezra Cornell during their partnership days when they likewise planned the city's Jackson School. The home, upwards of two and one-half stories high, was converted into a four-unit apartment house by realtor Quayle Cannon in 1938 or thereabouts. Alas, at this writing it's not fully rented. The builders were Elmer Darling and Frank McGurrin. Darling, back in the '80s, was the chap who thoughtfully bought a sizable chunk of real estate on the underdeveloped Avenues, and became largely responsible for the Darlington Place development or addition. Extension of the new electric trolley line along Third Avenue east from E Street helped the "suburban" growth of the Darling properties beginning in 1889 or thereabouts.

The big house is something of a lesson in stylistic mixture. It is sheathed in shingles—and thus is properly labelled a "shingle-style" home of that turn-of-the-century period. But Ware and Cornell also used modest Doric columns to support the gabled front porch, and the open tower atop the curved shingled area very likely boasted Doric columns when first built. Semi-classic? Sort of!

Newell Beeman, the first occupant of the mansion, was involved in mining and railroads—but his major claim to fame, in the 1880s, stemmed from his place on a uniquely Utah commission. He apparently helped to set up the test oath required of prospective voters under the Edmunds Act of 1882. Unless Utahns swore obedience to this antipolygamy statute, they could not vote. According to the history books, 12,000 citizens were disenfranchised due to refusal to solemnly swear obedience under the "infamous Edmunds Act."

There are other lessons to be learned on the Avenues concerning local history and architectural styles. One of the district's finer intersections is the crossing of R Street and First Avenue. 1037 First Ave., on the northwest corner, is a two-story, onion-domed, brick and wood home in prime Queen Anne style. In fact, architects say it is one of the finest Queen Anne structures in town, marked as it is by fish-scale shingles on the round tower, a hip-roofed bay, an oddly projected cornice, and a broad, curved porch.

Frederick A. Hale, a prominent architect of the period, is listed as the probable designer in the textbooks. Edwin C. Coffin, the original owner and occupant, moved in in 1896, when he was a major downtown manufacturer's representative and investment broker.

Just across R Street, at 1055 First Ave., is another fine Queen Anne-style home, this one dating from 1890. It displays a tall, narrow rectangular tower and a simpler, broad but less romanticized porch on its lower level. Obviously well pleased, its first owner, businessman John Hall, occupied the home for forty years. Today's owner, Bert L. Dart, keeps the house looking immaculate, freshly painted in white. All in all, it looks as pristine and "queenly" as the round-towered house across the way, the latter occupied, I believe, by Mrs. Hardy Nolyn.

By the way, realtor-builder Elmer Darling turns up here once again. He set construction crews to work at 1055 First Ave., when his Darlington development was in its infancy. Fortunately, the two R Street Queen Annes are painted white, not blue.

# Gay Nineties House on Logan Avenue

MARCH 18, 1990

There are, a poet tells us, "books in the running brooks, sermons in stones, and good in every thing." While I'm a little uncertain concerning good in all things these stressful times, I'm ready to testify that sermons, or at least history lessons, can be found in buildings if you search them out. Which brings me to the matter of the splendid-seeming house at 918 Logan Ave, the pressed-brick, multi-shingled, oddly roofed affair sketched in the adjoining column.

    Standing as it does on an oversize lot, with carriage house graced by a tidy cupola at its rear, this Logan Avenue residence (no, I don't know who lives there) is three stories tall, both higher and more distinctive than its neighbors. In addition, its brickwork, porch shingles and carpentry are almost exuberant, being prime examples of the "gay nineties" architectural style so different from the staid boxiness of too many latter-day residences.

134

Most important, from the standpoint of this lazy columnist, a very lucky start at "researching" the Logan Avenue house brought the happy discovery that the home had already been painstakingly studied by the state's preservation office for inclusion in the National Register. Historian Roger V. Roper reported rather fully on the building in the winter issue of the *Utah State Historical Quarterly* in 1986. His study, to which I'm much indebted, makes clear two very intriguing nonarchitectural facts concerning the 1891 house. Its initial owner was a territorial judge, one John W. Judd, a Tennessee native who served on the Territorial Court of Utah a single year from 1888 to 1889. (More of that a bit later.) The other matter of importance is the building's location in the "Perkins Addition," our city's prime example of a "trolley-car subdivision." It is as well a prime example of zealous drum-beating by real estate developers eager to garner top dollar for suburban land. Unsuccessful advertising, I must add.

The Perkins Addition, extending along both sides of Logan Avenue and 1700 South, ran from 900 to 1000 East in Salt Lake's "southern suburbs," conveniently served by a new electric trolley-car line that operated between downtown and Sugarhouse. There were similar trolley-induced real estate developments in the same era, of course, but the one in question seems to have been the only such project developed by overeager out-of-staters such as Gilbert Chamberlin.

Coming from Denver, where he had built similar residential subdivisions, Chamberlin had dollars enough to pay widow Sarah Gibson $2,500 per acre for her five acres of farmland. He promptly subdivided the acreage into ninety-eight lots priced at some $400 a lot. Hope springs eternal in the breasts of developers, and Chamberlin estimated his efforts would net him over $5,000 an acre. But for reasons that shall be forthcoming, he "managed to sell only a few lots from that particular parcel."

After naming the tract for one F.M. Perkins, who was an official of the Western Farm Mortgage and Trust Co. of Denver, Chamberlin told local newspapers he planned to invest more than a million dollars to "improve the property handsomely" while constructing fully 300 first-class residences. He pledged trees, lawns, sidewalks and pavement for "the most convenient, the most beautiful, the most sought after addition" in the city. His newspaper advertisements soon stressed "pure, healthful, invigorating" air free of industrial or railroad smoke, and even a lack of "miasmatic germs." His hard-sell ads, aimed at "providing fine home sites" for the "salaried classes," were no better or worse than the flowery wordage offered by other realtors, then—or now.

Alas, he seems to have run afoul of the then-current Mormon antipathy for non-LDS neighbors and outlanders. Church leaders preached against such land sales of long-held property as that which brought the widow Gibson a modest fortune. No matter how he labored, Chamberlin could sell nary a lot to a member of the prevailing faith. The hopeless realtor reported in 1890, "Mormons seem ever ready to sell but in eighteen months we have not made a single sale to a Mormon."

There is, of course, a slight chance the slow sales resulted from the transplanted Colorado styling of the homes in the Perkins Addition. True, the thirteen homes built by Chamberlin were all of pressed brick shipped in from Golden, Colo. But this foreign-made brick was considered so superior to local products that Salt Lake brickmaker John P. Cahoon journeyed to St. Louis, where he bought $85,000 worth of equipment for manufacturing similar pressed brick for later use by his Interstate Brick Company.

Chamberlin's houses, like the one on Logan Avenue, certainly were not outwardly displeasing. Each had two-story front porches, distinctively patterned trim on the eaves and specially patterned gable shingles. As a result, the dozen remaining today are rich in elements architects label "Victorian eclectic," and are easily recognized in the Logan Avenue neighborhood.

Not only did each have a formal parlor, dining room and kitchen at the rear, with bedrooms upstairs—they were "technologically advanced." All had newly perfected electric lights, hot and cold running water, tub baths and "modern" furnaces plus built-in china cabinets, sliding doors and a modest amount of stained glass.

As for John W. and Eliza Judd, the previously mentioned territorial judge and his wife, they occupied the house at 918 Logan until 1898, when the Confederate Army veteran returned to Nashville, Tenn., to serve on the Tennessee Supreme Court. Earlier, in 1889, he had resigned his territorial judgeship for the private practice of law in Salt Lake. Of course, in those days, when the practice of polygamy incensed Congress, newspaper editors, cartoonists, priests, clerics and a wide variety of "gentiles," the judges sent to Utah to uphold federal laws were among the best-hated of mortals in Mormon precincts.

It could be that by selling what is still the largest home on the block to a territorial judge, realtor Chamberlin sealed the fiscal fate of his subdivision. Coming from Colorado, he was perhaps unaware that boycotts could and would be imposed against his subdivision despite his well-designed houses and the speedy electric trolley line down the corner.

And the Judd family had another distinction. They employed the first black woman ever seen in the suburb, a "live-in" nursemaid named Charity, whom neighbors said was "exotic."

# Sugarhouse Business District

MARCH 17, 1985

Nowadays, with the raising of sugar beets and the processing of the annual crop no longer of prime importance to Utah's economy, Millard Malin's Sugarhouse Monument at the intersection of 2100 South and 1100 East has a somewhat forlorn look. True, Sugarhouse Square has been repaved, the sidewalks extending to the four compass points from the heart of our city's long-time furniture sales center have received the red-brick treatment, while portions of 1100 East have been (inexplicably) narrowed.

Once-bustling Southeast Furniture has been neatly remodeled to accommodate a variety of smaller shops and offices. The very sizable Granite Furniture, Sterling Furniture, and adjunct businesses still draw newlyweds and more sedate seekers after dining room and bedroom suites. First Security Bank has built a commodious office building opposite the monument. But Sugarhouse, many residents and businessmen report, is scarcely thriving—holding its own, perhaps, but not exactly thronged with shoppers or baby-carriage-pushing family folk.

Sugarhouse is still "on the railroad track." Boxcars from Georgia and other assorted furniture-making states are still switched onto the D&RG siding, but not in the number recalled by old-timers who lived here when a small railroad yard, a line extending up Parleys Canyon to Park City, and a spur to the nearby brick factory were profit-makers for the railroad—and economic conveniences for Sugarhouse businesses.

Rail freight haulage dwindled years ago, but neighborhood shops such as Keith O'Brien flourished yet a while, along with a mix of small but well-stocked stores. Then, rather gradually, despite turkey premiums and Sugar Days contests, one of Salt Lake's better "close in" districts began fading. At the moment, its best hope for revival—and survival—would seem to be plans for a major shopping mall, plans that have been announced, aired, shelved and announced again, plans dependent not upon architects but upon bankers, upon financial institutions that must agree upon the profit-making potential of the mall and the viability of Sugarhouse. If the plans are dropped, failure for Sugarhouse may be a self-fulfilling prophecy.

The situation has its parallels, of course. Shops in such once prosperous metropolitan suburbs as Bryn Mawr and Evanston, New Rochelle and Sausalito have had difficult times—if only because of changes in the population composition of Philadelphia, Chicago, New York and San Francisco. Increasingly, the construction of major shopping malls in ring after ring of new bedroom suburbs service motorized office workers, attract young family folk who commute to and from jobs via freeways. To yuppies, outlying home developments are as accessible by car as the closer-in districts once were to young commuters who rode rapid transit trolleys. Hence, close-in commercial centers developed at geographical crossroads a half-dozen miles from downtown are obsolete.

Could it be that the close-in neighborhoods, of which Sugarhouse is one of Utah's prime examples, can never again regain their business-oriented status? Certainly Sugarhouse should not be allowed to revert to the status of rural crossroads. But perhaps more effort should be made to bring new residents—rather than new shoppers—to this very pleasant part of the valley.

Sugarhouse has a college—Westminster—plus a public library, plus its own post office. Its square is lined with attractive buildings housing branch banks and a sprinkling of restaurants, not to overlook its very busy Snel-grove's shop and ice cream plant.

The community has spacious Sugarhouse Park, now maturing as its trees gain stature. There are picnic spots, as well as a pleasantly scenic small lake, for nongolfers, while Forest Dale and Nibley are on the periphery for neighborhood golfers. There are tennis courts, a swimming pool, a boys club and an adequate supply of schools including Highland High, the newest in the city school district. There are such amenities as family-owned bakeries, markets, neighborhood ma and pa stores, automobile service stations, cafes, and even a district police substation.

With the downtown business district of the metropolis less than twenty minutes away (by UTA bus as well as by car), Sugarhouse appears to me to be as well situated as any Salt Lake City neighborhood. Perhaps it is not as picturesque as Marmalade Hill or the Avenues, but it abounds in solid bungalows and sizable, lawn-rimmed homes, built before today's cookie-cutter wooden tract home consumed the land in West Valley, Sandy and Kearns. If some drumbeater arranged a Sugarhouse home and garden tour, quite a few golden oldies would turn up, although in quite a few cases the original clapboard siding or fish-scale shingles have been covered with aluminum siding or asphalt. Sugarhouse suffers, in some minds, by being middle class. The eye beholds a bourgeois cityscape, a mix of post-World War I styles, a scatteration of Victorian remnants, a neighborhood blessed or cursed by only one or two large new apartment buildings.

Locals can point out one or two splendidly fenced, carefully gardened and meticulously painted polygamous homes. Like any older neighborhood, there are a few contrasting, rundown structures occupied by a few remnant hippies. It is, thankfully, a district graced with trees.

There are venerable trees on lawns and along the streets forming leafy green arches in summer. They do, of course, bring down a power line or two in winter. There are streets and houses offering fine views of Wasatch foothills, other streets where the views are less expansive, closer knit; where residents sit on a front porch, look up and down the block and enjoy the quiet sights of a middle America most residents of larger cities don't realize is still extant. Whether rimmed with ice, or fluttering with midsummer green, whether bare of foliage or bright with autumn color, the Sugarhouse trees interact with the equally old houses, reminding occasional visitors that early residents of these quiet streets cared, as do latter-day renters or home buyers.

Here and there in Sugarhouse there are vacant lots that could be filled with small apartments, or with single-family dwellings or duplexes. Downington, Garfield, Allen Park Drive, 900 East, 1100 East, Browning, Highland Drive, Redondo, Roosevelt—whether named for poets or presidents, for geographical feature, for neighborhood builders or merely mathematical dividing points, the Sugarhouse streets, leaf-strewn in autumn, slushy in spring, are havens of quiet on summer Sundays, all the very warp and woof of the real Salt Lake City. Inhabited in the main by people who love it, or at least like it, it's a community that profit-hungry major builders have, fortunately, bypassed for larger tracts more capable of "development."

Perhaps a shopping mall near its heart is a necessity for the viable residential neighborhood we label Sugarhouse. If so, it is hoped, it will be a well-designed mall, suited to its locale, one which won't wreak havoc on the existing struggling shops, the present traffic pattern, the parks, the scale, the "tone" of Sugarhouse.

EDITOR'S NOTE: In the ten years that have passed since this column was written, several sizable franchised restaurants and shops have created a busy new Sugarhouse.

# Westminster Heights Bungalow

MAY 1, 1994

When folks who take a special interest in matters historic and in the city's curious mix of architectural styles venture to explore Salt Lake City's non-familiar neighborhoods, they may be journeying—unawares—halfway 'round the globe to the Indian subcontinent.

Witness, for example, Westminster Heights in Sugarhouse, the principal goals being a number of so-called "California bungalows" on Westminster Avenue, between 1300 East and 1700 East. What's the connection with India? Well, as a bit of exploration in the pages of your dictionary, atlas or encyclopedia will explain, the term bungalow stems from the Hindi "bangla," meaning house. The simplest definition encountered explains, "a bungalow is a house in the Bengal style, usually one-storied and of a type developed in India characterized by low, sweeping lines and a wide veranda." Thus, in your mind's eye, you may picture Errol Flynn in red coat and pith helmet lolling on such a veranda, downing cooling libations while preparing to lead heroic Tommy Atkins and his regiment in a rousing defense of the Khyber Pass.

When the celluloid-inspired clouds dissipate and your image of India dims, you may peer at today's sketch of the California bungalow at 1369 Westminster Ave. and see no signs of India. You may begin to wonder how a sizable group of such dwellings ever sprouted in Sugarhouse.

The operative name in this case is Dunshee, or, to be more specific, Clark and Earl Dunshee, brother real-estate developers who acquired some fifty acres of property above Westminster College in 1905. After subdividing existing orchards and farms, they turned to "pattern books" showing architecture and plans of Southern California bungalows. The thought was this style might attract upper-class Salt Lakers who would find this new look attractive enough to result in a multitude of sales.

Obvious to the Dunshees was the fact that plans for these low-slung bungalows would be altered to fit Utah's winter climate.

The bungalow development caught on rather slowly because trolley-car lines leading to downtown businesses had not yet reached Westminster Heights. The area gradually caught on, in part, because this high southeast location was generally free of smoke and smog.

By May 1913, the *Salt Lake Tribune* reported sales were rising in the bungalow neighborhood. A year or two later, businessman Henry Cohn built the home at 1369 Westminster Ave. Beautifully restored and brought to its present state, the house seems certain to impress.

Cohn, who entered the wool business after an association with Frederick and Herbert Auerbach, lived in his "Swiss style" California bungalow for five years, then sold it to the L.L. Ewing family for $4,000. After many more years, it passed to present owners Rick and Laurie Summers.

In plan and exterior look, the house is an almost exact twin of a California design by Arthur Heineman, but its floor plan is "flipped." While many Westminster Heights bungalows are built of fieldstone, this house is built of bricks fired unevenly, giving a random, uneven look. To conform with the "flipped" floor plan, the Summers home was given a continuous front porch plus a side stairs. The home has exposed beams typical of the California plans, an open porte-cochere on one side, and decorative chains attached to the beams of the roof over the front porch.

The interior woodwork is gumwood, lightly stained, giving an airier feel than in many such interiors of the same period.

For affluent purchasers of the time, the Dunshees or their contractors installed inglenooks around fireplaces, bookcases, window seats, buffets, breakfast nooks and the like that remain intriguing features of Westminster district homes. Whether "mission" or "Swiss chalet" in style, they seem "Indian" in look to most Salt Lakers. By-the-by, back East the term "bunga-low" denoted not a sizable, stylish home, but a cheaply built, shack-like beach cabin. What's in a name?

*Drawing Courtesy of Georgia Sullivan*

# Historic Trolley Square

JANUARY 1, 1994

Salt Lake City has been blessed since its inception by its exceptionally wide downtown streets. Thus, it strikes some strolling residents as a bit odd that the town never built pedestrian bridges across its major thoroughfares. True enough, a few such structures cross busy freeways or state highways where children must walk to or from schools. There is a tunnel under downtown State Street providing an exceptionally expensive link from ZCMI to Social Hall Avenue. But no network of bridges connects downtown buildings to ease pedestrian passage at busy traffic hours.

If you journey to such a metropolis as Cincinnati, for example, you'll find much of its downtown district tied together by a second-story walkway. The busiest sectors of the walkway are linked by cross-street bridges. As a result, nearly twice as many shops exist in the busiest sectors of that

Ohio city as can be found in comparable towns. There are stores on the street level and abutting the second-story walkways.

To my knowledge—and I'm open to correction—Salt Lake has just a single real cross-street bridge. It's the steel-girdered affair linking the south side of Trolley Square with a large parking lot. If I recall correctly, this bridge was something of an afterthought. Trolley Square first opened to the shopping and food-ingesting public in 1972–73, but its pedestrian bridge was erected ten years or more later.

Trolley Square's owners being history-minded, their bridge has a curious history all its own, one completely unconnected with public transit at that.

Fully 150 feet long, the bridge spanning 600 South Street, midway between 600 and 700 East, is in itself a long distance from home base. It was hauled, piecemeal, to its present location all the way from Tooele. This serviceable walkway originally was built as a conveyer trestle and was designated a "thickener bridge" by its owner-builders, the International Smelting and Refining Co.

The bridge, according to a historic marker testifying to that fact, carried the drive mechanism for the thickener operations of the IS&R mill, which handled ore from Oquirrh Mountain mines. The operating company was subsidiary of the Anaconda Mining Co., whose principal product was copper. One guesses, possibly incorrectly, that lead, zinc, silver and even gold were mined, along with copper, in that part of the Oquirrh Range.

Today the bridge is carpeted and roofed, and even has side panes of glass, providing a comfortable crossing to and from the second-floor level of Trolley Square. To natives of New York City, the stairway leading to and from the Trolley Square parking lot across 600 South is somehow a reminder of the stairways on the Sixth Avenue elevated lines that served Manhattan residents a half century ago. This is as it should be, since Trolley Square has taken some pride in its link with its transportation heritage.

Of late, two original trolley cars, their bodies used as shops or food stands, seem to have been removed from the premises. But the pedestrian bridge has its own ghost of a trolley.

You can best glimpse this odd reminder of Salt Lake's original light-rail lines by viewing the bridge at night. Neon tubes, glowing a bright red, outline the body, windows and wheels of what appears to be a trolley car crossing the bridge. It's really just an advertisement.

Since its beginnings under the rather visionary Wallace Wright and his associates, there have been other attractive historic elements at this intriguing Utah "theme park." For example, the big bay window and other portions of the long-vanished Culmer Mansion now grace sectors of the square. The Culmer Mansion, built in 1882, stood at 158 N. Main until it vanished abruptly a half century ago.

The Trolley Square complex centers on the streetcar barns and repair shops railroad millionaire E.H. Harriman ordered for his Utah Light and Railway Company in 1906. The company grew from a merged trio of streetcar companies whose rails once laced the city. One of those antecedent companies had used horsecars at its birth—but the site has an earlier history. It was known as the Tenth Ward Square in 1889, and was used for Utah's first Territorial Fair under the auspices of the Deseret Agricultural and Manufacturing Society.

Nowadays, after you've crossed the glass-enclosed, carpeted pedestrian bridge, you can thicken your tummy by inhaling cookies, clear your throat at the Juice Express, and put on few more pounds at Schmidt's Pastries, the Candy Barrel, the American Taco Fiesta or Charlie Chow. If the tiled floors and cutesy names such as Potions and Lotions or Fowl Weather Friends wear you down, you can rest awhile at Joe's Shoe Repair Shop while having your soles and heels thickened to proper dimensions.

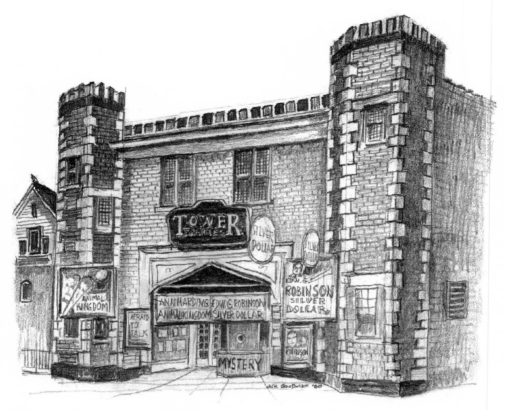

# The Tower Theatre

NOVEMBER 18, 1990

Don't search our town for the battlements and stonework of the unmoated castle in the drawing illustrating today's column. You won't find this not-too-masterly representation of the Tower of London gracing 900 South at 900 East any longer. Did the architect of this, the original Tower Theatre, seek to emulate the semi-Tudor style of London's Tower Bridge, the ingenious structure just below the Pool of London? Built in 1921 of solid-seeming brick and stone, the Tower Theatre looked this way until the 1950s, when its rather grim facade was replaced by the smooth tile and simple marquee of the neighborhood movie house we were familiar with until the marquee lights were turned off two years ago.

A bit of research into the archives of the world of celluloid indicate that the photo from which the drawing was made was snapped in 1933—that being the year during which Ann Harding and Leslie Howard could be seen locally in *The Animal Kingdom* and Edward G. Robinson was being his usual semivillainous self in *Silver Dollar*, a not-too-epic an epic in which he toyed with the affections of Bebe Daniels. To be perfectly truthful, the Tower of 1933 was formally titled the "Tower Talkies," since it could boast of synchronized sound, beginning with the Al Jolson *Jazz Singer* days.

One claim to fame was the fact that the Tower Talkies was this city's first air-conditioned movie house. Of rather more importance was the fact that this semimagnificent motion picture palazzo was Salt Lake's first sizable "art theatre." To be sure, the Cinema Arts theater, just a few steps east of the Cinegrill and "movie row" on 100 South, was our first venue for Art films (with a capital A) and for the showing of foreign films. Gordon Crowe, who long ago fled the city of Saints for the sidewalks of New York, opened Cinema Arts (below street level with comfy seats acquired from a shoe-selling emporium). He was succeeded by youthful George Gregerson, then a newcomer from the land of the Danes. *Tight Little Island, Miss Julie* and *Skipper Next to God* were some Cinema Arts offerings in those distant days.

Came the late 1950s and early 1960s, and film-TV mogul Sid Cohen, an associate of KALL/KUTV's George C. Hatch, acquired the Tower—art-deco front and all. Before you could say Jack Robinson or even Rene Clair, the neighborhood house became an "Art house," with, if memory serves aright, Tania Karol as manager. Soon coffee and homespun chocolate tidbits were served in the lobby during intermissions, and patrons could while away idle moments gazing upon paintings by Alvin Gittins, Edie Roberson and other contemporary artists.

The Tower flourished as an art house for at least a half-dozen years, a period when patrons could enjoy (and argue about) films by Orson Welles and Ingmar Bergman, by Polish producers and French directors, films with Indian, Japanese and even American actors and actresses. Alas, TV helped scotch local box-office seekers of *Lust for Life, The Lady Vanishes, The Informer* or reruns of Chaplin and Marx Brothers fare.

As you may know via recent reports by *Tribune* film critic Terry Orme, a considerable effort is under way to transform the now dark Tower into an art house once again. At present, little thought is being given to the resuscitation of the long gone "Tower of London" facade. The rather bland but friendly building's present face and marquee can be utilized at less expense once the revival house is revived. A group of folks addicted to better film fare than is usually found at shopping malls or on the tube have banded into a group called the Independent Film Foundation, and are beating the bushes in search of the $150,000 deemed necessary for a bare-bones reopening of the Tower. Led by Greg Tanner, operator of the all-too-small Cinema in Your Face on 300 South, erstwhile music-maker Marty Steinberg, filmmaker Mark Allen and film student Nikole Thayne, the organization has tossed a partially successful block party as a fund-raiser. The event was handicapped by rather atrocious weather, but was assisted by stomach-warming edibles and drinkables from the Brackman Bagel Bakery just across the way.

At the moment, the cinephiles hope for funds sufficient to patch the leaky roof, cleanse the interior and permit reopening the Tower on a lively, livable scale. After all, the Blue Mouse has been shuttered and Cinema in Your Face is too small for a viable operation. The city and its suburbs are believed to have a sufficiency of folks who like their movie fare a bit more thought-provoking than the run-of-the-mill stuff available at neighborhood malls. Building owner Harold Hill of Hill Real Estate has adopted a wait-and-see attitude towards foundation fund-raising efforts. Let's hope for the best.

Hill is, of course, no neophyte insofar as building rehabilitation is concerned, being the power behind the renovation of the Judge Building and the Clift Building at opposite corners of Broadway and Main. If the present modest plans work out, the Cooper Roberts Architecture firm has a rather solid set of future plans ready for a thorough redo of the building's interior, including a small second screen in the present balcony area.

One rather intriguing thing about the "Save the Tower" project is that the movie house's very presence has helped keep the East Central Community district viable. In addition to the aforementioned bagel shop, the Chameleon Artwear store and the Crackers Antique establishment are just across the way. There's a barber shop, Eldredge's Lawn Mower repair store, Cahoots and Nathan Read's next door. The long-lived (and one hopes prosperous) Jolley's is on the southeast Ninth and Ninth corner. Spend a few minutes in the vicinity, and you'll come to realize this is a young people's neighborhood, one in which an art house could survive, no matter what the style of its facade might be.

EDITOR'S NOTE: The Tower Theatre has opened as a movie house again, although some of the shops mentioned have closed or changed.

JACK GOODMAN '94

# Splendid, Shady Gilmer Park

MARCH 13, 1994

If you are among those of us who've wondered how and why some sections of the city developed more rapidly or slowly than others—and, more important, how they became areas in which better-than-average homes abound—why streets are especially pleasant and landscaping is obviously important to residents and why the value of homes remains high, you can find the answers to most such questions in long-lasting Gilmer Park.

This neighborhood lies between 900 South and Harvard Avenue (1150 South) and between 1100 and 1300 East. If you stroll or drive through it, your first discovery is the "pitch" of the land. It rises rather sharply from flat 1100 East to the beginnings of the east bench. But it is nowhere as steep as the thirty-degree slope today's city and county planners supposedly set to demark the east-bench hillsides on which home construction is banned, a ban not too well enforced.

As the sharp-eyed instantly realize, the shade trees in which most homes are sheltered are old—at least a half century in age. But Gilmer Park had its beginnings more than a century ago, back in 1888, when John T. Gilmer and wife Mary E. bought about half of the area from farmer Alvin F. Guirvits. Mr. Gilmer, a financially successful mine operator, was also a mail-hauling contractor and partner in Gilmer and Salisbury Overland Stage Company. Mrs. Gilmer, a leading suffragette, was a founder of the Ladies Literary Club and active in supporting the Sarah Daft Home for aging women.

A year after their purchase, the Gilmers built the equivalent of a country estate, complete with a curving uphill drive and a boundary line of Lombardy poplars. An old Utah Historical Society print is enlivened by a well-turned-out horse and carriage. But in 1889, the rural house and property were leased to the newly established Salt Lake Country Club. Many of today's Country Club members think the Forest Dale course was their first—but they are wrong. The Gilmer land was their initial playground; the move to Forest Dale didn't come till 1907.

When the golf club moved to Sugarhouse, the widowed Mrs. Gilmer and her son Jay formed Gilmer Realty Co. and began subdividing. By 1909, the first lots were sold and homes built, with others subdivided in 1919 by Gilmer Realty, Taylor Evans Woolley, Evelyn Burton, J.G. Vincent and George E. Merrill. Nearby trolley-car lines, plus development of the automobile, helped accelerate home-building.

Meantime, Gilmer family members abounded—Jay T. Gilmer moved into the house in today's drawing in 1910. The home at 1038 S. 1200 East was designed by architect Frederick A. Hale. Mary Gilmer lived with two sons at 949 S. 1100 East, while a Gilmer Service Station began pumping gasoline on the southwest corner of 900 South and 1100 East.

Earlier, LeGrande Young obtained the remainder of today's Gilmer Park. His home occupied the site of today's Church of Jesus Christ of Latter-day Saints Garden Park Ward house. Young planted oak, plum, apple, pear, elm, poplar and horse-chestnut trees on his land.

Meanwhile, Red Butte Creek and local springs added to the parklike air, and soon LeGrande Young's children built homes along streets or lanes. Young sold his acreage to John C. Howard, president of Utah Oil Refining Co., leading Mrs. Howard's brothers, Burton and Joseph Musser, to build homes on east Harvard and east Yale avenues.

Simultaneously, the neighborhood became an "architects' haven."

Taylor Woolley, architect and owner of some land in the "park's" beginning, became responsible for laying out the streets and lots along Gilmer Drive. He had been a student of famed Frank Lloyd Wright in Chicago and Europe, and was enamored of deep setbacks, retaining walls and elevated "natural" yards. An "Architect's Row" developed, with Woolley's home at 1222 E. 900 South, and Woolley partner Clifford P. Evans's at 1266 E. 900 South.

Each architect, while respecting the parklike landscaping and curved streets, built in different styles. Gilmer Park includes Prairie, Period Revival and Bungalow-style homes, according to architects who know the neighborhood. There have been changes, of course. For example, the 1910 Jay Gilmer home at 1038 S. 1200 East and pictured here has a new tiled roof, a new peaked entry and windows shaded by hoods that have greatly changed its original look.

But through the use of good architects, multilevel landscaped grounds, handsome walls and fences, a forest of trees and neighborly respect for the environment, Gilmer Park remains what it has been for many years, a pleasant residential sector of the city.

# Rose Park

JULY 17, 1994

If you are a Salt Laker of ancient age, you may recall that housing in our town—and across most of the nation—was virtually nonexistent when the Second World War came to an end in 1945. Affordable housing, that is. Youthful veterans released from the armed forces made their homes with their parents or in-laws, or crowded into subpar rentals. Some lived underground in roofed-over basement dwellings they hoped would someday become the foundations of above-ground houses.

Americans, being ingenious, quickly found solutions to fit the need—and you can imagine a mass example of what resulted if you'll wander the pleasant streets of Rose Park, roughly between 400 North and 1500 North, and from 900 West to the Jordan River or Redwood Road.

No streets are named for Alan Brockbank or Ed Holmes, or the Stayner-Richards, Steenblik or Doxey-Layton firms. Instead, the streets,

154

whether straight or curved, bear such names as Pearl Harbor, Centennial or Florabunda. Likewise, there are no neighborhood memorials to Abraham Levitt and his sons William and Alfred. Unsung heroes of a sort, the Levitt family had purchased 4,000 acres of potato farmland near Hempstead, Long Island, and eventually mass-produced 140,000 low-cost homes back East. They had learned, while building housing for shipyard workers, that a dozen concrete foundations could be laid in a single day, that bulldozers could replace horses and scoop-shovels, and power hand tools such as saws and routers could boost productivity to record levels.

The builders of Rose Park worked in two phases with two major housing materials—wood or brick. They never quite mechanized construction methods to the Levitt tempo, but they did pretty darn well, finishing more than 3,000 homes in less than a decade. And they sold those homes for about $7,000 apiece. Viewing the success of Rose Park, banks loaned builders sizable sums for new tract houses within and outside the city limits, with some federal aid, to be sure.

Just about the only folks displeased by mass housing were the few architectural critics then extant. The *New Yorker* magazine's Lewis Mumford complained that the nation's builders were producing one-class communities of look-alike houses fated to become slums. Paul Goldberger of the august *New York Times* thought such quickly built communities of "ticky-tacky houses" were "an urban planning disaster."

If you round a Rose Park corner and encounter VerDon Parker or Kent Mayberry (who occupy the left-hand and center houses in today's sketch), they view their neighborhood's homes in a very different light. Parker bought one of the first such homes in 1946 and has lived there ever since. Mayberry is a comparative newcomer—just twenty-five years in his brick dwelling.

"Ninety percent of us first purchasers were vets," Parker recalls. "My house cost $8,670, and while my wife and I raised two kids, we paid off sixty-three dollars a month. Some neighbors had more children of course—the Jackson's across the way had eight." As he and his neighbor tell you, "we didn't have paved streets or sidewalks at first, but were the biggest ward in the LDS Church."

One of the first things Parker did was "put in a full basement. I worked for Utah Power and had a steady wage. I could walk to work, and the neighborhood kids walked to Onequa School—now torn down—or to Rose Park Elementary. The bus line only came to 400 North and 900 West, but neighbors soon had cars. We had a garage like most of the new houses, and got together with neighbors to pave their driveways. We had driveway parties to celebrate."

Mrs. Parker, her home now ringed with big trees and given "a family pride" by its gardens, recalls her first purchase was for "Venetian blinds, since we had no shades." Now, like many Rose Park homes, those windows have aluminum shades. Air-conditioning units are common, or a rooftop cooler, such as the one on the adjacent Mayberry home.

The neighborhood visitor soon realizes many of such homes have extensions, backyard sun decks and porches, aluminum siding, extra rooms, shade trees, flower gardens, a variety of fences; there are new bay windows and picture windows, small greenhouses, barbecue shelters. The only real problem such a homemaker as Mrs. Parker can now recall was shopping. "The only nearby store was Macey's; otherwise you managed to go downtown."

This columnist interviewed Alan Brockbank, a one-time president of the National Homebuilders Association, back in 1986, not long before the former died. "Rose Park posed a few problems, but our architects Lloyd Snedaker and Jack Clawson had planned homes that would last well, and could be expanded." Much of the land on which the community was built had been vacated, owned by Anaconda Copper Co. and Pippy Iron Foundry.

Brockbank recalled Mayor Earl Glade and the city commissioners at first refused permission for curved streets. "And we had trouble with the bricklayers—Interstate Brick Co. made some oversized brick we thought could speed up the job. Finally men laid the larger brick."

Nowadays, driving or walking around Rose Park, you may marvel that the one-time "look-alike, ticky-tacky, cookie-cutter houses" are now unlike their neighbors. White and red, buff, yellow, russet, surrounded by trees and ample lawn and flower gardens, the homes in the city's first postwar subdivision look different indeed. And, if you can find one for sale, its price will be in the neighborhood of $85,000 or $95,000. Alas, "For Sale" signs are virtually nonexistent.

Such is not the case out in West Jordan or Draper or the Bountiful foothills. There, huge new homes are priced in the $700,000 range—and have a very oversized, ticky-tacky, cookie-cutter look.

156

# CHAPTER 7

# Meanwhile . . . the Churches

# Trinity AME Church in Central City

NOVEMBER 20, 1988

It's certainly not the largest church in Salt Lake City. Fact is, it might qualify as one of the smallest. But Trinity African Methodist Episcopal Church at 239 E. 600 South makes up for its lack of size in the down-to-earth good works of its parishioners. And Trinity AME has a very considerable history as well. With its neat, trim appearance—outside and in—this modest one-story building, marked by a tall, shingled cross-topped steeple, might qualify as the edifice you imagined when, as a youngster, you sang of "a church in the wildwood," sang of a "church in the dell." True, the Trinity AME Church that motorists whiz past on 600 South is of sturdy red brick construction, while the one recalled in that melodic old song was a rustic brown affair.

Perhaps more important is the fact that this congregation has carried

159

on its good works since the 1880s, and not just in matters religious but also in the church's role as a focus of neighborliness in the Central City district.

The Rev. Curtis F. Sewell, pastor of Trinity AME, takes considerable pride, along with his coreligionists, in the history of the congregation as spelled out by the Utah Division of State History when the modest building was placed on the State Register of historic structures a decade ago. "Trinity African Methodist Episcopal was organized during the 1880s by the Rev. T.T. Saunders. This congregation has served as a focus of black religious, social and cultural activity in Utah from territorial days till the present. In 1907 this property (at 239 E. 6th South) was acquired and a church designed by Hurley Howard was constructed through the sacrifice and energy of the congregation under the Rev. T.C. Bell." Restoration and renovation of the building undertaken under the Rev. D.D. Wilson was unfortunately necessary again following a fire on July 5, 1985.

However, the history of black settlement in the Salt Lake Valley extends to that much-celebrated day a century earlier, when Brigham Young's original company came down Emigration Canyon on July 24, 1847. Among the men in that first wagon train to arrive in Zion were Green Flake, Hark Lay and Oscar Crosby, listed on pioneer rosters as "colored servants." However, not a few mountain men, "free trappers" of an earlier era, were blacks, including such a notable pathfinder as James Beckwourth, whose early adventures in the Cache Valley were followed by his discovery of what became Beckwourth Pass in the Sierra. This route was later followed by the Western Pacific Railroad near the Feather River Canyon. Parenthetically, the coming of the railroads brought an increasing number of black citizens to Utah, especially porters and other employees who worked in Pullman cars and dining cars out of Ogden as well as Salt Lake City. And for many years, black troops were stationed at forts in Utah to keep the Territory's trails free of marauders.

Today's Trinity AME, looking much as it did when its original walls rose in 1907, has a simple interior seating some 125 people. There's a modest organ, raised seats for the well-practiced choir, simple but colorful stained glass windows and plaques testifying to the services of an F & AM Lodge, the Women's Progressive Club and the Elks Lodge. The names of several past and present members of Trinity AME will be familiar to many Salt Lakers—Nettie Gregory, Oscar Jackson, Charles, Mabel and Bernard Gordon. "Unfortunately, as in all Central City churches, many of our best members move to the suburbs, or, due to hard economic times, leave the valley," reports the Rev. Sewell. One who is especially missed is former State Senator Terry Williams, who left Utah for employment in California. But Albert Fritz, longtime NAACP leader, and local political leader Marvin Davis remain in the valley.

"We may not see them here often, but this is the 'Mother Church,' the first black church in the state," the pastor points out. Historically, members of the little red brick church have been linked, down through the years, with the AME Church that had its beginnings in Philadelphia 200 years ago, when black and white congregants came together at the altar rail to band for freedom of worship unfettered by color lines.

Some of the present worshipers at the 600 South church "commute" to it from suburban homes, others live close by in a neighborhood of apartments and tree-shaded, modest, older dwellings. It's interesting to note that despite the facilities offered by the sprawling Central City Multi-Purpose Center, tiny Trinity AME serves a significant role. "We preach the gospel, help feed the hungry, help clothe the naked, help house the homeless, help find jobs for the jobless," the Rev. Sewell says with considerable pride.

"We've always had the same goals here, the same mission."

# Ex-synagogue / Current VFW Post

JANUARY 2, 1994

Large initials over its central entrance doors identify the 1½-story brick building as "Veterans of Foreign Wars Post No. 409." But even a cursory glance at the structure at 833 S. 200 East tells observers this must have been a church.

Wrong. This is indeed a building erected for a religious institution, but it was designed as a synagogue for an orthodox Jewish congregation named Sharey Tzedek. It was begun in 1919 and completed in 1920 by general contractor John E. Anderson for a small, none-too-successful Jewish congregation termed a "splinter group" by local historians. Its members broke away from the Montefiore Synagogue in 1916, but the congregation was only active until the years just preceding World War II.

The structure stood vacant until 1945 or 1946, when it was sold by a nearly defunct board of congregants to a new VFW post headed at that time by Guy Snyder and Post Commander Lloyd S. Grover. Its present Post Commander, Jack Grover, is the son of that earlier Post No. 409 commander. Unfortunately, Cmdr. Jack Grover holds out little hope for the continued existence of this VFW unit, and as a result the former synagogue structure may be doomed.

"We don't keep open on a regular basis," says Cmdr. Grover, adding that with the death of the post's World War I members, and the "dropping away of interest" on the part of the World War II, Korean War and Vietnam veterans, membership in Post No. 409 has dwindled sadly.

"The main problem is apathy, a second problem has been the maintenance of the old building in the face of vandalism," Cmdr. Grover adds. There are, for example, no visible windows in the one-time synagogue. When built, it had circular windows at its front, apparently containing colored glass with a traditional six-pointed star. "There is still some colored glass in some windows visible from inside, but we have had to cover all the widows with metal panels due to vandalism," says Grover.

In its heyday, Congregation Sharey Tzedek synagogue had eight rooms, some in the basement. The dedication service on March 28, 1920, featured an address by Utah's lone Jewish governor, Simon Bamberger. While not a member of the new congregation, Gov. Bamberger had been a founder of the B'nai Israel Temple. It still stands (used for other purposes) on 400 East identified by its large, dark dome.

Built at a cost of just $32,000 on a lot that cost $1,200, the orthodox synagogue structure featured a traditional "Bihma" in the center of its main floor worship hall. Containing a Torah scroll (the Old Testament in Hebrew), this was used as a reading desk and altar by Rabbi Joseph Strinkomsky and congregation members who took part in services. Main floor seating was strictly for males, with women worshiping upstairs in a gallery that may have been curtained, ultra-orthodox style. Congregation members taking leading roles in its formation included Sam Hayden and Morris and Ida Gorelick. Abe Guss was a member with Reuben Kaplan listed as the final board president of the short-lived congregation.

Today's VFW Post 409 uses a kitchen and some of the unchanged smaller rooms in the structure, with a downstairs entrance also in use at times. The gallery, with some railings still in place, has been preserved but is closed.

On the exterior, the north and south side walls were divided into window bays by plain, projecting pilasters. A flight of steps leads to paired central entry doors framed by brickwork forming an arch. Parapeted walls rise on the west facade which has a small, hexagon projection that may have supported the interior ark.

The Utah Historical Society terms the Congregation Sharey Tzedek Synagogue building significant "for its historical association with Utah's pluralistic community." Long before the construction of today's Kol Ami structure at the southeast end of the city serving the combined membership of Montefiore and B'nai Israel, Sharey Tzedek at 833 S. 200 East was a congregation of relative newcomers to the city. Most members were eastern European- and Russian-born Jews who formed a small Yiddish-speaking enclave. The membership, which followed old-country rituals, briefly supported a kosher butcher as well as a rabbi. Its members chiefly lived within a few blocks of Sharey Tzedek. These orthodox Jews not only read services in Hebrew and spoke Yiddish, but they also were forbidden to ride to Saturday or holiday services according to their tenets.

Prior to the sale of the building to the VFW, many elderly worshipers had died, while others were familiar enough in the ways of the land to which they had emigrated to become at least partially satisfied with "reformed" services at B'nai Israel or the "almost Orthodox" services at nearby Montefiore Synagogue.

Vast changes in the former Soviet Union have brought several hundred new Russian immigrants to the city. They join a number of the Lubavitcher sect who have established a presence in the city. A new synagogue may be in the offing someday.

# St. Patrick's Catholic Church

SEPTEMBER 6, 1992

In past years this column has focused on many churches and temples. One more worthy of attention despite its small size and lack of "status" is St. Patrick's Catholic Church, which has occupied its site at 1702 W. 400 South for almost a century.

This St. Patrick's is different in grandeur, fame, cost, and architectural richness from St. Patrick's Cathedral on New York's Fifth Avenue, the nation's first major cathedral built in Gothic Revival style. Begun in 1858 and completed in 1879, the edifice, occupying the Manhattan block-front between Fiftieth and Fifty-first streets, was designed by James Renwick. Nowadays, its twin granite spires, rather similar to those of the Cologne Cathedral, remain lacy, lovely and impressive, dwarfed though they are by the sixty-story mass of Rockefeller Center directly across the street. It properly remains a magnet for cathedral appreciators who may never journey to

Europe to study the masterworks of man such as Westminster Abbey, or the soaring structures at Rouen, York and Exeter.

To the unseeing or nonseeing, Salt Lake's St. Patrick's Church will seem sadly lacking in grandeur. There is no true nave, transept or crossing, no lovely Lady Chapel or vaulted ceiling. Fact is, our local St. Pat's might even bring to some minds a memorable, if slightly inebriated, Fulton Fish Market trawler captain. This seafarer told Joseph Mitchell (the *Herald Tribune* and *New Yorker* magazine's peerless reporter), "I never go to church. I did enjoy the old hymns, the gloomy ones, but the sermons drove me away."

On a more positive note, the St. Patrick's on our town's west side was, according to the Utah Historical Society, "probably designed by the firm of Ware and Treganza, and constructed at a cost of $10,000 by A.J. Gillis."

Although it was completed in 1917, the "War to End All Wars" delayed its dedication until 1920. Today architects label it as significant for its rather rare (for Utah) example of Spanish Colonial Revival style.

Study its fine bell tower surmounted by a crucifix, its stark white brick walls, dark wooden entry doors, the bright red tile roof and porch topping, and one instantly recalls old mission chapels in Monterey, Santa Barbara or Santa Fe—churches that still glow in the bright western sunlight despite partial destruction by earthquake, fire and floods. They've even survived the revolts of Native Americans displeased by the way of life brought them by mission friars before the years of our American Revolution.

Father Donald E. Hope of Salt Lake's St. Patrick's reports other bits of local, regional and Catholic history when you visit the church he serves. The site once was owned by the San Pedro, Los Angeles and Salt Lake Railroad. In the years when Bishop Scanlan and Father William Ryan chose the structure's location, many railroaders were among its possible congregants.

Then, as now, the city's west side was "working-class" in composition. German brewery workers were employed a block or two away at Fisher's. Trolley motormen, railroad engineers and brakemen were often of Irish descent. Tracklayers and switchmen, iron puddlers at nearby foundries, teamsters and countless other day laborers were often Italian-Americans. Those were times when few felt overly annoyed by the designation of some citizens as hyphenated Americans.

Within the local St. Patrick's, there are five windows on the east side, five on the west, each in modest, pale green stained glass. Each bears the name of a neighborhood parishioner. There's not a socialite among them, no "lace-curtain Irish," all godly, religious neighbors.

There are, as in all Catholic churches, Stations of the Cross, carved, in this case, of a lightly burnished wood. Again, statues have been given to honor departed neighbors. The simple altar is being repaired, enriched with handsome dark reddish tile from the Cathedral of the Madeleine uptown. "We're going to be short of that cathedral tile," says the Rev. Hope, somewhat sadly. "The folks over in Tooele heard of the available tile first and got there before we did."

Most importantly, he points out, this St. Patrick's, although not a cathedral, remains a neighborhood church, with an important role in a neighborhood that is noteworthy for change. "We have no choir singing in English," he reports. "But we have both a choir that sings and prays in Spanish, Mexican Americans, and a choir whose language is Tongan."

It's a case of Americans all, immigrants all, west-siders all, and all parishioners of St. Patrick's. This church is, in a manner of speaking, the city's own Ellis Island.

# The Holy Trinity Greek Cathedral

DECEMBER 20, 1987

The sights and sounds of Christmas have been everywhere in the city these past few weeks—or has it been months?

Understandably, a great many Utahns may be more than mildly fed up with the twinkling lights, electronic chimes, plastic stars, flocked trees and overly jolly Santas that have come to symbolize Christmas in our mall-sprinkled land. But, if you're tempted to join E. Scrooge and mutter, "Bah! Humbug!" to the glitter and glitz, I suggest a visit on Christmas Eve or Christmas Day to the Holy Trinity Greek Orthodox Cathedral at the northeast corner of 300 South and 300 West. It is not festooned with colored lights, not even decorated with a dozen or two wreaths, nor graced with a red-tagged Montana Christmas tree.

Neither the 7 P.M. Christmas Eve service nor the 10 A.M. Christmas Day service is likely to attract a television cameraman. Those electronic

168

reporters are much more likely to turn up at midnight mass at the Cathedral of the Madeleine, to tape brightly lighted Temple Square or to "capture the holiday spirit" at one of the edifices in the rather more "stylish" churches where familiar oratorios or carols will be sung. All Holy Trinity can offer its parishioners and visitors will be age-old services of the sort conducted in Greek Orthodox churches since the very beginnings of the Christian era.

Outwardly this cathedral, dedicated in 1924, looks very different from others in the valley. Designed by Pope and Burton, it occupies a site purchased from the Sweet Candy Company for some $20,000—a sum enormously difficult to raise when most parishioners were small shopkeepers, Bingham miners, Midvale smelter workers and other recently arrived immigrants, or their first-generation children. The 550-seat Cathedral-church they built and decorated with their hard-earned dollars is the state's purest example of Byzantine architecture, built in a style traceable to far larger Saint Sophia in Constantinople dating to 533 A.D.

Our city's Greek Orthodox cathedral is enhanced by a half-dozen arch-topped columns flanking its 300 West entrance—but those columns are concrete, rather than more expensive marble or granite. No matter, that same facade is graced by twin, tile-rimmed, well-proportioned towers topped by the requisite crosses. Best seen from the southwest, the dark brick edifice is set apart from others in the city by its sizable but rather low dome, a dome pierced by twelve windows and supported by the traditional dozen pillars, columns symbolizing the twelve apostles.

However, as in many larger cathedrals, Holy Trinity's beauty and worth are best appreciated from inside. Of course, during the holiday services (mainly in Greek, but partly in English) you may be caught by the audible symbols of the Orthodox faith, intrigued to hear The Lord's Prayer in a strange tongue and made the more understandable by cards outlining the Nicene Creed, cards printed in the classic Greek alphabet, in the modern Cyrillic of today's Greece and in familiar Roman-style typography. Above and behind you, a forty-voice choir will be singing unfamiliar hymns in polyphonic fashion stemming from Byzantium, hymns in the main unfamiliar to most of us.

No "processional" of the sort to be found in a Catholic or Episcopal cathedral moves down the aisles during the service. Nevertheless, there's a very splendid, almost theatrical look to any service in Holy Trinity. On Christmas Eve and Christmas Day, Father Joachin Hatzidakis, Father John Kaloudis and Father George Politis (I believe I've listed them by seniority) will wear the white, richly ornamented, full-length robes symbolic of their calling as they stand facing the altar and its traditional cross.

"We offer our prayers as representatives of the congregation, we therefore face the altar and cross with them," explains Father Hatzidakis. The priests read from the Gospel, a privileged member of the congregation is chosen to read the Epistle and following the sermon there is a presentation of the gifts of bread and wine to all members of the congregation who come forward.

But it is the decor of Holy Trinity that will be the focus of attention of most newcomers to the otherwise rather modest cathedral. The ceiling of the dome is a rich blue, almost more vivid than the sky. Frescoes of the evangelists, paintings that, in their rather rigid styling, take on the appearance of icons, decorate the pendentives—the supports of the spherical dome. At the cathedral's front, a brightly painted central panel represents the Last Supper, while side panels, equally bright in color are lit, during daylight hours, by sunshine streaming through those twelve windows in the columned dome.

A central mural above the altar, again surprisingly rich in color, represents the Holy Mother and the Christ Child. Left of the altar an Epitaphios, a flower-covered, shrinelike structure, represents Christ's tomb, while on the right is a far more elaborate Epitaphios of carved and gilded wood. A bishop's throne testifies to the fact that this has long been the see and mother-church of the Intermountain Region.

An icon over its entrance reminds churchgoers of Christ's entry into Jerusalem. An Alpha and Omega are placed before a tomblike centerpiece fronting the altar, while the striking blue of the dome and the rich royal red and gold wall hues are reminders of the Kingdom of God.

As noted, there is little of what we may deem to be "Christmas decor" at Holy Trinity. There are no strands of electric lights, but votive candles glow and flicker just beyond the entryway. Saints limned in stained glass look down from the dome upon a setting that is the same this week as in any nonholiday.

Richly colored stained glass windows of considerable size placed in the north and south walls will remind many visitors of immigrant Greek families that have immeasurably enriched the city and state. There are windows honoring the Cayias family, the Louis Strike family, the Gianos family. And one window was presented by "West Jordan and Midvale, Parishioners," the hardworking, devoted men and women who came to a raw new land bringing with them an ethos—a work ethic.

Their building remains an edifice needing no "Tannenbaums," no chimney-descending St. Nicholas, none of those colorful but not too meaningful Anglo-Saxon or Teutonic icons from those more recently civilized lands far north of the Greek isles.

Nevertheless, the drawing accompanying this paean of praise for the Greek Orthodox Holy Trinity Cathedral is this columnist's effort to recall the woodcut or engraving style of such northern European masters as Dürer, Holbein, Breughel, and Grünewald—artists who pretty much passed their images of the Christ child and holly-hung mangers to the lesser artists of Merrie Olde England and these United States.

# Cathedral of the Madeleine

DECEMBER 21, 1986

As this is written, the wherewithal for a white Christmas has not arrived, meaning S. Claus won't be followed by small boys on Flexible Flyer sleds. However, our oversupply of evening mist—a polite term for air pollution thick enough to chew—softens the hard edges of even the new concrete office buildings our city has acquired of late.

And the installation of a half-million or more large and small pastel lights around the valley has given our metropolis a pleasant seasonal glow. When giving thanks for large and small favors, please save kudos for Thomas Alva Edison, the inventive chap who let there be light.

While countless visitors stroll through Temple Square to "oh" and "ah" at what imaginative picture-caption writers annually label a "fairy-land of lights," your seasonal inspection of the Mazdas twinkling in the Main Street environs should also include a drive up or down South Temple.

If so, don't overlook the rather less glitzy, but essentially satisfactory, night-time appearance of the Cathedral of the Madeleine.

In truth, our city's largest Catholic house of worship is floodlighted nightly throughout the year. But to sentimentalists of any or even of no religion, the cathedral's illuminated facade and twin towers, as well as its fine interior decor, seem to take on added grandeur at this season.

These nights, those rather heavily incised stone towers meld into the mist in almost airy fashion. Viewed from any angle on East South Temple a bit east or west of B Street, the facade, enriched by the multicolored glow of the centerpiece Rose Window, is especially compelling.

If you are in good physical shape, you'll benefit from the walk up steep B Street to First Avenue for the view from another vantage point. Turn back and look out at the light-spangled city, with the darkened cathedral bulking large against the pattern of homes and streets. Seen from uphill, the curve of the chapel and chancel blend into the geometrical ridge of the copper-clad roof and its single narrow spire.

The masonry tops of the tallest towers, silhouetted against the misty sky, remind us of churches or cathedrals in villages, towns or cities elsewhere in the world. Most were built in ages past, when men, although untutored (by our terms) in mathematics and science, managed to rear immense stone towers skyward in reverent fashion, seeking, one must suppose, to come as close to God as possible.

Battered by artillery shells and bombs in countless wars, cathedrals and churches were often the first buildings repaired and restored in London or Louvain, in Rouen or Rome.

Floodlighted or not, Salt Lake's Cathedral of the Madeleine is hardly a candidate for the Guinness book of records. Its spires are far from the tallest; it has no amazingly large dome or broad floor span. Occupying as it does only a portion of a less-than-large avenues block, this house of worship would be crowded indeed if more than 1,200 or so parishioners attempted to occupy its pews. Nor is its organ the mightiest in town, while its modest choirloft couldn't accommodate the nationally known musical aggregation so long a magnet in the domed Tabernacle a few blocks west.

And yet the Cathedral of the Madeleine looks the part—it being the approximation of an old-world ecclesiastical structure in this region. Architects will remind you this is not a pure Gothic structure, nor is it truly Romanesque. Along with its admixture of both those honored styles, this cathedral presents more than a dab of Germanic heaviness, which should come as no surprise, since its initial architect was German-born Carl M. Neuhausen.

Upon Neuhausen's death, Bernard Mecklenburg, whose name gives a solid clue to his ancestry, took over. It was Mecklenburg who seems chiefly responsible for the final design of the lofty roof and the ornate twin towers. But a third architect, John Comes, worked the final embellishing touches into the structure, and it was Comes who brought Felix Lieftuchter onto the scene to handle the decorative work.

Again a Germanic influence—since Lieftuchter, a native of Cincinnati, was trained in Munich in a mural tradition ensuring that painted walls and panels did not intrude upon the overall effect of a traditional interior.

Thus this cathedral, like so many abroad that took centuries to build, is a blend of architectural styles, a layering of influences. And, like many such structures overseas, this cathedral came into being because a notable personage insisted it must be built. Not a Sforza, not an English ruler, not a pope.

This being the one hundreth anniversary of the establishment of the Salt Lake vicarate, it is incumbent to note that Lawrence J. Scanlan, an Irish parish priest with the humble beginnings of so many of his fellow immigrants, was chiefly responsible for the Cathedral of the Madeleine. Arriving in Salt Lake in 1873, "without a penny in his pockets and patches on his coat," this powerhouse of a cleric was shortly to be named the territory's first Catholic bishop.

Little more than a dozen years after his arrival he was insisting that a proper site for the building of his dreams was atop a hillock on Brigham Street. By 1905, ten years before his death, he had not only built the first parochial schools and a Catholic hospital open to all—but was able to preside at the dedication of the present cathedral, unfinished though it was.

This holiday season, Salt Lakers attending the annual midnight mass will look down the rows of columns rising high above the nave toward the traditional altar, pulpit and bishop's throne. Studying the dimly lit, gold-leaf-embellished murals, the stained glass and stations of the cross, at least a few visitors will muse a while about the need for peace on earth and good will toward all men.

The cathedral walls, the ageless symbols of worship, the misty skies outside, pierced by a few beaconlike stars, speak of the season at least as well as the bright, all-too-often plastic decorations in the malls and merchandise marts scattered across the valley.

EDITOR'S NOTE: A three-year restoration chiefly involving such exterior matters as deteriorating stonework and a new roof was completed on the cathedral in 1991 at a cost of $1,115,000. A more ambitious program concentrating on the colored glass windows, the murals and the general interior completed in 1992 cost some ten million dollars.

# New England-style Unitarian Church

NOVEMBER 10, 1985

It has always seemed odd to me that members of Utah's dominant church, although building houses of worship in extraordinary numbers, so rarely turned to the architecture of their native New England or New York state when designing their church structures. Understandably, early Church of Jesus Christ of Latter-day Saints meetinghouses were simply rectangular boxes with gable roofs. But in Vermont, New York state and other areas that gave birth to this native American church, meetinghouses had—long before the 1847 Mormon migration—been topped by slender steeples, graced with porticos, and otherwise given a touch of Neoclassic styling. Colonial churches are numerous even today in Back Bay Boston, in suburban Connecticut and elsewhere in the Eastern states.

    As a result of this curious lack of architectural spillover into Utah, we suffer from a scarcity of church buildings derived from the style of Christopher Wren and his American followers. In fact, there seems to be only one such ecclesiastical structure in all of Salt Lake City, and it is of fairly recent date. It is, of course, the First Unitarian Church on 1300 East at 600 South. First Unitarian is a warm, reddish brick, Georgian-Colonial-seeming affair crowned with the requisite white wooden tower and shapely spire reminiscent of that belfry tower of the Old North Church toward which Paul Revere peered before beginning his famous ride.

Designed by Salt Lake architect Slack W. Winburn (working with the Boston firm of Smith and Walker) the Unitarian Church was not built until 1927, and Eliot Hall, the addition south of the main structure, wasn't completed until 1960. Since the Unitarian faith had its beginnings in Boston, it's understandable that the congregation looked to its proper architectural ancestry, especially so because Utah's scanty supply of Unitarians had endured considerable difficulty in finding a permanent home.

The congregation worshipped in the LDS Social Hall on State Street, in Odd Fellows Halls on Post Office Place and in the Jewish Temple on 400 East before building its own Unity House at 138 S. 200 East in 1904. But when funds were found for the present more adequate and handsome building on 1300 East, the Unitarians erected as pleasant a church as can be found anywhere in the valley.

Considered as a whole, it is, perhaps, a bit "out of balance" due to the Eliot Hall addition. Nor are the proportions of the church textbook perfect. To my mind, the handsome steeple is a mite too low, although admittedly topped by one of our town's finest weather vanes. The front porch, graced by four tall wooden columns, seems a bit narrow from some angles—the portico is, after all, fully two stories high. But the tall, well-proportioned arched windows, the sloped roof, the brickwork and the corner quoins seem just right to me and to many who have studied the building.

The interior is equally handsome. Behind those tall supporting columns there's a vestibule flanked by a pair of especially graceful curved staircases that lead to a narrow rear balcony. Inside, those high arched windows light a very dignified nave. This being something of a replica of a New England church, the interior of the structure is understandably plain. There's a modest cornice; the chancel with its lectern and pulpit are properly proportioned; and the walls and pews are painted in the rather neutral ivory so characteristic of Colonial churches. The black trim on the pews seems a bit harsh, but the graceful chandeliers glint like old silver. The interior and exterior are somehow harmonious—just right for a congregation of New England ancestry and history. The building is small, seating perhaps 500, but it's the sort of hall that warmly welcomes members and outsiders alike to the lectures, concerts and other events that have given the Unitarian Church a rather unique character in the city.

Recently the exterior of the church, including the white wood of the steeple, its portico columns and window and door trim has been acquiring a fresh coat of sparkling paint. Now the building front gleams like those far older, rather more historic churches some of us remember glimpsing through Vermont maples or beneath the Berkshire hills. By the way, during the painting process, Minister Richard Henry suddenly noted the disappearance of one of the four fennels—the urn-like architectural elements at each corner of the base of the steeple. Unnoticed by most church-goers, it had fallen and lodged in the fence at the base of the tower.

While the Unitarians felt no need for a Paul Revere-style lantern, a bell was sadly lacking until the late 1970s when one was shipped from France—there apparently being no proper bell makers left in our land, even in New England.

Mulling over the lack of traditional white-steepled, well-proportioned "Colonial" churches hereabouts, I've remembered another one—a real beauty too—down in St. George. Deep in Utah's Dixie the Saints indeed recalled New England scenes and built an especially handsome red sandstone tabernacle back in 1871, a few years before the first Unitarian services were held in the territory.

# The Buddhist Temple on First South

FEBRUARY 20, 1994

On one of those gray, imitation-London days with which our town is periodically afflicted, fog nearly hid the upper stories of the tall apartment tower on Salt Lake's near west side.

The scene was brightened more than a little by the gleaming Oriental-style entrance and simple walls of the Buddhist Temple at 211 W. 100 South. This is not an old edifice, of course—many Salt Lakers of other faiths recall its dedication in March 1962. Nearly a block long, and just two stories in height, it is (I am told) architecturally unlike most Buddhist temples in Japan. But, as I never have traveled in the Orient, its style and simple lines somehow represent Japan to me.

The canopy over the entrance doors midpoint in the long facade helps give the outward aspect of the temple its properly Oriental look. The canopy swoops in a graceful curve unlike the arched or straight-line protective

179

elements above European-style doorways or modern Americanized versions of such rain-shedders. There is a simpler pair of entry doors a dozen yards farther east, doors topped by five windows just beneath the roofline. These windows, with their simple dividers, also help give the structure its Japanese look.

The interior of the temple is the religious heart of the structure, providing a proper setting for the traditional shrines many thousand miles removed from the usual centers of that religion.

The most eye-catching object in this house of worship is an elaborate altar, constructed of hundreds of small, hand-carved pieces of hardwood, carefully fitted together and covered with gold leaf. The altar was delicately pieced together by members of a Japanese family specializing in such work for some three centuries.

There are other symbolic representations in the Buddhist Temple—one depicting Shiman, the founder of the Buddhist sect followed locally. Another teacher followed is Rennyo, the eighth abbot of this branch of Buddhism.

Virtually everything within the temple has symbolic meaning—the burning candles represent the light of wisdom; incense being burned purifies the soul as well as the air. Flowers, carefully placed and chosen, symbolize the lack of permanence in the lives of humankind. The heavy, burnished gong, when struck, gives emphasis to portions of the sutra chanted during services—carefully chosen from the 84,000 scriptures in the teachings of Buddha.

The religion is some 2,500 years old, founded by "the awakening one," Prince Siddhartha, in 566 B.C. in India. A traditional "Hana Matsuri" service marks the birthday of Buddhism every April.

To the average Utahn, the history of the Japanese people in Utah, with special reference to problems they have overcome, should be as important as their chosen form of religious worship.

According to historian John S. McCormick, few Japanese were in Utah before 1884, when the Japanese government repealed its centuries-old ban on emigration. Late in the 1880s, the few Japanese in Utah found employment in railroad construction, like the Chinese before them.

The 1890 census tallies showed 467 Japanese immigrants in the state—including eleven women. By 1920, there were 3,000 Japanese in the state. These hardworking immigrants already were facing severe racial prejudice in communities where they had become farm laborers and then farm owners. Immigration continued until the 1923 Oriental Exclusion Act, largely a product of the West Coast "yellow peril" fears inspired by the Hearst press. By then, some Japanese were prospering through the shipment and sale of Utah celery, while several hundred were employees at the Kennecott Copper Co. smelter at Garfield.

A Japanese Buddhist Church, founded in 1899 in San Francisco, was followed a dozen years later by the founding of the Intermountain Buddhist Church, sponsored by immigrants who felt the need to worship in familiar form. Initial services were in the Kyushuya Hotel at 168 S. West Temple, in a neighborhood long a center for shops handling Japanese foodstuffs and merchandise. On June 1, 1924, ground was broken for a church building at 247 W. 100 South, with the Rev. K. Kuwahara as its leader.

The building was demolished in 1962, when constructing the Salt Palace made for major neighborhood changes. Earlier, the Japanese Buddhist community suffered considerably with the outbreak of World War II. When all people of Japanese ancestry were moved from their West Coast homes and businesses, some 1,500 came to live in Utah, while more than 8,000 were shipped to Topaz, Utah, for internment.

Many Topaz deportees stayed in Utah. With the earlier immigrants, they went on to overcome the unwarranted prejudices of their neighbors— many of whom were, of course, immigrants themselves.

In many ways, as thoughtful Utahns came to realize, the Salt Lake Buddhist Temple is a memorial to Japanese who came to the city in the early years.

CHAPTER 8

# Schools Sprout and Adapt

# Rowland Hall-St. Mark's School

JANUARY 20, 1991

Even when you've attained maturity, a visit to an elementary school can prove instructive—and a stroll around the campus of an institution that is a century or so old can prove especially so. A case in point is the Rowland Hall-St. Mark's School, where such labors as a unifying paint job, the tidy restoration of a passel of old-timers and the construction of some stylish frame "skeletons" by a thoughtful group of modern architects have served, in recent years, to "tie things together."

If you don't mind a mite of hill-climbing, or have a car capable of uphill travel, you need only head for the square block in the Avenues Historic District for a look-see all your own. No noisy teenagers will bowl you over during your stroll. The institution long since took over a public, junior high building to better meet the needs of more active older pupils. However, small fry of the "lower school" still make full use of the historic structures in the block bounded by A and B streets on the west and east, and by First and Second avenues on the north and south.

A modern monolith, the DeWitt Van Evra Building, occupies much of the First Avenue frontage. Ignore it for later study, remembering it is useful for classroom purposes.

Originally, Rowland Hall School for young women was housed solely in the Watt-Haskins home, a two-story gable-roofed affair built largely of adobe in 1862 and enlarged in a somewhat Georgian style about 1871. George Watt came to Utah from Nauvoo, Ill., and completed a mission to England in 1850, but after considerable service at the *Deseret News* he left the Mormon Church, joined the Godbeite group and moved to Kaysville. He sold his home to banker Warren Hussey in 1869 or thereabouts.

Hussey, an Episcopalian, along with several like-minded Christians, persuaded the Rt. Rev. Daniel S. Tuttle to come to Utah and establish Christian missions in this "godless wilderness." He was to become bishop of the Episcopal Missionary District of Utah, Idaho and Montana. One early missionary, Thomas W. Haskins, lived in Hussey's house while serving as principal of St. Mark's School in St. Mark's Church on 100 South.

Haskins put a truncated roof on the house, added a sizable section at the rear, and by 1880 turned things over to a Rev. Kirby, who, according to National Register files, "received title on behalf of his mother-in-law, Mrs. Rowland." Hence, obviously, the name "Rowland Hall." The Watt-Haskins house, remodeled and added to half a dozen times, was used for classes (female) while boys struggled along downhill at St. Mark's Church.

Skipping a few decades or so, we learn that attorney Joseph L. Rawlings, a founder of the local Democratic Party, built a house (now on the school grounds) in 1887. Businessman Joseph E. Caine built a home down the street in 1888, while Priscilla Paul Jennings built a house on the block in 1890, some years after her husband, the city's one-time mayor, had died. Jennings, by the way, built the much more famous Devereaux Mansion on South Temple in what is now the Triad development.

The Rawlings home was bought by Rowland Hall in 1922, the Caine house was purchased in 1965 when St. Mark's School reopened, and the Jennings home became school property that same year. But the most significant building project on the little campus began in 1900, when Felix Brunot donated $35,000. Bishop Abiel Leonard hired an architect (Theodore Davis Beal) and, insufficiently funded, work began on a new classroom and a chapel.

By 1906, there was a new bishop, F.S. Spalding, and the classroom structure took shape in the rear of the Watt-Haskins house. But not till 1910 was there money enough to build the chapel seen in the center of today's sketch with the old Watt-Haskins building on the left. The chapel was built by contractors David R. and George A. Smith to the decade-old designs of architect Theodore Beal.

The chapel, situated between the Watt-Haskins building and the 1910 classroom addition, is set back to create a small three-sided courtyard. Inside the second-floor sanctuary, the chapel's interior has exposed wood trusses, a large leaded-glass window at the south end, dark wood pews and red brick walls.

The south front of the older buildings linked to the chapel have dormer roofs, bracketed cornices and quoins, all in a modified Georgian style. There's a second-story fanlight window on the right-hand structure placed under a gable Georgian-style.

Aside from the new 1970 classroom building on First Avenue designed by Snedaker, Budd and Watt, an obvious attempt has been made to unify the campus, chiefly through the use of gray paint with white trim. Indeed, Lloyd Snedaker's valiant effort to link old and new is obvious in the De-Witt Van Evra structure. The archway through which visitors approach the "old campus" frames the chapel and its neighbors, while the shallow mansard roof and even the gray brick detailing of the new somehow echo Rowland Hall-St. Mark's history.

The simple white frame structures dotting the campus (two appear in the sketch) were built a half-dozen or so years ago when the architectural firm of Hallet, Hermanson and Associates, undertook, rather successfully, to brighten the campus with well-thought-out play equipment, outdoor classrooms and the like. The major frame structures lack solid roofs or sides, but serve to join a clever paint job in unifying the diverse one-time homes and classroom buildings. Rowland Hall-St. Mark's illustrates what the efforts of thoughtful architects can accomplish down through the years.

# Westminster's Converse Hall

JANUARY 1, 1989

If you've strolled or driven past the Westminster College campus during recent weeks or months, you may have taken note of the careful and much-needed renovation and restoration work under way at Converse Hall, the Jacobean-style, turreted building that has been the institution's architectural centerpiece since it first rose in 1906.

Designed by Utah architect Walter E. Ware, it was named for John Converse, president of the Baldwin Locomotive Works, who was happily persuaded to donate $20,000 for the handsome $27,000 structure.

Those who take time to give Converse Hall more than a hasty look can learn much about architecture, escalating building costs, changing tastes and even botany by browsing a bit, and, more especially, by chatting with Steve Crane, architect in charge of the $1,200,000 restoration project.

To begin with, there's the odd matter of botany, or nurturing nature heedlessly or too well. "Vines were the greatest threat to the building's exterior," Crane reports, a statement worth pondering by graduates of "Ivy League" universities here and overseas. "Vines engulfed the entire northern facade, wrapped over the parapets, grew onto the roof. Over many years, the growth cycle and capillary action of the vines combined to deteriorate the building's mortar, masonry and stone." Crane assures the public that Converse Hall, in its new dispensation, will be freshly landscaped, sans vines.

One major architectural lesson you can learn by carefully eyeballing the eighty-two-year-old building has to do with paint. Paint preserves, but it does not necessarily enhance. Tedious hours and a multitude of dollars have been spent removing the peeling pink-beige paint that once brightened—or disfigured—this campus landmark. Scholarly Walter Ware, one of the region's most prominent architects soon after the turn of the century, selected an English style that had evolved since the founding of Oxford and Cambridge, a style long deemed especially fitting for an academic structure.

Its octagonal towers, parapets, crenellations, carved stone, corbeled brickwork and decorative Tudor windows all "speak" to generations of easily influenced nonacademicians of proper-seeming collegiate architecture. Obviously, what's good enough for Princeton and Yale should be good enough for modest Westminster College of Salt Lake City. But unfortunately, as your earlier recollections of Converse Hall may make clear, that oft-applied pastel-pink paint canceled architect Ware's detailed ornamentation, hid his careful articulation of major elements and nullified the contrast of the original glowing-red brick with the stonework of medallions and corner quoins.

When interior and exterior renovation work is complete, when steps, walks and driveways are repaired, when the rusticated red-stone foundations have been carefully grouted and cemented, when roof leaks, weathered gables and warped moldings of the Hall's decorative windows have been repaired—will the labor and dollars expended pay off? What will those dollars, provided by a gift from Berenice Jewett Bradshaw and by a low-interest federal loan, have bought if expended on a new structure?

Converse Hall will now house twenty new classrooms and associated facilities for the arts and humanities. Would a new replacement building have served the college and its public in better fashion?

Let me turn, for a partial answer, to another campus, another city, another era. In 1831, the year of its founding, New York University built its first academic building on Manhattan's Washington Square Parade Ground. It, too, was a multi-towered, English-revival affair. In its tower rooms Samuel Finley Breese Morse developed the telegraph, artists such as George Inness put paint to canvas, Walt Whitman visited fellow poets, professorial inventor/artisans worked on such abstruse affairs as the Bessemer steel process and the screw propeller.

Unfortunately only a bronze tablet now marks the site of that first NYU building. At the turn of the century, beguiled by the practicability of the new, the university demolished its "old Main," replacing it with a ten-story steel-framed affair having all the outward characteristics of an office building. Its College of Commerce and School of Education were soon housed in similar high-rise structures. Indeed, NYU shortly remodeled typical loft and office buildings in the Washington Square neighborhood to meet its needs. Not until the years following World War II, when a fake "colonial" law school building and the huge, much-debated red sandstone Bobst Library took shape, did NYU, one of the largest of the nation's privately endowed universities, give thought to a unified campus. It was far too late to salvage a major piece of New York and the nation's academic heritage, a building that would have enhanced NYU's prestige.

Now—back to Salt Lake City and Westminster College. About two years ago, after extensive surveys, hearings and considerable soul-searching, Westminster officials felt compelled to demolish old Ferry Hall, a column-fronted, increasingly decrepit campus landmark named in honor of Col. William Ferry, a Park City mining investor who had donated the entire sum to purchase the campus on 1300 East.

The decision to tear down the long-shuttered firetrap was happily followed by good news—family funds were on hand for a new Bill and Vieve Gore School of Business Building. Designed by architect Michael Stransky, the Gore Building now stands on the old Ferry Hall site and contains a dozen new classrooms, a 150-seat lecture hall and requisite faculty offices. While its east-facing wall unfortunately stares blankly at passersby on 1300 East, the building's west facade offers a better notion of the functional look one may expect when other new buildings rise on the campus.

A three-story-high reflective glass entryway in the Gore Building brings the indoors and outdoors into a pleasing relationship for students, faculty and visitors. Five tall, slender columns reminiscent of bygone Ferry Hall soften the austerity of the unembellished stone walls and the contrasting red brick flanks. The new structure is in scale with such comparatively modern Westminster buildings as Bamberger and Hogle halls. Another major virtue—it is unobtrusive enough to permit Converse Hall, when renovation is complete, to continue as the focal point of a pleasant college campus, an academic "park" that does not obtrude upon the surrounding residential neighborhood.

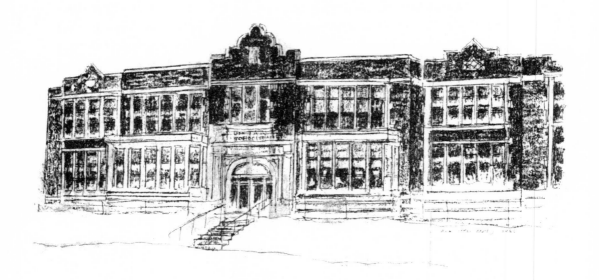

# Uintah Elementary School

JANUARY 26, 1986

With a skiff of snow accenting its roofline, broad window ledges and trim, the Uintah School looks especially inviting on a winter's midmorning. Not a child in sight—although any parent passing by would know that at recess or when classes are dismissed, swarms of brightly garbed kids would be tossing snowballs at their peers. In fact, anyone entering the school's broad entrance could spot a crop of snow-soaked mittens hanging in the heating vents—a very practical use for the vents that may not have occurred to architects, plumbers and contractors back in 1913.

Having seen the passage of seventy-two winters or so, and having echoed to the passage of countless children in its broad halls, the Uintah School is the last of its breed, sole survivor of its type still in use in the Salt Lake City School District. Down through the years there have been additions fleshing out its north and south sides and a pair of temporary structures edge its ample play-yard. But the casual visitor, and, I suppose, most parents coming to attend PTA sessions, can find little in the Uintah School to fret about. The halls in the central section are so wide that, having been carpeted as a sound-absorbing measure, they can be used as dance or quiet play space by the small fry. And the building's twin kindergarten rooms, on the ground floor level flanking the main entrance, are just about the sunniest, brightest rooms visible in any city school. Each is fronted by five huge windows, with an extra pair of windows on either side of the street-facing bays. As Principal E. Dilworth Newman cheerily points out, the rooms make ideal greenhouses—for growing plants or children.

Fact is, a visit to the Uintah School raises questions concerning its modern counterparts which, all too often, are being built without windows or with the tiniest of clear-glass panes. Don't today's kids like to peer outside at trees and grass, passing buses or passing dogs? Surely the outdoors is distracting, but the interior of our modern schools, especially the new Emerson School, which is built partially underground, might predispose some youngsters and teachers to claustrophobia. In any event, every room in the old-fashioned Uintah School has notably large, notably deep, multipaned windows—plus shades that can be drawn to hide the setting sun. Perhaps the radiator pipes knock and squeal on occasion, but then the blower motors of more modern educational installations can sound like boiler rooms aboard naval vessels speeding under forced draught.

When originally built in 1913, Uintah's thirteen rooms made it one of the larger schools in the city; a 1927 addition, giving the building a total of twenty-five classrooms, made it one of the most useful. Now it has a sizable multipurpose room added in the 1970s for cafeteria and gymnasium purposes, plus the necessary offices to serve thirty teachers and 650 youngsters in classes ranging from kindergarten to sixth grade. For the information of ever-angry taxpayers, the original Uintah cost $85,000 including an auditorium that could be converted to a "dancing ballroom by merely removing the folding chairs." All this plus metal troughs beneath the bay windows, installed for "botanical purposes."

According to early news items Principal Newman dredged from his files, "real estate companies were so optimistic of the future of the district" near the school (at 1227 S. 1500 East) that they "furnished ties with the street car company to take children to school." But way out in this benchland country crisscrossed by Yale, Harvard and Princeton avenues, "winds from the canyons swept across the fields ferociously. The east winds, carrying snow from the mountains, would drift level with the high yard and pack it solid across the street. . . . snow fences along 1500 East were no defense. . . . street cars were stalled several blocks away, many hats were lost, many feet were frostbitten and many teachers fell exhausted after reaching the door." Alas, this wintry clipping bears no date, but the winter in question may have been that of 1916, when A.B. Kesler was principal. Too early, of course, for attendance by Uintah's sole man in space, U.S. Sen. Jake Garn, one of its more prominent graduates. But very likely Sen. Garn did enjoy "the curtain for the stage, three radios, a duplicating machine, a recording radio and several sets of encyclopedias supplied by the school PTA before 1940."

From the standpoint of architecture, the Uintah School poses something of a mystery for Carl Childs, inspector of buildings and grounds for the city school system. The name of C.L. Lewis turns up on the blueprints for the 1927 addition—but there's no name upon the 1913 plans. Never mind. The dark, brownish-red brick, laid in bonded courses, has held up well. The decorative emblems atop the main entrance and each wing look fresh and new. The Uintah School and its look-alikes in cities and towns across the nation have served generations of pupils well. Douglas School, of equivalent age, while no longer part of the city system, is used by Salt Lake County's Autistic Children program. The older Oquirrh School, with its high attic and semi-gables, dates from the 1890s and has been converted to office building use. From the look of things, the city's taxpayers got a considerable bargain when the Uintah School was built on its five-acre site—there's even room for a playground and for parking.

One minor mystery remains. The name of the school carved over its door is Uinta, minus the letter "h," although the official spelling is Uintah. One theory is that the Indian tribe out Fort Duchesne way was accorded that spelling by the U.S. Army Bureau. Of course there was no phonetic spelling way back then.

EDITOR'S NOTE: Since this column appeared, Uintah School was torn town and a new one erected on the same plot. It opened for students in the fall of 1993.

# University of Utah's Kingsbury Hall

JUNE 10, 1990

Question: Aside from their obvious affinity for the performing arts, what do the Hanya Holm dancers, the Budapest String Quartet, Paul Robeson, Marian Anderson, Yehudi Menuhin, Grant Johannesen and Artur Rubinstein share in common? And John Gielgud, Vincent Price, John Houseman and Orson Welles? As you may have deduced from the accompanying drawing, all the above, and many, many more such notables, played in, performed in or trod the boards at sixty-year-old Kingsbury Hall.

An efficient job of "name spending," utilizing a list gathered by the indefatigable but recently retired Paul Cracroft, would pretty well fill this entire column. It would include other such practitioners of the lively arts as Count Basie, Woody Herman and Ella Fitzgerald representing the world of jazz; Sherwood Anderson, Thomas Mann, Bertrand Russell, Theodore Dreiser and Robert Frost representing literature and letters, and Drew

Pearson, Lowell Thomas and Eleanor Roosevelt (as a columnist) appearing for the Fourth Estate.

Am I correct in thinking the University of Utah campus was a livelier place, or at least more of a magnet for the thinking public in the days when Kingsbury Hall ranked as our town's own Town Hall? And there was no television, no Channel 7, to compete for the attention of folks who considered most Hollywood films (rightly or wrongly) as so much pap.

On May 8 the Utah Symphony played a Fiftieth Anniversary Concert in Kingsbury—which was altogether fitting and proper. But it is likewise fitting and proper to remind you that Kingsbury Hall was completed and officially dedicated ten years earlier than the date of the initial Utah Symphony concert. The need for an assembly hall on campus had been obvious as early as 1900—but then, as in more recent times, the Utah State Legislature could be a mite niggardly in funding educational structures.

By 1922 the U.'s President George Thomas was pleading, almost on bended knee, for a hall capable of seating 2,000 students and faculty members simultaneously. The Board of Regents agreed, but not until 1927 was the Legislature cajoled into a loan of $250,000 (with much of the sum going to the School of Mines) as funding for the new hall.

In a move debated with considerable heat, it was decided the architect should be selected "on a competitive basis." Specifications called for "a seating capacity of 2,000, a stage and dressing rooms, with classrooms admissible but secondary." The location on the north side of the campus circle was selected, likewise the building's name, honoring the university's president emeritus. And of considerable importance, the architectural style as stipulated must conform, in general terms and appearance, to that of the John R. Park Building at the top of the circle.

Today visitors, faculty and students agree, in the main, that the architects selected, Edward O. Anderson and Lorenzo S. Young, did very well indeed, as did the building firm of William J. and Vernon W. Dean. The completed structure was dedicated on May 22, 1930. The cost—just $275,000. On first sight, this very useful structure, its outer wall and columns faced with a light buff-colored terra cotta, looks rather Grecian or Roman in style, especially if you glance rather hastily at its cornices, dentils and decorative friezes. But a careful scrutiny indicates, to the surprise of some visitors, that the four portico columns and adjacent porch elements are topped with Egyptian-style motifs, handsome, well-proportioned, but a bit odd for such a structure.

Somehow for those of us a certain age, well-worn Kingsbury Hall, inside and out, has a warmth we've never felt at Pioneer Memorial Theatre. The latter is sumptuously furnished, as one patron once put it to me, "rather like an overdone funeral parlor." One reason for Kingsbury's attractiveness perhaps, would be its broad, rather battered front steps. At intermission time Kingsbury patrons, in the days before we were apprised of the dangers of smoking, would hasten outside, sit or stand on those steps during clement weather and smoke our Chesterfields, Camels or Luckys while discussing the evening's performance. If rain or snow fell, we could crowd beneath the portico, with the pillars providing some shelter from the wind. Or, if winter weather was really bitter, the corridor at the rear of the house was comfortably overcrowded by patrons who seemed little bothered by the haze of smokers who squeezed just inside the doors.

Today, paintings of "locals" who graced Kingsbury in what many of us recall as "the good old days" hang in the hall. Two are portraits by Alvin Gittins—displaying his usual flair—of Maurice Abravanel and Willam Christensen, men who in truth introduced fine symphonic music and excellent ballet to the city and state. Nearby there are paintings of Maud May Babcock and Emma Lucy Gates Bowen, who endeared themselves to Utah audiences through the theater and vocal music, respectively. It would seem to me a portrait of C. Lowell Lees should hang next to those of "Mr. C." and "the Maestro," but unless I'm mistaken there's a painting of Lees at PMT.

In the lobby, a plaque properly takes note of the members of the Board of Regents who pressed for the construction of Kingsbury Hall, and who thereby gave a substantial boost to the arts in Utah. They include Robert H. Hinckley; Oscar W. Carlson, Wilson McCarthy, James H. Wolfe and J. William Robinson. A radio network executive, an educator, a railroad president, an attorney, a congressman. Others who pressed for construction would include Gail Plummer, Prof. Elbert D. Thomas (later a United States senator), Joseph F. Smith of the speech department, Marion Redd of the drama department, and, in late days, Keith Engar.

When navigating the steep aisles at Kingsbury, or when waiting for the houselights to dim, patrons can't help but notice the twin murals alongside the proscenium arch designed and painted by Florence E. Ware. She did a considerable amount of teaching as well as painting, both on campus and off, thereby leaving her mark on artists of succeeding generations.

The murals, like many other art works of the period, were financed as a federal works project under the WPA, headed in Utah in 1936 by Judy Lund Wassmer. Each panel, seventeen-feet square, is oil on canvas. The pair, if read from left to right, will tell you much concerning the "Evolution of Drama Through the Ages" as viewed in the 1930s. If you seek them out, you can find African dancers, Greek tragedians, Chinese and other Oriental performers, and even Anglo-Saxons engaged in composing and singing ballads of Beowulf.

The mural panels also take note of painters, sculptors and composers equipping them perhaps a mite simplistically, with the requisite trade tools--brushes, chisels, lyres and the like. Modern times (of the 1930s) were not neglected by Ware, who included Kleig lights, up-to-the-minute movie cameras, microphones and such like paraphernalia in her panels. As is fitting and proper, William Shakespeare occupies an especially important spot in the lower central portion of the right-hand panel, but less notable but recognizable buskers, including a court jester, Punch and Judy puppets, masked actresses, jugglers and even Wagner's Parsifal can be spotted.

Kingsbury Hall, inside and out, remains something of a haven—indeed a mecca—for Salt Lakers who avoid the role of TV couch potatoes.

As Shakespeare still reminds us, "there are books in the running brooks, sermons in stones, . . ." Next time you're at Kingsbury glance upward between the columns to read the mottoes selected for our considered appraisal by the late Dr. S.B. Neff of the English department.

Above the west door is Walt Whitman's nearest approach to prayer: "Praised be the fathomless universe for life and joy, and for objects and knowledge curious." Aeschylus reminds us (above the center door): "Learning is ever in the freshness of its youth, even for the old." And, above the right-hand, eastern portal, this message from Socrates: "There is only one good, namely knowledge; and only one evil, namely, ignorance." The carvings remain crisp and clear more than a half century after a workman's chisel bit into the stone.

*Drawing Courtesy of D'Arcy Dixon Pignanelli*

# East High School Entrance

NOVEMBER 13, 1994

When the late James Hammond, president of the Salt Lake School Board, laid the cornerstone for the city's splendid new East High back on Sept. 14, 1912, he called the new structure "our first modern high school structure, one that will last and last and last."

As if to prove him a man of more than a little foresight, a landmark portion of the eighty-two-year-old building will remain to stir the memories of graduates—even though a functional, modern-style building is rising to replace the old. That is to say, a very recognizable reminder of "Old East" will continue to stand on 1300 East if members of its scores of graduating classes succeed in raising one million dollars.

Chat with almost any graduate or student of East, and you speedily learn what the fuss is all about. When the present city Board of Education decided a new, more functional high school is needed up on 1300 East, nostalgic alumni, a cadre of neighborhood residents and a sizable batch of architects and artists said, in effect, "Don't, whatever is done, tear down the ornate center of the 1300 East facade!" That is, of course, the English-style, "collegiate Gothic" tower that has distinguished the main entrance ever since the architectural firm of Eldredge and Chesebro designed the turreted building—which cost $700,000 in 1912 greenbacks. Since then, another $450,000 was spent for a proper gym, complete with lockers and showers, in 1952—but that was just a starter.

Came 1964 and the arts, science and homemaking took priority, with $685,000 spent to update their areas. Next came cafeteria remodeling, library remodeling, new metals shops and a "resource center." Somehow the elderly building found space (with a bit of stretching) for all, while the acreage to the west accommodated track, tennis and football facilities for red-and-white Leopard teams.

All good things very nearly came to an end in 1972, when a major fire gutted much of the main building. Another library redo, plus a $250,000, twelve-hundred-seat auditorium project, put the building back in much the shape today's students know it. But the old bugaboo of earthquake proofing still remained, while the arrival of the electronic, computerized communications age all added to a perceived need for a completely new East High.

Which leads us back to the million-dollar plan to make that central, collegiate-style tower a useful memorial to the older, long-lived East High. The FFKR firm (Fowler, Ferguson, Kingston, Rubin) has drawn plans under which the turreted four-story center will be preserved as a landmark monument, serving as an entry and back-drop to a sizable outdoor amphitheater. Richard Evans, Rhoda Ramsey and other trustees of a new Student/Alumni East High Monument and Park fund see it as a useful center for alumni gatherings, reunions, open-air recitals, dramas and all manner of neighborhood events.

"The broad stone ledge, plus 1,500 folding chairs, plus space on the lawn facing the stage, all make this a usable landmark," trustee Evans asserts. And the Monument Board reports "lots of interest, lots of community aid" for the project. Reagan Outdoor Advertising has contributed twenty billboards to advertise it. Folks at Quality Press (one suspects many are East High graduates) are contributing printed mailing materials. Mailings are already going out to 15,000 names, called "just a beginning" because the project volunteers have now acquired a list of some fifty or sixty classes of Salt Lakers who attended East.

Board members make clear the community is invited to participate in their project, while the present Salt Lake City School Board has approved the outlines of the FFKR plan. At this early stage, pledges for $150,000 are in hand from city residents "who recognize an important part of the community will be gone if the landmark history of East High is not preserved."

As endorsed by such organizations as the Utah Heritage Foundation, the existing front entry and its marble stairwell area would be preserved and flanked with a breezeway, to serve as an entry to the outdoor stage and storage areas. The stage would reach west to within 200 feet of the new East High building. As many Salt Lakers are aware, that structure is rising on the grounds of the former athletic field. A new field, complete with grandstand, is already in use east of 1300 East. Trustees assure this columnist there will be no drive for tax funds, with City Board of Education approval predicated on the fact that the dollars needed will be escrowed in advance.

"Now," says one elderly East High alumnus, "if they can also restore 'Mary's Place' and bring back Mickey Oswald." Mickey was, of course, a noted East High coach. Mary's Place was the slightly disreputable off-campus shop at the 800 South corner where students long ago could (it was whispered) purchase such illicit items as cigarettes.

# Spanish-style Columbus School

AUGUST 9, 1987

For the capital city of a state initially visited and explored by venturesome Spaniards, ours is a metropolis exhibiting few signs that the culture of Castile ever played a role in Utah life. Happily, Catholic padres, Escalante and Dominguez, are remembered by bronze figures at "This Is the Place" Monument. They've been rather neglected in most history texts since they came this way in 1776, a year highlighted in most such volumes for more significant events in Philadelphia. But in San Francisco and Santa Barbara, in Santa Fe, Pasadena and Phoenix, "mission style" architecture, with its abundance of red tile roofs, shaded courtyards and patios, thick adobe walls (old and new) and mujadeen or Spanish-Moorish domes help most westerners recall that Spain and Mexico once flew their flags over nearly a third of the old "forty-eight."

While I've never checked every street and byway of the city, the sole major structure I've found proudly proclaiming its Spanish antecedents, architecturally speaking, is the aptly named Columbus School, at 2530 S. 500 East. Fact is, the building has proved so successful and long-lived for educational purposes that one wonders why it was never duplicated.

The records show that the handsome central tower and two flanking wings were opened on January 17, 1917, after scarcely a year under construction. The building has served Salt Lake City parents and taxpayers ever since. Architect C.S. McDonald obviously did a sound, practical job for Board of Education President William J. Barrette and his successor, President Oscar W. Moyle, who served in 1916 and 1917 when the Columbus School was rising on its 4.68-acre tract.

At this point, a bit of conjecture or speculation may be in order as to why architect McDonald and school board officials "plumped" for a Spanish-styled building so unique in our town. Back in those days, Spanish look-alikes had freshly risen in San Diego's Balboa Park, and the Columbia-Pacific Exposition must have been fresh in the minds of many architects, sculptors and painters. In any event, McDonald's modified mujadeen schoolhouse decorated with brick, tile, plaster and terra cotta was completed on the southern fringe of the city for the sum total of $77,100. I've been unable to learn the cost of the land, but the Board of Education records in the building and grounds office, kept by Mary Rowlandson, report "the land was formerly part of the MacKay Farm annexed to the city on May 29, 1916." Obviously, urban sprawl was in the wings keeping pace with construction of trolley lines and paving of once rural roads to suit the growing needs of motorists and their Marmons, Franklins and Maxwells.

The Columbus School's unique, archway-pierced tower is the central element in a building boasting a total of fifteen rooms plus the necessary library, principal's office, manual training center and restrooms. The nine teachers, principal and busy fire-tending custodian made for quite a payroll —their salaries and wages were less than $100,000 for 1917 in good, noninflated, gold-backed dollars. The names of a few teachers and supervisors may bring back fond memories to old-time residents of Salt Lake City who studied the three Rs at Columbus School, planted the Arbor Day trees now adorning its front lawn or who saluted the Stars and Stripes raised each morning on the flagpole just beyond the central tower. A.J. Becker was district "penmanship supervisor," Anna Louise Corbett supervised the teaching of "needle skills," Edith E. Kendell was principal (as of 1923) and busy Libbie Godbe taught seventh grade classes totaling forty-one young-sters.

In those long-gone years, a single male teacher, one Clay Allred, joined with Ruth Anderson in helping fifty-eight kindergarten tots don and doff their boots, snowsuits and Tim's caps in snowy weather, while Mary Hog-lund's grade-three youngsters in room VI drew prizewinning posters urging parents to buy war bonds to help lick Kaiser Bill. In most years, Columbus School coped with the educational needs of some 500 neighborhood small fry. It opened with 246 boys and 220 girls in its fifteen classrooms—figures that were reversed in 1968, when Columbus School's traditional role was abandoned and its neighborhood kids dispersed to other elementary schools.

But today, or at least in the autumn when city schools will again be in session, the halls and rooms of Columbus School will not be silent. Its chief use these past twenty years has been to serve handicapped youngsters, chil-dren with a variety of learning difficulties—all coming for daily training in outside life to the Columbus Community Center headed by the Salt Lake City Board of Education's Drew Peterson, a specialist in such programs. Its large-paned windows, high ceilings and well-used, somewhat old-fashioned rooms and corridors have a cheerier look than can be found in many stark and sterile newer school buildings. At any rate, as motorists who drive to and from work on 500 East can testify, the youngsters who gather on the lawns and beneath its shade trees while waiting for buses or for parents seem happy with, and well served by, this seventy-year-old school with the unique Spanish appearance.

The proudest moment for the Columbus School, and the pleasant neighborhood of small homes it has served so long, came in 1974, when its faculty and student body excitedly greeted President Gerald Ford. The nation's chief executive, accompanied by Jake Garn, our town's mayor of the moment, came to view and applaud the work under way at Columbus to serve a too-long-neglected segment of the city's school-age population.

# Lincoln Junior High's Demise

DECEMBER 18, 1988

Some buildings are unlucky. One local case in point is the handsome but outmoded Lincoln Junior High School, now being battered into mountains of dust and brick and piles of twisted steel on the northeast corner of State and 1300 South. Its Egyptian-style pillars and columns, its warm-hued terra cotta and brick facade, will have become mere memories in another few days as the Bland Clearing Co. cranes and bulldozers load the bare bones of a no-longer-useful school onto mammoth trucks for dumping at some unknown site.

Lest you've forgotten, Lincoln Junior began life as the city's South Junior High in 1920 during an era when the "Junior High" movement was new and promising. According to George N. Childs, assistant superintendent of Salt Lake's expanding school system, the parents of the 750 pupils moving into the gleaming new building designed by the architectural and engineering firm of Scott and Welch would soon realize that "there's no question but the junior high movement will prove one of the most distinctly beneficial advances ever undertaken in our city." And South Junior High, one of several new schools made possible by a $12,130,000 bond issue approved by voters in 1918, was later kept abreast of new developments through a 1926 addition designed by Cannon and Fetzer that included ten additional classrooms, an "auditorium with balcony," a cafeteria and a "gymnasium with balcony." Finally, in 1956, the architectural firm of Young and Hansen supervised a thorough remodeling and a further addition without marring the State Street and 1300 South facades that gave the building its long-lasting distinctive look.

Unfortunately, a post-World War II boom that brought construction of a dozen new schools in the Salt Lake City School District was followed two dozen years later by the shutdown and sale of a host of old and new schools alike. The city school population peaked in about 1965 with 43,000 pupils. Yellowing clippings of stories by the *Salt Lake Tribune* Education Editor John Cummins and Lavor Chaffin of the *Deseret News* reported the 1965 completion of Parkview Elementary and earlier construction of Franklin, Indian Hills and Matheson Elementary, Northwest Junior High and Highland High. But the roster of shuttered schools was suddenly outpacing new growth ever more rapidly. Declining enrollment brought the closing of Oquirrh, Grant, Columbus, Stewart Training, Jackson, Forest, Riverside, Onequa, Sumner, and Irving Junior High.

Out in the county, the Granite School District and other suburban school systems sought to cope with an influx of pupils, but Salt Lake found itself with an oversupply of vacant buildings. Educators began recalling the fate of the one-room schoolhouse of John Greenleaf Whittier's poem, "a ragged beggar sunning."

Lincoln Junior High's turn came in 1976, when the city school board sold the building to Autonomy, Inc., for $600,001. Soon there was word of a rescue for the still handsome structure. The Bonneville Broadcasting Corp. was said to be planning to use the building, with its classrooms, auditorium, gym, cafeteria and shops as a new Broadcast House accommodating KSL and KSL-TV. That plan went out the window with word that Adnan Khashoggi's elaborate Triad Center would include a spanking new KSL and KSL-TV Broadcast House. The vacant Lincoln Junior High was tossed into the corporate gullet of Triad—which proved unable to find a tenant or purchaser for the school and its four-acre site. Vandals soon destroyed most of its windows and the building became a neighborhood eyesore.

Triad went bankrupt, and the building stood, an empty, scarred shell, until last month, when word came that the Stockwell Finance Corp. of Santa Barbara, Calif., would demolish the one-time pride of the local school system and replace it with a 400,000-square-foot mall featuring "factory outlet-type stores."

But as the building bites the dust, former pupils and teachers assure you that Lincoln Junior High was more than mere bricks and mortar. A few graybeards and matrons can even recall the ceremony when the institution's name was changed from South Junior High to Lincoln in 1936, more than fifty years ago. That was shortly after principal Devoe Woolf went to the big new South High as its first principal in 1931. This past week, Robert M. Woolf, M.D., recalled that his father had remembered his days at South Junior as among the happiest in his career. Not without reason—a Board of Education annual report in that period showed the school had "just 2 cases of habitual truancy," one of the lowest in the city.

Pat Petty, who would later become a *Salt Lake Tribune* librarian, taught at Lincoln Junior from 1947 through 1949, when Joseph Driggs was principal. "It was a wonderful place, my first full-time job—I had just come to Utah from the Midwest," she remembers. "It was just after the war and jobs were plentiful if you were properly trained. My salary was a magnificent $1,620 a year. Very good, indeed."

Her science class pupils were well behaved, and the faculty members were friendly to a newcomer. She especially recalls shop teacher Marvin Powelson, and a Mrs. Ivy, Miss Argyle, and a Mr. World.

Advertising executive Howard Jorgensen's student days in 1946–47 were made memorable by the "raging river on sandbagged 1300 South, a flood that meant we couldn't get to school for several days." He gained valuable experience as editor of the school newspaper, aptly named *The Lincoln Log*. And as tangible evidence that Lincoln Junior High did indeed exist, Jorgensen household artifacts include an "absolutely indestructible metal dustpan" plus a sewing cabinet. "The woodworking and metal shops were in a separate building out back—and our first project had to be a camp stool. Mine didn't turn out too well, but that sewing cabinet I made for my mother was a real beauty," he states proudly. "I played in the band, too. Our teacher was Mr. Martin," adds Jorgensen.

Many Lincoln Junior High "old grads" remember the school's rather unique architectural style, especially the Egyptian motif of the decorative paintwork above the proscenium arch in the auditorium. Some former faculty members and students hazard a guess that the building's architectural embellishments may have resulted from publicity concerning discovery of the tomb of King Tutankhamen in the distant land of the pharoahs about the same time the building was blueprinted. Of course when South Junior became Lincoln Junior, considerable stress was placed upon the life and times of the Great Emancipator, with pictures of the bearded martyr in many rooms.

Just about every former Lincoln Junior High pupil contacted recalls memorizing major portions of the Gettysburg Address and reading the Emancipation Proclamation. Naturally enough, special programs in that Egyptian-styled auditorium were the order of the day when Lincoln's birthday rolled 'round each February 12th.

"It hurts me to see the building coming down," Pat Petty says. As for Howard Jorgensen, "at least I've saved that sewing cabinet and copies of *The Lincoln Log.*"

In addition to saddening Lincolnites with long memories, the building demolition work is obviously upsetting one of the city's largest flocks of pigeons. After roosting atop a south-facing cornice for years, the birds have been aimlessly wheeling and circling above the remnants of the structure. But there are always compensations. Patrons at the Coachman Pancake House, and tenants in the gray-painted apartments and offices of the nearby Laurelwood Village, express regret that some use couldn't have been found for the big school building. But they hastily add, "it was an eyesore, useful only to pigeons."

CHAPTER 9

# Downtown Falters and Stagnates

# The Centre Theatre

NOVEMBER 11, 1984

Word came from the real estate battlefront this past week that another major building on State Street will vanish from our midst in a matter of months, making way for (you guessed it) still another multistory office tower. How long has it been since you went a-movie-going to the Centre Theatre?

Quite a while? It is for that very commercial, noncinematic reason our town's classiest motion picture palace will soon have a date with a wrecker's ball, some claw-toothed bulldozers or perhaps a few demolition charges. Down will come the odd-appearing but appealing three-story pylon with its yellow letters; down will come the curved marquee, the concrete pilasters, marble trim and even that front-of-lobby ticket booth where uniformed cashiers exchanged tickets for your dollar bills when you squired your date

211

to see Clark Gable, Jimmy Stewart, or even watch Ronald Reagan kiss Claudette Colbert, Carol Lombard or even Jane Wyman.

To wax nostalgic for another paragraph or two—when I arrived in Utah's capital ever so many years ago, I knew instantly that the motion picture palace at the corner of Broadway and State was indeed a "class act." After all, one quickly noted it was not merely the Center Theater— this was the Centre Theatre, its spelling styled to befit the flagship of a major film chain. Of course, it was small-town stuff indeed when compared to the rococo Paramount or Roxy in New York, the State in Chicago, Graumann's Chinese in Hollywood, or similar mammoth houses in which overblown architecture was as important as seating capacity. But the Centre was the city's finest—spacious, stylish and comfortable.

And the Centre was, and still remains, one of Salt Lake City's few examples of Art Deco. Looking around town, I have a hunch that only the Charleston Apartments, up on 1300 East at 500 South, is an equivalent example of late-30s, early-40s Art Deco style, if only by virtue of its steel-framed corner windows. But heck, the Centre Theatre still has a terrazo circle in its front pavement, polished marble trim on lobby walls and metal frames perfectly suited to enshrine the phizzes of the Hollywood whizzes of the pre-TV era.

It's astonishing to recall that downtown Salt Lake City, as befitted the metropolis of an entire state, once boasted a dozen cinema houses of various size, price and ranking, with the Centre long considered the prime first-run "hard-top" of them all.

Oldsters even more ancient than yours truly tell me of the difficulty of making choices between the Paramount, Pantages, American, Wilkes, Victory, Hippodrome and Orpheum—all of which were shuttered before my day.

The Capitol, Gem, Studio and Orpheum survive as physical structures—the Orpheum housing the Promised Valley Playhouse and the Capitol providing a home to Ballet West. The Utah Theatre, where parents once parked their kids for a mad Saturday of cartoons, is the sole Main Street survivor now that the downtown Trolley has projected its last flicker. Downtown parking problems being what they are, the old-style movie house long ago became a dinosaur—the Utah has been twinned or tripled, while the multiplex screens in the Crossroads Mall are not "free-standing" picture palaces of the sort mother and dad knew.

It is too early to know how the Centre's replacement will look—but spies who have been peering at drawing boards in a much-respected local architectural firm promise that the office building will not be just another rectangular box set on end, for which we can all be grateful. It is also good to realize that State Street is increasingly viewed as viable, and that the lower floor of the new structure will have store space to rent that could prove attractive to local merchants. Of course, approximately a dozen stores on State and on Broadway will be vacated when construction of the new medium-rise replacement for the Centre Theatre gets under way, but with luck a few such displaced tenants will move over to Main Street, a thoroughfare increasingly decimated of its one-time proud and profitable shops.

The Centre Theatre has survived as a real movie house—and has outlived most of the drive-in "theaters" once dotting the valley. You might, if the Centre's bill intrigues you, if the spirit moves, and if you are in the mood for a popcorn feast, drop in at the Centre while it is still among us, as the saying goes. You won't see Gable or even John Wayne's ghost—but you will see a well-built movie house, complete with a balcony, clear sight lines, upholstered seats and the number of aisles deemed necessary way back when.

Take the kids—so they can tell their children they once visited a genuine motion picture palace.

# The King Joy Cafe

NOVEMBER 10, 1991

Will Salt Lake City's Main Street ever "come back," ever be as attractive to pedestrians, shoppers and hungry office workers as it was in the days just before and just after World War II? That's a question many, many downtown denizens find themselves asking one another when they gather for coffee breaks or at lunchtime in the last of the street's old-time spots—Lamb's—or in such comparative newcomers as the Judge Cafe or the even newer American Grill in the Clift House (the old Utah Oil building) at 300 S. Main.

When heading for Sam Weller's Zion Book Store, or for The Broadway Stage theater so bravely ensconced in the former Rialto movie house at 272 S. Main, one can't help but glance inside the vacant, long-time locale of Harry Louie's well-remembered King Joy Cafe. At least a fading remnant of card-carrying "newshawks" recall pleasant lunchtimes or dinner hours

214

spent with employees of the *Tribune-Telegram* or even of station KALL, briefly located a few doors north in the David Keith Building.

Oriental scallop decorations remain on the King Joy's modest overhanging entry at 264 S. Main. Indeed, the booths, where a generation or two of guys and gals employed downtown once sat while chewing the fat or munching fortune cookies, still remain in place. Outside, the concrete planter boxes, brick-and-tile pavement design and the partially denuded trees, testifying to a sudden spell of wintry weather, remind citizens of the efforts of Main Street plan-makers and rehabilitators to restore life to the once-bustling shopping street.

Alas, not only has the King Joy departed, so too have the promises and premises of idealistic planners, folks who believed rather simplistically that a reshaping of pavements (with the added fillip of flowers, shade trees, new streetlights and glossy bus-stop shelters) could reverse a twenty-year trend being felt on Main Street, not to mention adjacent sidestreets and equally depressed State Street. It now seems woefully true that the ills of the local downtown district duplicate the anguish felt in many other cities.

Harry Louie's King Joy Cafe (which moved to its Main Street location in 1965 when the J.C. Penney store and parking terrace replaced the Wilson Hotel on 200 South) outlasted a goodly number of shops and luncheon spots. The upscale Leyson-Pearsall Jewelry emporium comes to mind, as do Keeley's (with its Ironport approximation of Moxie), Crouch's delicatessen near the Federal Building, The Mint (where you could place a bet while you downed a meat pie), the Grabeteria up north on Main, the Peter Pan (complete with pool parlor) below the David Keith building and the Mayflower on Main upstreet a block.

There were others, of course—China Village, Alec's Cafe and Broiler, the Chesapeake, the Rotisserie, the coffee-shop counters in the Woolworth and Kress stores, and the better-than-average dining spots in Auerbach's and the Newhouse Hotel.

All are long gone and increasingly forgotten. Equally poignant, for mere men, the same blocks boasted a wealth of haberdashery shops. These included Arthur Frank's and Fife's, Hibbs, Mullet-Kelley's, Collins, McConahay's, Norm Sims the Hatter, Charles Felt's end-of-period establishment, and even a Rafter Shop in the basement beneath Lamb's still-existent restaurant. Main Street banks, law offices, accountancy shops, advertising agencies, insurance firms and the like must have employed more men than in the present Main Street era.

As for the women—a mere male can't even begin to recall the shoe stores, dress shops, fur stores, milliner stores, the pricey or low-cost "women's wear" establishments existing on Main Street two and three and four decades ago, during those simpler, premall times.

Main Street, indeed the downtown district, was no utopia in those increasingly forgotten days, of course. More and more shoppers complained of a lack of parking—in fact, letters to the *Salt Lake Tribune* often held that the elimination of angle parking and left turns had a deleterious effect on retail business.

Architects and planners, with a sizable quota of idealist/realists among them, expressed belief that adequate parking, along with brick- and tree-lined arcades and shopping malls, would brighten downtown's prospects.

Later, much later, as downtown sales were decimated (in part by the almost simultaneous construction of the ZCMI and Crossroads malls), came a belated realization that even the best of designs can't make a district flourish, especially in an era when the motorist is king—or queen. This was crushingly true in a city where a sizable slice of the upscale populace was convinced the suburban life would be a better life. Holladay and West Jordan, Draper, Bountiful and Layton—the once-green fields of Salt Lake and Davis counties were no longer distant realms given over to cow-grazing and fruit-raising. From the Eisenhower years on, new freeways and interstates would rim the city, bleed it of population, and sponge up its business dollars.

Of course, during far less than a lifetime, Salt Lake's downtown was graced by construction of a Beneficial Life tower, First Interstate Bank, the twin American Tower apartments, tall buildings topping the Crossroads and ZCMI malls, the Kennecott and University Club structures and, most recently, the Eagle Gate and the new Block 57 high-rise, occupied by UP&L employees plus a passel of lawyers. Soon, a glass-covered structure will open, replacing the Centre Theatre.

The old-time buildings that have vanished to make way for the newcomers are too numerous to mention, and their inhabitants seem to have vanished with them. Meantime, the construction of new glossy, glassy boxes in such locations as Fort Union Boulevard and 7200 South must about equal the space being provided for office workers on and near downtown Main Street. The workers and shoppers in the suburbs seem now to outnumber downtowners on an average day.

Meanwhile, fewer and fewer of us, peering into the vacant premises

216

that once housed the King Joy Cafe, will recall the fried rice, the pork noodles, the popular rice-enhanced Oriental dishes, or the establishment's American fare, including apple pie, chicken pot pie, and that strangest of Western dishes, chicken-fried steak. It was tasty, was neither chicken nor steak, but was indubitably fried.

The King Joy, business home of Harry and Helen Louie (his father had opened on 200 South), was long a second home to a hundred or two local attorneys, bankers, physicians, editors, reporters, clerks and clerics. After some forty-five years, the place is empty. Harry and Helen are retired, and sisters Mary and Jean and a bevy of children no longer come down to help during busy hours.

# The Lollin and Carrick Buildings on Main Street

AUGUST 26, 1990

At almost 8 o'clock on a weekday morning, downtown Salt Lake City's Main Street—the west side of the block between 200 South and Broadway—is still deserted, vacant of pedestrians. That being the case, it is a perfect hour for finishing a sketch of the Karrick Building, the rather ornate structure at 236 S. Main (on the right in the drawing), and the Lollin Building, next door south at 238 S. Main.

Usually not even a gal or guy wearing a jogging outfit and thick-soled sneakers is on hand to pause for a breath and read the historic marker on the facade of 236. The bronze plaque reminds a forgetful public that Lewis W. Karrick had the building constructed in 1887 after accumulating "a sizable fortune principally in mining interests."

But to most increasingly ancient city denizens, the century-old building is best recalled as the Leyson-Pearsall building, since that jewelry company leased the premises in 1905 and operated therein for over seventy-five years. Not too many years ago, Main Street would have been crowded at an early hour—office workers arrived by 8 A.M., although banks didn't open until later. A few white-collar workers or their prospective mates would have paused at Leyson-Pearsall to eye engagement rings displayed in ornate wooden window cases rimmed by reflective mirrors. A few of the city's nabobs would have stopped en route from George Osterloh's Ramp Garage to a banking floor or office—gazing fixedly at a necklace, a sudden reminder that a loved one was about to celebrate a birthday. Or was it an anniversary that was upcoming?

At any event, two dozen or so years ago, Main Street was busy in the early-morning hours and crowded at noontime. That being the case, what sort of store occupied the ground-floor premises in the Lollin Building at 238 S. Main? Of course bookman Sam Weller remains just down the street in the David Keith Building. But occupants of the Lollin Building (which a later bit of research shows dates from 1894) seem harder to recall. Light suddenly dawns, or perhaps a light bulb is switched on in my cranium as in old comic strips. The Main Street front at 238, now given over to the Great Wall Chinese Restaurant, was occupied for many, many years by the Hudson Bay Fur Company.

Remember Fred Provol, a chap related to Joe Dupler, who operated equally elegant premises in the *Tribune* building? Provol's Hudson Bay shop was in the Lollin Building from 1915 until 1965. Historian John S. McCormick further reports, in his *Historic Buildings* issued in 1982 by the Utah State Historical Society, that a Mrs. Ella Stickney Becker ran a millinery shop alongside the Hudson Bay Fur Company from 1924 till 1929. Did the Great Depression beginning that year also signal the demise of women's hats? One wonders, while recalling that Provol and Dupler never had to contend with picket-sign-toting protectors of the foxes, minks, sables and seals slain to keep a well-dressed generation warmly clad.

As for the architect who crafted those ancient structures that recall so many memories for the city's old-timers—he was among the best who ever worked hereabouts. The building at 236 S. Main, where Stan Russon and other salesmen discreetly displayed wares in Leyson-Pearsall's posh show windows, was built to the designs of Richard K.A. Kletting, who later blueprinted the Utah State Capitol. By the way, Lewis Karrick, who gave the building his name, was quite a fellow too. He not only owned the Troy Laundry and a men's store, he likewise organized the National Bank of the Republic. More importantly—or curiously—he formed a local militia called the Karrick Guards, served on the City Council, and ran for mayor on the Liberal Party ticket. Historians designate his Liberal Party as "anti-Mormon," which may be why "liberal" remains a word that brings displays of choler to some Latter-day Saints.

Architect Kletting enhanced his 1887 building with supportive cast-iron columns just above the second story, ornate stonework, central porches still enhanced by wrought-iron work and an elaborate cornice now shorn of twin pinnacles and a flagpole. But the general effect remains despite repainting and the much-changed lower storefronts. This was a handsome building and one of the prides of Main Street. Fortunately, Brain Inc. is keeping it trim and neat, with gray-painted closed shutters on the upper floors enhancing the general effect.

Not so the Lollin Building at 238 S. Main. Its upper-floor windows are drab and dark, and the curtained windows on the second story are stained and none too tidy. But its architect was also Richard K.A. Kletting—although the Karrick and Lollin buildings seem stylistically very different. The Lollin dates from 1894 and cost $13,000 or thereabouts. You can still read the incised "1894" in the decorative stonework midway between the second and third stories of this classic commercial structure. Kletting spaced its Roman-arched windows with Ionic columns between those third-story windows and added a wealth of deeply dentiled cornice work that still interests the eye.

John Lollin came to the United States from Denmark in his teens, stopped briefly in Omaha, then settled in Salt Lake, where he quickly learned the hospitality business. In the 1890s, he operated the famed Lollin Saloon at 129 S. Main and built the Lollin Building with its profits, along with funds coming from mining investments. A saloon, then the Davis Shoe Company, then the Hudson Bay Fur Co., lured the public to the Main Street building. Upstairs, a succession of dentists also attracted patients— Dr. James B. Keysor, Dr. Mark D. Bringhurst, Dr. Edward W. Ward and Dr. Calvin E. Clawson all occupied space upstairs in the ensuing half century or so.

Nowadays if afflicted with a toothache one heads for a dentist's air-conditioned office in a suburban mall, complete with off-street parking and a dental assistant competent at tooth cleaning. Once vacated by successive dentists, the upper stories of Main Street's two- and three-story buildings have remained empty. Just another reason for the decline of downtown.

*Drawing Courtesy of Arthur T. Swindle*

# The Utah Theatre

JUNE 12, 1988

What downtown picture palace, on the site of Salt Lake's first Masonic Hall and the Auerbach Bros. store, was opened in 1920 with a showing of "unequaled vaudeville" along with the movie *Pollyanna*, featuring Mary Pickford, "the nation's sweetheart?" What no longer pristine, sadly subdivided movie house shut its twin projection booths last March, following a dual offering of Joanne Woodward in *The Glass Menagerie* and an art film entitled *Whales of August?*

If you guessed Utah Theatre at 148 S. Main, you may butter yourself a batch of home-popped popcorn as prize. Then please shed a tear or two in memory of the bittersweet days when you and a long-forgotten soulmate clutched at each other in a darkened balcony while warfare raged (courtesy of Fox Movietone News) and you wondered why Claudette Colbert and

Clark Gable did not tear down that flimsy curtain in *It Happened One Night*.

Alas, the Utah Theatre of our misspent youth has vanished, a youth countless Salt Lakers could have likewise whiled away in celluloid dreams at any of thirteen sizable movie houses dotting the downtown district just before and after World War II. Way back then, a single chain, Intermountain Theatres, controlled the Utah, the Capitol and the Centre, all first-run houses. Likewise, the smaller Studio and earlier Victory.

Lest you are not a trivia fan, let's project a few names and addresses on the olio with our magic lantern. The Studio, which became something of a pigeon roost after shuttering, was at 161 S. Main, north of Lamb's estimable coffee house. The long-lamented Victory stood, until it went up in flames, at 48 E. Broadway, between Auerbach's and The Paris stores. To confuse history buffs a bit, this house opened as the Colonial but became the Pantages in a 1913 name-change honoring the vaudeville circuit that "wheeled" talent to the theater. When the Utah opened in 1920 on Main Street it was initially labeled the "new" Pantages.

The Broadway establishment promptly became the State but underwent another change in 1924 as the Victory. There, on the 300 South section that some of us still call Broadway, local cinematic history was made when the talkies arrived with Al Jolson opting to become a "Jazz Singer" rather than a synagogue cantor. Of a certainty, there was not a dry eye among the scattering of Yiddish mommas in the domed and doomed house. Over at 148 S. Main a progressive management hastened to install sound equipment.

A few more addresses may be in order, courtesy of the Utah State Historical Society and a University of Utah research paper by James Venditti. The Empire stood at 158 S. State, the Gem at 162 S. State, the Lake at 132 S. State and the State at 228 S. State. Then, the small Star was round the corner at 72 E. 100 South. Marie Floor's husband, Andy, ran both the Star and the Lake. The latter, becoming the Lyric and later Promised Valley Playhouse, now features live theatricals. Mrs. Floor, by the by, is frequently found behind the counter, not of a movie house, but of Sam Weller's Zion Book Store.

Back on Main Street, in addition to the Utah, patrons seeking top films could find them at the Uptown at 53 S. Main, a site sacred to bargain hunters ever since being bulldozed for the ZCMI store in 1971. Initially, in its sixty-year existence, the Uptown was the Empress, a vaudeville house until a name change in the 1920s. Then it was dubbed the Empress-Paramount, then just plain Paramount.

In this jumble of changing names and vanishing addresses, let us not lose sight—or the site—of the Broadway at 63 E. Broadway, and the Rialto at 272 S. Main. The latter became a Trolley Theatre before its demise. Just to compound the confusion, old city directories tell us the Lyric on State Street occupies a building that once served as the St. James Hotel. And just outside the downtown district, the Blue Mouse (where you brave the local police to enjoy off-beat, but excellent films) began life as Gordon Crowe's Cinema Arts theater, with patrons occupying seats fortuitously purchased from a shoe store chain.

The last major "hard-top" built downtown before the advent of drive-ins such as the Motor-Vu, was the Centre, still commanding the northeast corner of State and Broadway. This still stylish survivor opened in 1937 and was the scene of the August 23, 1940, premiere of *Brigham Young,* an event marked by searchlights and a Hollywoodish parade in which Tyrone Power, Linda Darnell, Mary Astor and Dean Jagger rode in open-topped limousines along Main Street.

But the more elderly Utah Theatre retained its adherents, especially parents who "parked the kids with Pincus." Charlie Pincus was the affable, inventive manager of the Utah, who saw to it that Saturday morning and afternoon matinees featured cartoon clubs, healthy Tarzan films and a plentiful supply of "oaters" or cowboy films. Mothers left their youngsters in the safe halls of the Utah at 10 A.M. and collected them after shopping and lunch. Fathers could do the same before toiling in the yard—or napping.

Before being hacked horizontally into a double-screen, Plitt house with 826 seats in its No. 1 sector and 631 seats in the No. 2 division, the Utah, despite its unimposing store-front and marquee, boasted tall columns and rather intriguing friezes styled in vague "Hollywood Italian Renaissance." It was never as truly architecturally distinguished as, let's say, the wondrous Ogden Egyptian Theatre—a gem that should become the crown jewel of Ogden's redevelopment. The Utah was simply a good, workaday, money-making, downtown movie house. It cost just $250,000 to build—but obviously earned its keep many times over.

# The Brooks Arcade

APRIL 22, 1990

Want to see a depressing sight? Not matter how sunny or pleasant the spring day, a stroll along the north side of Broadway between Main and State will teach you that Progress with a capital "P" seems to require two steps backwards before today's Salt Lake City can achieve one solid step forward. Reading from west to east, the pedestrian will encounter the now empty residences of businesses, memorialized in such self-explanatory store-front names as The Bride's Shop, Broadway Music and the Ding Ho Chinese Cafe. Other establishments that have relocated or closed include Littlefield's (a longtime purveyor of hearing aids) and Nanci's, which sells feminine wear. All are closed or closing, as a result of the long-lived hassling, arguefying, planning, refining, redefining and financing of our town's Block 57 project.

A few intrepid entrepreneurs remain, lingering on prior to the next phase of tearing down and building up. The barber pole (that striped ancient symbol of a bloodletting healer) still twirls outside Perry's Barber Shop, while people can still have their shoes shined and hats blocked at Jim's. The Broadway Cafe remains open to devotees of low prices and large portions at Fifty-three E. Broadway. But the most hopeful of the old block's commercial parishioners deal in shoes, new and old. Dick Wirick, operator of the Oxford Shop at No. 9 these past thirty-five years, says he "still loves doing business on Broadway." And the longest lived business on this stretch of Broadway exists in that rather grim, rather gray, rather grimy building called the Brooks Arcade, occupying the State Street corner. It is, of course, Joe Bolinger's Broadway Shoe Rebuilding shop, which Joe's father opened back in 1911.

But what of this old corner building, the Brooks Arcade? While solid information is hard to come by, city officials indicate that it will be spared when the iron ball next swings. I'm told the upstairs floor and interior of the big structure in today's drawing are in woefully sad shape. But that solid-seeming stone facade remains rather solid, is indeed historic and can be retained as a front for any new construction on the Broadway State corner.

To history buffs, as to some architects, the Brooks Arcade is indeed worth preserving. Curiously, when designed by Samuel C. Dallas and William S. Hedges just one hundred years ago, it was planned for merchant/investor Julius Gerson Brooks as a six-story building, one of the city's largest and finest. But a financial depression set in, and when completed the Brooks Arcade was just three stories tall. It was a splendid structure nonetheless. If you can block out the sight of the depressing, vacant store fronts, peer aloft at the facade and you'll see why students of architecture consider this a prime example of Richardsonian-Romanesque.

Henry Hobson Richardson was one of the nation's leading architects in the period of transition between High Victorian and more modern styles. As for the local firm of Dallas and Hedges, it also designed the McCune Mansion, the McCormick Mansion, and the vanished Boyd Park building on Main Street.

The upper stories of the Brooks Arcade remain topped by bands of incised cornices, topped in turn by railings and a corner flagpole. The facade, of heavily rusticated sandstone, is enhanced by dentils, basket-weave and bracket-work cut stone many now view as quaint. Windows on the upper floor are rounded off by arches. Those below, now displaying years of grime, were doubtless large enough to afford considerable light and air to tenants in bygone days.

The past tenants of the new building were many, including doctors, dentists, music teachers and even a Swedish language newspaper. During the years 1896 to 1920, one John W. Miller operated a hotel on the upstairs floors, but business and professional tenants returned when the hotel closed.

Two of those tenants made the history books in very different ways. One was Salt Lake's most prominent abortionist, Dr. Frank Moormeister, whose wife, Dorothy Dexter Moormeister, was most foully and mysteriously murdered at midnight, February 21, 1930. She was last seen alive at 6:30 P.M. that wintry evening when she exited the Brooks Arcade offices of her estranged husband to drive off in the family Cadillac. The big sedan was apparently used to run over the unfortunate Mrs. Moormeister in the barren lands just west of Taylorsville. The car was found the next day abandoned in Pioneer Park. No one was ever convicted of the crime.

The other prominent tenant was Herbert S. Auerbach, a distinguished businessman/historian whose scholarly life ended peacefully in a spacious top-floor Arcade apartment in 1945. He had purchased the Brooks Arcade in 1913, which seemed only fitting because he was the grandson of builder Julius Gerson Brooks.

From 1936 until 1945, Auerbach was president of the Utah State Historical Society. He was also a composer, musician and published poet, a graduate mining engineer and member of countless boards in the Salt Lake business world. He was also a state senator and for many years served as president of the Auerbach department store, which occupied the opposite corner.

Obviously lots of history was made behind the grimy stone facade of the Brooks Arcade. Is the building worth saving? You be the judge.

CHAPTER 10

# Newcomers to the Downtown Scene

# One Utah Center

JANUARY 19, 1992

Now that it's finished, how do you like it?

Sean Onyon was asking friends that question the other day—with the "it" in his query referring to the One Utah Center building bulking large on the southeast corner of Main and 200 South. Onyon, lest you've forgotten or never knew, spent the past two years or thereabouts as project architect for the big structure. The major architect of record is, of course, Niels E. Valentiner of the firm that bears his name. Valentiner was the chap hired by the owners, the Boyer Co., to handle the task of designing the largest job to come down the pike hereabouts in a good many years.

Standing tall among downtown Salt Lake City's office buildings, its height of 458 feet 9 inches makes it the second-highest building in town, topped only by the Church Office tower east of Temple Square.

How to answer Onyon's question? Having changed my own mind concerning the structure as it rose, I must admit to liking it. I do, however, keep wondering what the color, the overall color, of the building is—it varies so according to the light and the hour of the day. Its granite facing was quarried and cut at Marble Falls, Texas. And according to Mr. Onyon, who should know, this granite, when polished to a "thermal" finish, takes on that glowing lighter russet hue. When given even more polish, the stone becomes darker.

How the granite will fare when weathered by a dozen or so years of temperature inversion, smoke, fog, chill winds, snow, rain, and similar rough treatment one never really knows. Remember the sad look of such "brownstone" office buildings as the old Union Pacific at Main and South Temple or the handsome Dooley Building on West Temple? The weather did them in, causing eventual discoloration, spalling, and dangerous icefalls.

According to the Valentiner folk, the original intent for One Utah Center was a twenty-story structure. However, by the time the old J.C. Penney store on the site began to vanish, Roger Boyer had not only signed Utah Power to a sizable bundle of rented space, but he also had leases from some of our town's most prestigious law firms in hand. Hence we now have a twenty-four-story building, complete with a pointed pyramid crown that is lit at night, plus four gables and even a penthouse. Office tenants tell me the building is working well.

Which speaks well for the Jacobsen Construction Co., several hundred building-trades workers, construction boss John Wright and project manager Kevin Brown. It's no easy matter, this business of building even a midheight skyscraper. There were fire codes and electrical and plumbing codes to meet, elevator shafts to put in proper place, restrooms, innumerable closets, heating, electric outlets—all to be blueprinted, all to be fitted out, all to work properly.

Of course completion of One Utah Center has not ended the deep thought being given by city planners to the multitude of outside problems raised by clearing all of Block 57. The old pawn shops on 200 South have vanished, along with Señor Pepe's, Tannenbaum's, Gallenson's and Wolfe's on State Street. Next, the elderly and far-from-lovely buildings on Broadway will meet the big steel ball, bulldozers and similar wall-bashers. The handsome Utah Bank on Main Street is gone, and the Kress store will follow in the wake of Woolworth's. Broadway Music, the Oxford Shop, Skaggs Drug, Warshaw's brave attempt at reversing the downtown tide,

Schubach's Jewelry, the Magazine Shop—all will go, leaving a handful of fading memories.

Not too many years ago, the city officials and downtown planners told pessimistic shopkeepers that repaving Broadway and State Street sidewalks with patterned brick, plus the installation of shade trees, plus the installation of a statue or two, would revive the none-too-viable downtown district. Alas, nothing quite worked. Suburban shoppers stubbornly refused to come back downtown, and Block 57 became a ghost. All that will be left of the old-time structures will, very shortly, be the Brooks Arcade.

However, Block 57, now renamed the Utah Center, is being underlaid with a vast parking area, an underground parking complex that must be as large as or larger than that beneath San Francisco's Union Square. Of course, Union Square has its Macy's, the St. Francis Hotel is close by, and numerous shops, pancake houses, bookstores, upscale restaurants and downscale eateries can be found just across the way from Union Square. Panhandlers too.

The One Utah Center building already has a main-floor eatery. Prudential Bank is opening new offices in the structure. And you can ride elevators from the shiny lobby into a vast area of parking stalls too numerous to count. Above the parking plaza—after or even while the Broadway buildings are becoming rubble—new grass, curvaceous paths, leafy trees, flowering gardens and flowing fountains will lure potential shoppers, sightseers and an army of clerks, stenos and even CEOs from new and old buildings nearby. Those folks will sit on benches for lunchtime concerts while downing edibles and will enter revivified stores for a spate of shopping. Or so the planners hope.

Well, Brussels has its square of floodlighted, gold-tinted old buildings. New York has its Plaza, where General Sherman and Winged Victory ride against Fifth Avenue traffic. London's Trafalgar Square displays Nelson's column topped by a statue of the heroic victor of Albion's naval wars. And, in the center of the City of Light, all the Paris boulevards radiate to cafes, tabacs, hotels, even to an iniquitous nightclub or two where scantily clad (or unclad) French chorines do the can-can.

Our present magnets? Across from the former Block 57, visitors will find a first-rate bookstore, a brave theater, a brace of fast-food emporiums, a shop dealing in large-size menswear, and not too much else. Morning, evening or noontime, in bright or lackluster light, in snow, rain or sunshine, our town's newest big building looks pretty darn good. Now if the powers that be (and I don't mean Mayor Deedee Corradini) would only restore the gaping, empty-windowed Hotel Utah. And Auerbach's. And Makoff's. And the men's shops that once lined Main Street. And the restaurants of which Lamb's is the last remnant. Then we would have a bright new leap year indeed.

Jack Goodman

# Ethnic Charm at Broadway Plaza

OCTOBER 20, 1991

Shelmerdine Court is not exactly easy to find—especially since the nine or ten homes that once graced this short thoroughfare have vanished. This court, alley or lane begins at 230 E. 300 South and vanishes from view in the parking lot just west of the geometrically shaped modern structure known as the Broadway Plaza. It's just east of the ten-story concrete apart- ment building called the Broadway Towers.

"Broadway," lest you are a nonknowledgeable recent arrival in Salt Lake City, is the rather overblown designation of 300 South in its passage east to west across our town's business district. Shelmerdine Court turns up again in the far reaches of the city, out in the vicinity of 3000 South, to be exact. But that's another story.

In its heyday, the Shelmerdine Court alongside today's Broadway Plaza was an outlying center of "Greek Town." Quite a few of its vanished houses were occupied by folks who once called the Peloponnesus peninsula of the Greek Kingdom their home.

At first glance, there's no sign of a Grecian neighborhood remaining in this sector of 300 South today. Older Greek residents still cluster in the shadow of the domed Holy Trinity Greek Orthodox Church a half-dozen blocks west.

But if you buy your toothpaste or have your prescriptions filled at the Broadway Shopping Center and Pharmacy occupying the modest plaza at 242 E. Broadway, you are certain to encounter Gus Sotiriou and his brother, Tom, the registered pharmacists on the busy premises. Fact is, if you chance to be afflicted by a disease of the skin, you may find yourself in the offices of Leo Sotiriou, M.D., a family son.

As many downtown denizens know, the white-haired pharmacist brothers and their associates own and operate the family grocery store in which the pharmacy occupies its modest corner. Established by their father, Chris, theirs is the sole such shop for miles around, meaning dwellers in nearby apartments and central-city homes and many workers at the Heber Wells state office building keep the doors swinging. They often exit carrying such exotic items as Greek olives, Israeli pickles, or falafel from Arabic lands. Plus, of course, bread, Grecian cheese, paper toweling, greeting cards and soda pop.

The modest shopping center and pharmacy had its modern beginnings when builder Joe Howard erected the black glass and stark white concrete structure in 1972 to plans drawn by Alfred Newman Beadle, a Phoenix architect. But since the pharmacists' business acumen extends to ownership of the twenty-nine-unit Broadway Eden apartments across the way (a porch-fronted structure that dates back to 1913) and since the Sotiriou family includes sister Marge plus a new generation of professionals, their story, with that of their compatriots, is worth examining.

As Gus Sotiriou reminds customers, residents in the Shelmerdine Court neighborhood once included James Sdralis, who owned the popular Silver Dollar Cafe, apartment owner Alex Halles, and businessmen George Dimas and Sam Gianis, who owned the Eden Apartments until the pharmacist family took over.

Chris Sotiriou, father of today's shopkeeping family, came to Utah like thousands of "outlanders," to work in the mines. Many Eastern Europeans were hauled directly to the Carbon County coal country from Manhattan and Hoboken piers where immigrant steamers docked. But Chris wound up in the hardworking "Greek Town" of Copperton near Bingham, where thunderous blasts rocked the rickety houses.

After a while, the mining of copper hardly seemed a career—there were opportunities in the valley. The big city also attracted the Lambs and Floors, the Strikes, the Korologos clan, the Speros and Papanikolas families. Immigrants all, Americans all, they found funds to open shops, restaurants, boardinghouses, even movie houses, often living in quarters behind or above their small business establishments. Children went to the Washington School and Salt Lake High (now West High).

Like most ethnic groups, Greek families "clustered," many of them in the old Covey-owned apartments just west of the Holy Trinity Greek Orthodox Church, across from Pioneer Park.

Within just a few years, a portion of the Greek community had moved east to the Shelmerdine Court neighborhood. Chris Sotiriou's grocery opened and flourished at 242 E. Broadway with the youngsters all working therein. The old one-story neighborhood grocery where the brothers worked became the present-day shopping center and pharmacy in 1972.

The tall new structure reflects the American dream come true.

# Warehouse District Renovation

MARCH 15, 1992

The opening of the new Delta Center has brought basketball fans in considerable numbers streaming to the city's west side—and, one hopes, at least a few among them have been at least somewhat attentive to the changes that have taken place in that sector of the city these past dozen or so years.

New restaurants, the renovation of elderly hotels, the repaving of several streets, new parking structures and new uses for old railroad stations are only part of the story.

One important change, not so evident unless you knew the old buildings, is the transformation of a number of structures in the "warehouse district" into office buildings.

If you've never wandered the area, you may not have been aware that a Salt Lake City Westside Warehouse District exists and that a portion of it has been properly designated as "historic." Originally, the area in which

238

some fifteen major warehouse buildings still exist was residential and had been since the town was "platted." An 1889 map shows the First Baptist Church stood on the corner of 300 West and 200 South surrounded by one- and two-story dwellings. But a rapid change was spurred by the construction of railroad spurs from the main-line tracks that had been laid on 400 West. Old photographs show warehouses bearing signs such as "Ham and Meat" or "Wool and Hides" and such mysterious materials as "Findings."

Quite a few old-timers may remember the buildings used by Cudahy Packing Co., Symns Grocers, Kahn Brothers Grocers, Keyser Warehouse, the Crane Building and Salt Lake Stamp Co. The latter three buildings still stand, while it is the largest of the Keyser Warehouse structures that appears in today's sketch bearing the Westgate Center label. Along with the Crane Building, it is perhaps the most important of the "new" Warehouse District structures.

In actuality, the Keyser Warehouses were a trio of buildings with construction extending over a twelve-year span, beginning in 1909. Their addresses are 312, 320 and 328 on west 200 South—and today the linked buildings are known as the Westgate Business Center.

Entered at the eastern end of the warehouse complex, No. 328 has undergone the most impressive visible transformation.

Occupied in the main by the Utah State Office of Education's Division of Rehabilitation Services, its east-facing side wall has been pierced by ten bow-fronted reflective-glass window panels, set in columns two and four stories in height. A cast-stone, angular archway on this same facade forms the main entrance to the rebuilt structure, used as the entry from a broad parking plaza.

The south-facing section of the structure, its red brick and metal properly cleaned, is broken into a trio of bays, with the windows of each bay made of gray or black glass panels—the sort of windows that cannot be opened, giving outsiders a hint that the structure is air-conditioned.

The architect for this, the last of the Keyser warehouses completed, was William A. Larkin, who was likewise responsible for the three-story structure at 320, immediately west. The Westgate building at 312 was completed in 1920; the one next door was built a year earlier. But the westernmost of the trio, completed in 1909 at 320 W. 200 South, was the work of a different architect, David C. Dart.

As a result of the Westgate Business Center modernization for office purposes, it is difficult to realize the units are of different dates and that two architects handled the project. The molded cornices atop each section, the cornices above the street level of the structures, along with the window shapes, help give the Westgate a unified look.

Nowadays the older units are occupied, I believe, by operation offices and other adjuncts of the Union Pacific Railroad. But the initial tenants, while mostly major firms, did not include a railroad in those earlier years.

The General Electric Supply Co. occupied much of the building at 312 for fully forty years, from 1929 until 1969. According to John McCormick's volume on the city's historic buildings, the central structure housed (for various times) Sears Roebuck, Hood Rubber, Richmond Machinery and Mountain States Supply. The Curtis Candy Co. and McGahen Brokerage are listed as past occupants at the older, five-story structure to the west at No. 328.

And who was Keyser? A native of New Jersey, he reached the city in 1868 and soon was in such diverse enterprises as cattle- and sheep-raising, tanning, lumbering, mining, real estate and insurance. The first building was built as the warehouse of the M.A. Keyser Fireproof Storage Co., but the other two were designed as rental properties from the start.

On today's city maps, the Warehouse District blocks are designated Block 61 and Block 66, and as a great many local businessmen can testify, it was a sizable and rather risky fiscal venture to take on a project such at the transformation of the Keyser Warehouses into the Westgate Business Center. This was a neighborhood, not too many years back, of vacant buildings, broken sidewalks, potholed pavements and unused, half-buried railroad tracks.

Now, along with Westgate, there's an up-to-date Crane Building, a brightly painted Sweet Candy Co., the handsomely rebuilt Henderson Block at 357 W. 200 South and, of course, the restaurants and art galleries centering on Pierpont.

Whether the recession will permit more of such venturesome progress is a question. Perhaps we'll see new efforts spurred by a new city government. Perhaps low-interest bank loans for further Warehouse District projects will be forthcoming, or rehabilitation funds from federal sources can become a solid possibility before the magic year 2000 is at hand. But it will need more than dreaming to remake all of west-side downtown.

# The ZCMI Center on South Temple

OCTOBER 13, 1991

As one might expect, there was a considerable effort preceding the recent Church of Jesus Christ of Latter-day Saints general conference to cleanse the downtown sidewalks at South Temple and Main streets of construction clutter attendant on remodeling the ZCMI Center, most popularly called the "ZCMI Mall."

Due to the hasty work outside and inside Salt Lake City's first downtown mall, visitors to the busy corner could at last see the shape of the "infilling" of the infamously windswept walkway alongside the ZCMI store on Main Street, as well as the larger construction job on South Temple.

In the latter case, the broad plaza between the O.C. Tanner storefront and Deseret Book's old locale has been filled by a sizable four-story structure topped by skylights and ringed with pillars. This new covered space will house a new, glistening-bright atrium and food park. The ground-level area has been designed by ZCMI Center officials to attract at least as many hungry Salt Lakers as the ultra-busy, lower-level fast-food oasis in the rival Crossroads Mall on the west side of Main Street.

Alas, now that pedestrians get a wall-to-wall view of what's been built these past two years or so, the average mall-stroller seems of the opinion the ZCMI Center planners can be equated with the Aesop's fable concerning the elephant who labored and brought forth only a mouse.

"Lots of fancy new marble flooring," said one chap seated at the Jim Conner shoeshine emporium where the rebuilt mall joins the Eagle Gate Towers's jigsaw-puzzle lobby. "Four new palm trees too, but not much else to show for the construction mess." One Deseret Book Store patron reported, "It's harder to get into the bookstore from South Temple; otherwise, there's not much change." And "it's just as hard to find the rest rooms," one old codger assured me.

Those slightly cynical mall-goers are not quite correct.

There have been changes—but whether they'll bring the crowds of the size that seems always to flock to Crossroads must remain in doubt. Answers may come at Christmas-shopping time—if major construction work is completed by then.

Pedestrians foresee two advantages—if the weather cooperates. Ever since the 600,000-square-foot ZCMI Center opened in mid-1975, passers-by on both Main Street and South Temple have been plagued by winds that blew down from the buildings and into their faces. The winds were pleasant zephyrs in summer, but during winter rains or snowstorms, those breezes could blow umbrellas wrong-side out, penetrate coats and parkas, and generally make walking past the entries pretty miserable. Filling in those hollow channels should eliminate much of the wind-chill factor abreast of the ZCMI Center.

The old flight of outdoor steps leading east from Main Street between the ZCMI and Kennecott buildings has gone—replaced by two dozen new steps sheltered by skylights and guarded, as it were, by a half-dozen columns on each side. Out front, a modest steel-and-glass area is topped by a triangular entablature of cast stone, matched, around the corner, by the entrance to the food court.

Here on South Temple, the cast-stone structure is topped by another rather plain triangle, and is linked to the building once occupied by Deseret Book by a broader steel-and-glass front rising some four stories in height. This, too, is enhanced by rows of equally tall columns. The whole ensemble west to O.C. Tanner's windows should look neat—if not beautiful—when construction work is at last complete.

But the rebuilt mall's interior raises quite a few questions concerning that elephant-mouse matter. The 35,000 square feet of atrium space, added to the original 600,000-square-foot mall, was originally announced in expansion plans by Zions Security Corp. divisional manager Richard Coles back in 1989. At the time, a "fast track" construction method was to ensure completion by November 1990.

Now almost a year behind that schedule, the project was originally estimated to cost at least ten million dollars. Its present dollar reckoning seems almost impossible to discover.

The project's architects, the firm of Feola Deeninhan Archuleta of Glendale, Ca., and John Brunt and Associates of Salt Lake, and prime contractors, Okland Construction Co., have made every visible effort to permit present mall tenants to stay in business during construction. They've also tried hard to keep auto and pedestrian traffic moving smoothly.

However, their task has been an almost-impossible one, made especially difficult by State Street tunneling and construction work at the vacant Hotel Utah across South Temple. By the by, have you noticed the upright steel girders now in place atop the northern quadrant of the one-time hotel? These are, one hopes, the first signs of a rooftop restaurant soon to take shape.

Back in the ZCMI Center, plans call for a dozen restaurants and fast-food establishments under the atrium skylights on the South Temple side of the mall. But meantime, the new center court of the mall is so marbleized, so bright and glossy, as to make one assume the food-court area will be more of the same. There are twin fountains in the court—call them tasteful or tasteless, depending on your viewpoint. Two new elevators now rise high above the "grand court." The twin elevators have brightly polished metal doors, fronted by a wealth of onyx and marble.

There are four palm trees in the court—you may or may not believe they add to the decor. The new Main Street side makes possible a wider, and perhaps grander, entrance to the old ZCMI. And the gray-and-green tile floors, well-shined brass railings, the neat escalators, are all fine indeed—perhaps too fine.

New shops will, landlords are certain, arrive to fill out new vacancies. But unlike local merchants who have vanished from Main Street, there's little nostalgia expressed at the passing of ZCMI Center shops that are no longer on hand to serve the public.

One wonders, walking through the new/old mall, whether it's not too neat, too orderly, too clean, too well policed to attract as much business as the more messy, less glossy Crossroads Mall across the way. If you were a teenager sporting a Mohawk hairdo, wearing ragged jeans and a black leather jacket, which mall would you hang out in?

# Crossroads Plaza Facade

MAY 23, 1993

If you think the view in today's sketch looks more like a theatrical stage set than a three-dimensional building, you are right. Go to the head of the class if you've recognized the facade of the 1869 Amussen Building pinned like a mounted butterfly to the Crossroads Plaza and its twenty-four-story Commercial Security Bank tower.

Since completion a dozen or so years ago, the mall has changed one "anchor" store, and as Main Street customers, fast-food munchers and oddly garbed teenagers know, the commercial institution fronted by the remnants of the Amussen Building has become the Key Bank.

When the carefully reproduced facade of the 1869 old-timer was grafted onto the plain brick wall of the mall at 50 S. Main, most architectural historians were irked by the skin-graft in which a precious historic structure was effectively "overpowered" by a high-rise.

Carl Christian Amussen's jewelry store was built by the construction firm of Folsom and Romney, who had set up the first steam-driven planing mill in the valley. William Folsom, a pioneer architect, designed a building renowned as the first fireproof structure in Utah Territory—almost as great an achievement as his Salt Lake Tabernacle and Manti Temple.

When it was pulled down, along with neighbors housing such locally prosperous shops as Zinik's (sporting goods) and the Grabeteria (really fast food), Amussen's old jewelry emporium had long given way to the Richard's Candy shop. It was also famed as the last remaining commercial building in the city built before the railroad came.

Constructed of cut red sandstone, it had large show windows of plate glass, the first in the city. Its balcony served as a bandstand for popular Sunday concerts. The owner, who originally spelled his name Asmussen, was a native of Copenhagen, Denmark, had sailed the seven seas, been a gold miner and had been persuaded by Brigham Young to purchase the Main Street property for a jewelry store.

The Crossroads Mall upon which the Amussen facade is now a mere appendage contains many more shops than once lined Main Street. Quite a few of the commercial establishments within the mall walls are mysterious indeed to doddering ancients such as myself. Haroon's—what's that?; Ypsilon—that name is equally mysterious. The Hot Flash, Mon Cheri, the Gamekeeper, Lotsa Hotsa—a guy needs a guide. There are all manner of passages leading to parking ramp levels. There's even a lane to something named Marriott. Oh well, youngsters who know what a Lotsa Hotsa is might wonder what Zinik is, or even a Grabeteria.

More important than puzzlement and nostalgia for days long gone is a learned discourse on the subject of malls by an eminent architect who bears the rather improbable name of Witold Rybczynski. Titled *The New Downtowns*, Mr. Rybczynski's opus reminds ignorant readers that "the malling of America" is no sudden phenomenon. It has taken almost a hundred years for the mall to become a feature of the urban and suburban landscape. Shopping villages begun by nonarchitects include Lake Forest Market Square near Chicago (1916) and Country Club Plaza in Kansas City (1925). The glass-roofed Galleria in Milan and a similar structure in Naples predate the turn of this century, and have been highly profitable.

Mr. Rybczynski believes Northgate on the outskirts of Seattle—which opened in 1950 featuring a carless central street, department stores and smaller shops—was the nation's first major shopping center by today's standards. By modern measurements, the Crossroads and ZCMI malls are pygmies.

For example, the West Edmonton Mall in Alberta includes a skating rink, amusement park, aviary, submarine ride and an artificial beach with rolling waves, attracting vacationers as well as shoppers year-round. The Mall of America, outside Minneapolis, is even bigger, enclosing 4.2 million square feet, attracting 100,000 visitors a day.

A French notable, the Duc de Chartres, may have started all this. The duke, chronically short of funds, opened his Palais Royale gardens and arcade buildings to the public—in 1784. His attraction may have helped bring on the French Revolution, as well as the malling of our nation and the world.

# Broadway Centre

JANUARY 5, 1992

Rest in peace, bygone Centre Theater. Welcome to the downtown district, newly arrived Broadway Centre tower. Despite past grumbling about the passing of the old big-screen Centre moviehouse, one must admit that the glassy, glossy, fourteen-story tower at the State corner of Broadway has cheered pedestrians and motorists considerably during our lengthy spell of sludgy, smoggy days. Even when the sun failed to bore through the murk, the reflective sheen of the downtown newcomer managed to brighten the familiar corner. During the most gloomy of days, the blue-black and grayish glass sheath, set off as it is by shiny anodized aluminum strips that accent both the vertical and horizontal aspects of the big building, have managed to reflect the ancient Brooks Arcade across State Street and the red-brick outlines of the rebuilt Auerbach structure just below.

At night, one suspects, when the nearly complete office structure is rented, bright lights in many offices will be reflected in the straight or curved glass walls of the tall building's well-proportioned structure. In past years, I've expressed marked distaste for most "glass boxes" that have sprung to life on 100 South and along suburban Fort Union Boulevard out in the county. However, the newcomer to our town's modest skyline is not a mere box. Peter Emerson, project architect of the Edwards and Daniels firm, along with design architect, Bruce Cameron, has eased the doubts that quite a few observers feel when viewing fragile-seeming, glass-walled structures. The architects have added interest, in the main, by giving the new building its rounded central core section, which contrasts nicely—and reflects—the two major rectangular wings.

While not as tall as downtown's bigger newcomer, the One Utah Center structure beyond that park-to-be over on Main Street, the graceful replacement for the vanished Centre Theatre has a rather handsome, and obviously expensive, granite-sheathed two-story base. That base, which gives the glass-fronted building a solid, well-supported look, is enhanced by aluminum flourishes including circular designs, column outlines, mullions and the like designed, I believe, by Richard Johnston, embellishment intended to recall the Art Deco "feel" of the old motion-picture palace.

While the vast, many-storied parking terrace linked to the new occupant of the downtown corner is not quite complete, the Cineplex Odeon, Broadway Centre's six movie houses have been opened, attracting sizable crowds to the once-busy corner. Despite a few initial complaints concerning difficulties in finding evening parking spots, those apparent problems should fade when the parking terrace opens. That terrace, being linked to the theaters and office structure (in part via a pedestrian bridge), means film fans should be able to park and head for their favorite cinemas dryshod. As promised, an initial look-see indicates that the decor of the lobbies fronting the six-plex relates, in color, carpeting, and some wall detailing, to the dimly remembered Centre.

It's rather amazing how quickly memory concerning vanished buildings falters. Can you remember the dozen stores that flanked the Centre Theatre on State Street or Broadway beyond the marquee? I have vague recollections of a Pine Cone eatery, a fur shop, and, early on, a big shop that sold record albums, pianos and electric Victrolas. Was there a butcher store as well? Around on Broadway, in the area now enhanced by granite and aluminum, there was a shoe-repair shop, a not-too-successful Swiss restaurant, and, in early years, a pet shop. Near the alley corner, in recent years, part of the area covered over by the parking terrace boasted a black-glass A-frame-shaped hamburger haven. Long important to gentile trencher-men, one of the shops a bit further east was occupied by Lu Dornbush's delicatessen. There a guy and a gal could absorb a corned beef on rye with a side dish of potato salad, plus a glass of Heineken beer, before heading into the Centre.

By the by, you can already see the dimensions of the new office struc-ture's lobby and the placement of the four tower elevators. All in all, it looks efficient, very "big city." But the well-remembered rooftop pylon of the bygone Centre won't ever be visible at the old site. The architects tell me it was "too deteriorated" when removed from the old stand to be sal-vaged.

CHAPTER 11

# Goodman's Favorite Five

# The Elks Club

MARCH 24, 1991

Unless you are a careful observer of small details on our city's buildings, there's little to inform you that the rather oddly situated structure at 139 E. South Temple was ever anything but an office building. But just above the long and cavernous tunnel—through which one can enter street level to down fish and chips at the Eat'N House, or to have one's hair trimmed at the shop labeled "A Barber" on the same level—a well-worn stone carving of an elk's head reminds forgetful Salt Lakers that this building was once the Elks Club—and a very splendid clubhouse it was.

Alas, as retired businessman Alton G. Thompson will tell you somewhat sadly, these premises—the entire building—once resounded to the lively sounds made by 2,500 members of the Benevolent and Protective Order of Elks. "We had an eighty-four-foot-square lodge room on the second floor for big meetings or dances," the past Exalted Ruler of the Elks recalls. Kitchens, dining rooms, bar, card rooms, exercise rooms—all were busy indeed from the day the building was dedicated on Nov. 3, 1923, almost until the changing years when the local lodge, along with fraternal organizations in every state, suddenly seemed outmoded and extraneous in a post-World War II world.

The Salt Lake BPOE had its beginnings in the 1880s, when the newly chartered fraternal group, Lodge No. 85, met in Shelton's Dance Hall, a structure long since torn down to make way for the Continental Bank Building at 200 South and Main. The Elks were soon meeting in larger quarters next to the now vanished Wilson Hotel on 200 South. Their next home was a temporary abode at the Odd Fellows Hall on Post Office Place— until $8,900 was raised for land at 59 S. State, where a spacious clubhouse was built. The order moved there in 1902—and shortly thereafter the local BPOE played host to a national convention. As many as 12,500 Elks swarmed to Salt Lake City, where they convened for several days in the Salt Lake Tabernacle, courtesy of the Church of Jesus Christ of Latter-day Saints.

The year 1912 was important for another reason, according to records preserved by past Exalted Ruler Thompson. "That was the year that inside toilets were installed in the State Street building."

But even such modern facilities proved insufficient to the needs of Elkdom, and the site at 139 E. South Temple was snapped up for $70,000 or thereabouts. While its cornerstone was laid on July 2, 1922, the building wasn't ready for occupancy for another year, after a fund drive that included a very lively circus netting $11,000.

If you've ever wondered why the building's main floor is a dozen or more feet above sidewalk level—well, the old Brigham Street mansions occupying the block before it was called East South Temple all stood at that level. Sidewalks, lawns and homes on the north side of the street were all considerably higher than those on the south side, a situation that has prevailed ever since the city's "boulevard" was first graded.

Thus the reason for the tunnel with its Elk-head arch. Ladies and guests who disdained stair-climbing could enter the tunnel and use an elevator to reach dance-and-dine areas, card rooms, meeting rooms and similar necessary spaces on the building's upper levels.

After World War II, the bloom was off the rose as far as lodges and fraternal organizations were concerned. The Moose, Odd Fellows, Masons and similar bodies found their membership rolls shrinking, and the Elks were no exception. Club founders such as Ferd Fabian, E.D. Critchlow, Hoyt Sherman and A.J. Dunn were no longer active, or had left, one hopes, for more exalted doings. There were fewer notable members, such as city treasurer Lou Holley or By Sims, whose hat store was a longtime downtown fixture.

There were not enough members to support such a large lodge building, "so we sold it for $750,000 in 1975, moved to 2960 Richards St., then to a new building on Fragment Drive," says Thompson. "There were so few members we had to give up our charter in 1987. But it's great to recall old friends, great to recall the war years when we often had a hundred or more troops sleeping on cots in the building, years when there was USO entertainment and refreshments for trainloads of kids."

The purchasing firm was called, I believe, Onondaga Properties.

At any event, the new owners made some remarkable changes in the building. As lively Salt Lakers of varying ages may recall, two movie houses were installed in the eighty-four-foot space formerly occupied by the ballroom. A glass-windowed penthouse was placed atop the structure, an addition marked by the logo of the Connecticut Mutual Life Insurance Co. A glassed-in greenhouse was put in place on the building's east side.

Most important of all to those of us afflicted with both a noontime thirst and a love for hearty hamburgers, an establishment named the Wasatch Front was installed on the eastern edge of the main floor. This bar and grill soon found favor with youthful lads and lasses from nearby brokerage offices, business establishments, shops and the Social Hall Avenue television and advertising offices. Prices were reasonable, the waitresses pert, and the bartenders and short-order chefs efficient.

Another eatery soon set up shop on the ground floor of the former Elks club, namely the Cinegrill. This establishment, operated by a gentleman named Cohne (with the musical assistance of Eugene Jelesnik), had been forced to leave its old quarters when "film row," a sector of 100 South just east of 200 East, was turned into rubble and then into a parking lot.

Cinegrill's management managed to instantly transport the bracing odor of garlic from the old location to its new home on South Temple. But for some reason, the Cinegrill did not last and was replaced by a posh restaurant or two. The movie houses and the Wasatch Front likewise faded from the ken of mortal man—and the old Elks Club structure was purchased, lock, stock, and brick walls, by Zions Security. No more bar and grill, of course. Respectability reigns at 139 E. South Temple.

# The Lion House, Beehive House, and Brigham Young's Office

MARCH 13, 1988

In sunlight or moonlight, snow covered or sunbaked, an admirably preserved trio of linked old buildings provides us a perfectly composed inner-city scene to tell us how things must have looked to Salt Lakers who strolled our streets a century or more ago. Despite the neighboring, clean-lined modern office tower to their rear, despite the bulky, heavy-columned church headquarters building to the west, the 1853 Lion House, the 1855 Beehive House, and Brigham Young's eminently practical "church office," linking his paired residences, still form a harmonious whole.

Singly or as an ensemble they give those who will take time to visit more than a few lessons in architecture and history, in such an intangible as "scale" and in the too often decried need for "preservation."

For starters, just suppose—those who have scoffed at the need for pre-serving our visible roots—just suppose the Lion House, Beehive House, and their connecting office structure had been demolished, one by one or as a group, when such almost equally historic neighbors as the now forgotten Tithing House became dust. Suppose the old red-brick LDS High School nearby had been saved as "more useful" than this historic adobe trio. Suppose the tall new Church Office Building instead occupied their South Temple Street site.

That pleasant, airy street would, of course, have become a canyon, walled in by the Kennecott and Eagle Gate Plaza high-rises, the elderly Hotel Utah, the oversized Greco-Roman Temple at 49 E. South Temple and a thirty-story church high-rise. No garden-fronted Beehive House, topped by a symbol of industry standing above a New England-style "widow's walk." No Lion House, with period-piece sculptured symbol and twenty gables at which generations of visitors gazed to muse upon Brigham's over-supply of wives and small fry. The downtown district, shorn of those three little beauties, would be a very different place indeed.

Fortunately for all of us, long before our recently acquired relish for doddering, elderly symbols of grandma's day, the powers that be in Latter-day Saints circles were afflicted (if that's the proper term) with both hero worship and thrift worship. In the thinking of the day, virtually anything relating to Brigham Young should be preserved—and even more so, should and must be preserved if it had utility. After Young's demise his Beehive House could (and would) be utilized by succeeding church presidents. Next when the structure ran down and seemed out of style, it could and would be used as a home for young LDS ladies from other towns and regions who came to Salt Lake City for schooling or work. By the time that use ended, the advantages of maintaining the rather dowdy house to show how Presi-dent Young had lived became apparent. It was refurbished completely and thrives to this day as a major tourist magnet.

As for the Lion House, it too proved a considerable attraction for sight-seers when vacated by the church president's considerable progeny. In re-cent times, after serving as a cafeteria-style mecca for thrifty downtown office workers, the Lion House's ample basement has been transformed into an attractive "club"—complete in the summertime with an arena for al fresco dining. A "no smoking/no drinking club," of course, thereby surpris-ing some visiting clubmen.

History aside, the three buildings Brigham Young ordered in 1853 have very real interest for local architects and builders. Young, by the way, was no slouch as a carpenter and some of the excellent joinerwork and cabinetry may have been of his own hands.

The authoritative WPA Guide to Utah (dating from 1941 and updated by Ward Roylance in recent years) reminds us that William Ward and Truman O. Angell, who designed the structures, were Utah's first pioneer architects. In the case of the Lion House, the basement walls are hewn of stone, the adobe walls of the two upper stories stand fully three feet thick. William Ward sculptured the symbolic lion (representing, this gentile supposes, the "Lion of the Lord" concept), just above the front doorway on East South Temple. The beast, far from being ferocious in appearance, is a "lion couchant" as the art scholars say—meaning the animal is amiably reclining. The upper story is made especially interesting by an oversupply of gables, or dormers, or peaks—ten on the east side, ten on the west.

The dormers must pose perennial problems for experts in shingling and roofing. Not to mention glazing, there being twenty Gothic-shaped multi-paned windows beneath those peaked gables.

It's intriguing to learn that the noted British explorer Richard Burton once gazed at the Lion House and reported: "It is tenanted by the 'plurality of wives' and their families, who each have a bedroom, sitting room and closet. . . . there is a Moslem air of retirement about the House, the face of woman is rarely seen at the window, and her voice is never heard from without."

Lest you get the wrong idea—the quotation is from the Sir Richard F. Burton who visited "The City of the Saints" in 1860.

The Beehive House, dating from 1855, seems to have been designed by Truman Angell alone. Its six-columned portico facing East South Temple, the matching columns on its east side, the twin chimneys, the wood-railed second-story porch and, of course, that "widow's walk" or "widow's watch," give the yellow painted adobe building a marked New England air. The "walk" or "watch" beneath the beehive-topped cupola matches those still common place in Nantucket and Martha's Vineyard, upper-story platforms where wives, telescopes at hand, looked seaward with considerable anxiety, hoping to sight an overdue whaler or clipper ship.

Indoors, nowadays, volunteer docents who guide sightseers through the house take considerable pride in displaying artifacts indicating that Brigham Young and his family lived in rather gracious style during the later years of his residence. The sparse furnishings in the Lion House, or those displayed at the Daughters of the Utah Pioneers Museum on Capitol Hill, are of more spartan style. Fact is, both indoors and in the curved extension to the north, the Beehive House is positively Victorian, rather than pioneer, in character.

Too often overlooked, the two-story adobe between the two residences was Brigham Young's office—and a pleasant-appearing workplace at that. Truman Angell designed it, finished it in 1852, but Brigham must have fussed considerably with latter-day details, including the built-in niches where records were pigeonholed, the stairway tucked behind a closet that leads to a small, oval mezzanine, and his handsome, practical pinewood desk. If you can talk your way into the little office building—do so. It somehow tells more about the man than his adjacent "official residences."

Of course, what we think of the original occupants of the three buildings—saints, sinners, or just plain folks—matters little. They, the buildings, are the most valuable in our town, the most significant remnants in the fabric of a vanished Salt Lake City. I hope they'll now remain visible for our children's grandchildren, lovingly preserved, no matter how many skyscrapers we mistakenly raise around them.

*Drawing Courtesy of Jasmial Freed Rich*

# The Armstrong Mansion

FEBRUARY 27, 1994

Sizable volumes, as well as several monographs, have been published concerning East South Temple Street—learned and scholarly works devoted to the history of the street and its multitude of mansions. Predictably, the Kearns Mansion, now the flame-seared home of Utah's governors, always ranks large in the list of mansions under the discussion.

The one-time homes of David Keith and Col. Wall also place high in lists compiled by local historians and seekers after significant architecture.

In my mind, at least, two South Temple dwellings have been unfairly scanted. One, the residence of Daniel C. Jackling at 731 E. South Temple, deserves special mention, although it is none too lovely a structure. Fact is, Jackling's home is plain and rather unbeautiful. But of all the men involved with mining in Utah, Jackling rates a topmost place in our industrial pantheon. More of the copper giant's home and history at another date. Today's column, however, as you may guess from the appended sketch, concerns the Armstrong Mansion at 1177 E. South Temple, on the northwest corner of S Street.

The Armstrong Mansion is not of ancient age, having been built, by some accounts, in 1911, or in 1912, according to other sources. In any event, it seems to me the finest example of a column-fronted, neo-Classic Revival building on East South Temple, perhaps in the entire city. There is a good reason for this, of course. This house had an outstanding architect, Richard Kletting. As just about any local architectural buff will tell you, it was Kletting who designed the Utah State Capitol, one of the better such structures in the nation. When I last looked long and hard at the mansion, work was under way to rehabilitate its foundations.

For many years, window shutters, doorways and other trim of the home were painted dark green. Recently, the entire home was upgraded––in my belief, at least––by a coat of glowing white, including all the trim. Its great glory is its two-story-high portico. There are four fine, tall columns seemingly supporting the portico, giving the home an undeniable "air," matching older mansions seen in the Southern states, the Midwest and New England.

Mark Angus, whose recent *Salt Lake City Under Foot* is a welcome guide to our town's historic neighborhoods, correctly notes one oddity in the Kletting structure. This mansion's entrance is not beneath the portico and between those pillars, but off to the side of the facade. Steps and sidewalks lead from the entry to East South Temple, but why Kletting or patron William Armstrong wanted the entrance placed where it is remains a puzzle to me.

Angus propounds a more chilling mystery concerning this Armstrong Mansion. According to the Angus account, "local folklore tells of a murder that took place here—the husband shooting his wife's young lover, who fell out the window and bled to death. Occupants say that at night they hear footsteps racing toward the window." At this writing I am 800 miles from the scene of the bloody crime and can't check on those footsteps. Are they merely the steps of some lovelorn lad hastening to catch a UTA bus before the last bus heads for the barn?

It seems fitting and proper to note that historian Margaret Lester, whose handsome Brigham Street volume is the local bible insofar as East South Temple mansions are concerned, has nothing to say about a ghost. She relates that William Wright Armstrong was born in Wisconsin in

1865, moved to Kansas, studied in Wisconsin, received a law degree (before there was a Badger football team), married Eva Lees of Irving, Kan., and settled in Nephi in 1890.

"He became a cashier in the First National Bank of Nephi," Lester reports. During his heyday, the mansion-builder had interests in the National Copper Bank, Bankers Trust Co., First National of Park City, the Salt Lake Hardware Co. and Salt Lake and Ogden Gas Co. But any television scriptwriter should be able to concoct a tale of a South Temple bride, a gas-company meter reader's doxy, or perhaps a trolley-car motorman's hapless attempt to flee from a pistol-wielding, aggravated husband.

One other slight mystery. My wife, Marjorie, attended the old Wasatch School just down the street from the Armstrong Mansion. "There was a young man named Minor Armstrong," she assures me. Why would a kid be named "Minor," not "Junior?" If he entered the Army and gained rank, would he be called Major Minor by his associates?

At any event, the Armstrong Mansion is very handsome indeed, and a major player on the East South Temple scene.

# The Alta Club

NOVEMBER 14, 1993

Outwardly, the three-story, hip-roofed building at 100 E. South Temple has changed little since it formally opened on June 1, 1898—unless you study its lengthy north-facing facade from across South Temple. You then can realize that the original structure was doubled in size (in 1910) by addition of a matching east wing.

This staid-appearing, Italian Renaissance Revival-style building is, of course, the home of the Alta Club.

Designed by Frederick Albert Hale, one of the city's premier architects, it rose almost as a challenge on the corner diagonally opposite Brigham Young's Beehive House, built for a club that unashamedly banned Latter-day Saints from membership when founded in 1883 as the city's preeminent social club.

Since the turn of the century, Mormons gradually have been wel-

263

comed to Alta Club membership. Indeed, despite its reputation for never varying in character or quality, there have been quite a few signs that the club will veer—sociologically speaking—to keep pace with changes in public attitudes.

For example, the Alta Club's bar, was, in effect, a nonearner of necessary revenue during the Prohibition years. That is not to say its members no longer imbibed alcoholic beverages. O.N. Malmquist, the 1974 author of the club's fulsome volume of historical facts, quoted some members still alert, alive and, one hopes, sober, as having obtained liquid sustenance via bottles garnered daily from the pockets of a mysterious white coat that providentially was always found hanging in a coat closet in the Hotel Utah.

There was also an era, in and around the years of World War II, when whirring machines, their facades featuring cherries, bells, bars and similar esoteric signs, provided considerable revenue to the Alta Cub treasury. Alas, the slot machines vanished long ago.

One major change in club policy—infuriating to some members—had implications to club architecture, custom and/or the valid rights of the so-called "weaker sex."

Architecturally, when the east wing was added in 1910, the original main entrance was moved from the State Street side to 100 E. South Temple (shown in today's sketch). The State Street entry became "The Women's Entrance." Not only was it thus designated, it was used as such, with the addition of a stairway women climbed for access to the main dining room. Mere men can use that entrance now!

As readers with short as well as long memories may recall, the possibility of lawsuit (and such cries as "O Tempora, O Mores") made it mandatory that women could join the Alta Club. Wives long had been welcomed with spouses or escorts in the dining areas. Now such members of the weaker, or stronger, or equivalent sex such as geologist Ms. Genevieve Atwood and our city's mayor, Ms. Deedee Corradini, have been welcomed to the fellowship of this no-longer-all-male fief.

Now, quietly and again without outward sign of change, work has just been completed on the club building's lower level modernizing the Alta Club via the installation of modern exercise, hot-tub, massage and shower areas—separate but equal, of course.

Jack Lossee, club president in 1992 when the exercise-area installation began, tells me, "The club has been seeking young members. Many youthful executives downtown want to lift weights, run on treadmills, and otherwise exercise."

True, the club has a splendid billiard room and an exceedingly comfortable library complete with newspapers, magazines, a fireplace and even rocking chairs. And there are more-than-adequate dining rooms, a bar and grill, and card rooms. But alas, the chief exercise these facilities offered members interested in development of muscles involved the lifting of glassware, forks, spoons and pool cues. "The only bicycles we saw were on playing-card boxes," one member mused recently.

When first formed to provide "the comforts and luxuries of home, together with the attraction to its members of meeting each other in a pleasant and social way," the club founders, mostly mining men, felt little need for exercise rooms. Founders included W.S. McCormick, J.R. Walker and J.E. Dooley, but business and professional men soon were represented. In more recent years, club presidents have included a Utah Power & Light official, contractors, attorneys, ranchers, bankers, brokerage-firm owners, surgeons and architects.

To most Salt Lakers, the Alta Club has seemed a bastion of Republican conservatism—and indeed it was said to contain Utah's highest concentration of F.D.R.-haters in New Deal days. However, notable members have included George Dern, secretary of war under Franklin Roosevelt, and Marriner S. Eccles, the chairman of the Federal Reserve system who helped succor Utah's banks. Both were Democrats, as were members Calvin Rampton and Scott Matheson, former Utah governors.

And, on the matter of gender, while present club president Zeke Dumke and manager Stephen Foristel are guys, the Alta Club bartender and barber, Doris Bohmand and Teri Talbot, are gals.

One more odd bit of history that should be recorded: Salt Lake City's first three-car, chain-reaction collision occurred in front of the Alta Club's State Street entrance early in 1906.

F.C. Richmond had a brand-new Pierce Arrow, E.L. Sheets drove his shiny Reo, and P.J. Moran had just purchased a Cadillac. The gentlemen agreed to dine together and show each other their expensive vehicles.

All arrived at the club simultaneously, went south to park—and lost control of their cars, each ramming one or both of the other brightly polished vehicles.

The members of the trio remained friends.

# The Kearns Building

APRIL 4, 1995

As architectural historians retrace the past, the realization is growing that Main Street reached its prime—both from the standpoint of business and of architecture—during the first decades of the twentieth century. Downtown stores seemed their busiest, sidewalks their most crowded, trolley cars their noisiest. And such tall structures as the Walker Bank Building, the Deseret Bank (now the First Security offices), the Judge, the McIntyre and Utah Oil buildings were rising.

Among them was the Kearns Building at 132 South Main, which still stands today as a centerpiece of the city's business district. Its owner-builder, Thomas Kearns, made his fortune in the silver-lead-zinc mines of Park City, became owner of the *Salt Lake Tribune* and served as a United States senator from 1901 until 1905. His terra-cotta-fronted building, designed by the Los Angeles firm of Parkinson and Bergstrom, was obviously influenced by the works of distinguished Chicago architect Louis H. Sullivan, sometimes viewed as the "father" of the skyscraper. However, it must be said that engineering developments, such as the Otis elevator and steel-frame construction were at least as responsible for today's buildings of far greater heights.

The Kearns Building, while just ten stories high, shows Sullivan's problem-solving in many ways. One puzzle architects were confronting was the need to give tall buildings clear-cut tops and bottoms, somehow linked via their middle stories. The Los Angeles architects, taking their cue from Sullivan, broke the Kearns facade with a half-dozen piers, and topped the vertical piers with arches enclosing the tops of paired windows. The roofline is formed by a strong cornice protruding well beyond the building's main surface. The cornice is decorated in much the same manner by mathematical patterns similar to those used so successfully by Sullivan in many of his major works. Taking these matters into account, John S. McCormick, in his volume on the city's historic buildings, notes the links between the Kearns Building and the Guarantee Building in Buffalo, N.Y., and the even more famous Wainwright Building in St. Louis, Mo. Both were built a dozen or so years before the Salt Lake City structure. Sullivan's lone work in Utah, the Dooly Building, vanished in 1964 when construction of the Salt Palace began transforming the near west side of the city.

As you pass by the Kearns Building, you come to realize that much of its detailing, in decorative terra-cotta, is well worth more than a hasty glance. The ornamentation under the wide cornice high above the street, plus the details above the window arches on the tenth floor, are a bit hard to see. But the fanciful figures enhancing the base of the piers are fully revealed at second-story level, as are the fanciful torchieres. All could lead you to decide that the decorative arts of the bygone era were superior to the plain, flat, mechanistic detailing of our latter days.

The Kearns building was renovated, inside and out, a half-dozen years ago, and its lobby, as well as upper story corridors and offices are worth a second look. One is happy that the structure still has at least a few tenants engaged in the mining business.